LIVING

THE

CODE

An American Outlaw in the Caribbean

Bill Goodwin

Published by Piscataqua Press
An imprint of RiverRun Bookstore, Inc
142 Fleet St. | Portsmouth, NH. | 03801
www.piscataquapress.com
www.riverrunbookstore.com

ISBN: 978-1-939739-83-4

Printed in the United States of America

LIVING
THE
CODE

An American Outlaw in the Caribbean

Bill Goodwin

Meeting Jack

The winter of 2006–07 was a bad one. Almost twelve feet of snow fell at our summer place in Maine, and there was a period of three weeks when the daytime temperature never got above five degrees below zero. Susie and I had long since fled to the Caribbean, where we would sail our fifty-foot pilothouse ketch, *Mariposa*, during the cold, dark months of the northern hemisphere. Some of our stoic Maine neighbors may have resented this cowardly escape, but we were comfortable with their thinly veiled contempt. It was worth the trade-off.

We had started that year's cruise in Isla Mujeres, Mexico, planning to transit the full 1000-kilometer length of the Mesoamerican Barrier Reef System, which is second in extent only to Australia's Great Barrier Reef. This L-shaped reef system starts at the northern tip of the Yucatan Peninsula, runs south along the Mayan Riviera and the coast of Belize, turns east at Livingston, Guatemala, and continues east all the way along the north coast of Honduras. It terminates at Cabo Gracias a Dios, where the landmass abruptly turns ninety degrees and the Nicaraguan coast begins to run south.

The Mexican government had recognized the tourist potential of Isla Mujeres and made sure it was safe for visitors. We saw people, even single women, walking unhurriedly through the town at ten o'clock at night. The beaches were similarly free of petty crime. European women sunbathed and swam topless without fear of being accosted. There were the usual beach vendors selling the usual Mexican handicrafts — carvings, beads, and hammocks — but they were easily dismissed by a stern stare and a slowly waving right index finger. Restaurants served authentic but cleanly prepared Mexican food so the gringos could eat without fear of contracting Montezuma's revenge, and the mariachi musicians didn't pressure them for tips. On the beach, though, music could be a real moneymaker. Every day a diminutive middle-aged man with a face like a deflated football, accompanied by a seven-year-old girl in a floral dress, came ambling along. While he banged a drum and crashed cymbals, she blew loud, random notes on a saxophone. They wandered in incessant, loopy circles around groups of beachgoers until someone paid them to go away.

Susie and I loved Isla, as the cruisers referred to it, and we stayed six weeks. It was so remarkable that we told both our sons to come down, although separately because of differing interests, and we met each of them at the airport in Cancun. From there we taxied over to the docks and took the ferry to the island. We left *Mariposa*'s dinghy at the ferry dock, filled it with their (mostly unnecessary) luggage, and motored out to the anchorage. Neither of them had ever lived on a sailboat or been on open water before, so we spent the first couple of hours orienting them to the realities of life afloat. Where to stow things in the limited space available, how to operate a marine toilet, why minimizing water use when showering or brushing teeth was necessary, when to expect the generator to be switched on for refrigeration and battery charging, what the water pressure pump sounded like, and how to get safely into and out of the dinghy are not usual concerns of people living in houses.

Our older son, Casey, loves scuba diving, and once he got squared away on the boat, he dived the reefs ringing the island every day, often twice. The dive shops even came out to pick him up at *Mariposa* in the morning and returned him, exhausted but happy, at the end of the day. He didn't care much for the beach, just wanted to get in as many dives as possible during the week he spent with us. The younger one, T. J., brought his girlfriend Joyce along. They just wanted to sit in umbrella beach chairs with iced buckets of Corona beside them, each bottle with its own wedge of lime. They went in swimming from time to time, but Joyce was not intimidated by the European girls. She kept her top on.

We made a point of introducing the kids to conch ceviche, not a dish commonly found on US menus. Joyce was not interested in eating giant ocean snails, but we all enjoyed having a drink at the beach bars, one of which provided seating on wooden planks tied at each end to overhead rods. We rented motor scooters and drove the perimeter road all around the island, stopping to take in the views of the cobalt-blue seas surrounding us, with foam-capped waves breaking on rocky outcroppings and clean white beaches strung like necklaces along sheltered shorelines.

Once the kids had gone back to the snow and ice, Susie and I returned to our developing friendships among the cruising community, frequently joining up for sunset drinks in one another's cockpits, going ashore for potluck dinners, and occasionally making sightseeing trips on the mainland to visit Mayan ruins or swim in freshwater cenotes. These pits, with their water surfaces fifty to one hundred feet below the top lip, are dotted across the Yucatan and have tunnels linking them. The Maya used them for transportation and trade; we used them for cooling off after a hot morning of climbing the pyramids of Chichen Itza. Jumping into seventy-degree water from platforms erected along the vegetation-draped cenote walls after sweating for hours in the heat and humidity of the tropical Yucatan was

Bill Goodwin

literally a breathtaking experience.

Then it was time to move on. As charmed as we had been by Isla, there was the whole rest of the reef system to see, new bays to explore, ports to visit, remote cays to anchor behind. Sailor's wanderlust had set in, and we began to provision *Mariposa* with enough frozen food, canned goods, cooking fuel, paper products, beer, wine, rum, gin, and tonic to last us for months. Provisioning this extensively meant several trips to and from town in the dinghy, and on one of those runs we ran into Betty and John, a British couple we had befriended. They were also planning to head south in the next couple of days, so we decided to "buddy sail" with them as far south as San Pedro, Belize. From there they would continue south to Livingston and go up the Rio Dulce to meet friends from England, while we would take a south-southeasterly course toward Cabo Gracias a Dios.

Once everything was securely stowed on our respective boats, we pulled our hooks — sailor talk for anchors — at first light on the appointed day and started the passage. *Mariposa*, a ketch with a mainsail, mizzen, and two headsails, was a faster boat than John and Betty's sloop, *Second Wind*, which was rigged with just a mainsail and a single jib. As a result, we outdistanced them substantially over the course of the day, but remained in regular radio contact. About midafternoon, John hailed us with the news that his water tank had ruptured. All their fresh water had gone into the bilge and been pumped overboard. I told John we had a watermaker and assured him we would keep them supplied all the way to Guatemala if necessary. Leaving them without drinking water on the passage from San Pedro to the Rio Dulce was out of the question, even if it meant Susie and I would have to change our plans. So each evening we headed into the same anchorages and dropped our hooks as close to each other as swinging room permitted. Then John lowered *Second Wind*'s dinghy and rowed over so we could fill whatever containers Betty had freed up. This way they could cook, take sponge baths, and have water to drink the next day. Helping each other like this is the norm for cruisers. We all know that sooner or later, everyone will have a problem and need the help of others. Nobody doubts that it will be provided without hesitation.

So Susie and I accepted the detour John and Betty's misfortune necessitated. Had we parted company in San Pedro, the northernmost entry point into Belize, we would have had a better angle on the wind as we headed for Gracias a Dios. A good angle is important to sailors, because sailboats can't go directly into the wind. They have to tack, zigging and zagging back and forth across the wind to gradually make progress in the desired direction. Going as far south as Guatemala meant that Susie and I would have to tack across the prevailing easterly trade winds in order to reach Gracias a Dios. Back in the late sixteenth century, Columbus had named the cape after he spent weeks slogging east off the north coast of what is now Honduras. When he could finally turn and run south along the coast of present-day Nicaragua with the wind abeam, he was said to exclaim, "Gracias a Dios!"

We continued with John and Betty all the way to the anchorage at Cabo Tres Puntas, easy striking distance to the mouth of the Rio Dulce. We filled their water jugs one last time that evening and, resigned to the long easterly passage, headed out the next morning. Compared to Columbus's passage though, ours was relatively easy. *Mariposa* had a fore-and-aft rig, a modern sailing hull, and a 120-horsepower diesel engine. His ship had been square-rigged, making it impossible for him to sail as close to the wind as we could. It had been essentially a motorless barge with a very inefficient sail plan.

Even stopping at overnight anchorages along the coast and in the Bay Islands of Honduras, we still made the cape in six days. From there, it was an easy beam reach to Isla de Providencia and San Andrés en route to the San Juan River in Nicaragua, where we would leave the boat and return to Maine for the summer. Miles up this deep, narrow rain-forest river was a "hurricane hole" where *Mariposa* would be sheltered from tropical storm surges and protected from the worst of the winds by the surrounding mountains.

Transiting the river for the first time, we were stunned by its beauty. One section of it snaked along the bottom of a three-hundred-foot deep canyon. The canyon walls were white limestone, draped with thick-stemmed vines with huge leaves. Colors exploded from tropical flowers where iridescent blue and yellow butterflies alighted to drink the nectar; squawking parrots fluttered overhead on their short, stubby wings; and pure white long-necked ibis stalked small fish in the shallows. Once out of the canyon, we were flanked by impenetrable-looking jungle, interrupted only by a few small villages carved out of the bush. It was hot, especially without the Caribbean breezes, but we were cautious about swimming because we had seen crocs in the swampy areas. The water temperature gauge on the instrument panel registered ninety-three degrees, so a swim wouldn't have provided much relief anyway. It took us three days against the current before we finally reached San Carlos, just downstream of the entrance to Lake Nicaragua.

The river there broadened into a lagoon three miles long and a mile wide in some places. Small palm-thatched *palapa* houses were spaced intermittently along its shores, and there was a ramshackle village with a U-shaped pier. High-bowed *panga* launches and dugout *cayuco* canoes were tied up, off-loading their catches of lake and river fish.

We motored past a few small marinas that catered to sailboat cruisers like us, radioing ahead to get directions to ours. It turned out to be a rustic little resort with about twenty slips, a few *palapa* style bungalows, and a restaurant/bar built on pilings that extended out over the water. Local fisherman were casting round, weighted nets near the docks while standing in *cayucos* that looked ready to flip their occupants into the river if they made the slightest uncoordinated movement.

The young men on the dock directed us to our slip, where the boat had to be sandwiched between two other vessels. I had to come in quickly to avoid the river's current sweeping me into the boat just downstream, so I favored the upstream side of the slip opening. What I did not know was that a counter current ran in the opposite direction close to the shore. As I slid into the slip, this unexpected current pressed *Mariposa* against an upstream piling and dragged the stainless steel boarding ladder, mounted at amidships, across it. The ladder was bent into an unusable shape. Once the boat was securely berthed, I asked the dockmaster if he knew where I could get the ladder repaired, and he gave me the name and location of a marine repair shop. I lowered the sailboat's dinghy from the davits at the stern, put on the outboard, and motored over.

When I found the shop's office, the owner, a short, stocky gringo named Dave, was in a heated discussion with another American expatriate. This fellow, Jack McCray, was holding forth about how the US government was screwing its citizens, ripping them off with taxes and ridiculous expenditures, all the while cutting back on their freedom of thought, choice, and action.

Jack, though vociferous, was an unprepossessing sort: medium stature, slim build, glasses, thinning sandy-red hair, and a wide forehead tapering down to a narrow jaw that appeared to be missing some teeth. But he was articulate in his rant, eyes flashing and hands gesturing emphatically, clearly unwilling to accept the owner's attempts to make any counterpoints. He was overgeneralizing, oversimplifying, and concluding each complaint with unanswerable or rhetorical questions. Rational discussion or argument seemed out of the question.

I wrote him off as an oddball who was trying to justify why he had fled the United States seventeen years earlier, as he said, to create a new life on a remote jungle river. I injected myself into the rant anyway, hoping that an interruption would provide an opening for me to address the shop owner. This was a miscalculation, because Jack just included me in his challenging diatribe. The owner and I fell silent in the hope he would eventually wind down. He did, at least long enough for me to make arrangements for the owner to come over to my boat in the afternoon and survey the damage. I exited the shop quickly, relieved to get away from the cranky expatriate and his one-sided vitriol.

Dave came to the marina and we scoped out the problem. He said he just happened to know a guy who did stainless-steel welding and could repair my ladder. When I asked how I could get in touch with him, he told me I had already met the man at his shop that morning. He gave me Jack's name again, and his phone number, and said I should work with him directly. Dave didn't want to be in the middle of it.

Given that Jack could likely solve my problem, my first impression of him changed dramatically. Sailors will put up with a lot when they find someone, however irascible, who can get them out enjoying their lifestyle again. Jack was apparently able to make this happen, so I called him right away. I told him (trying to keep the falseness out of my voice) what a pleasure it had been meeting him that morning and described the problem with the ladder.

"I don't work on boats," he said. "You'll have to take the damaged parts off and bring them to my shop. I'll see if I can fix them. If I can't, I'll make new ones."

A bit abrupt but clearly straightforward, so I asked how to find his shop, pointing out that I only had water transportation. He gave me directions, and I asked when his shop opened in the morning. He told me he got up at 5:30, so any time after 6:30 would be OK. I removed the damaged ladder parts so I could get an early start the next morning.

It was a dinghy ride and a twenty-minute walk through another ramshackle village to get to Jack's shop. I was astonished by what I found. He had a fully equipped machine shop tucked away in the middle of a rain forest. The clean concrete-block building was filled with automated drills, multiton stamping presses, and metal cutting lathes, while out on the river people were getting around in dugout canoes, sometimes propelling them (at least downwind) by holding up palm fronds. Some of them were also talking on their cellphones, which made the scene surreal.

Jack called me two days later and told me the ladder parts were ready and I could come pick them up. He described in painstaking detail everything he'd had to do to fix them: cutting, bending, welding, grinding, polishing. I thought, *Here we go, this guy is setting me up for a big bill.* But when I asked him what the charge would be for all this work, he said, "Fifty bucks." Now that was extremely reasonable, in view of the fact that anything having to do with boats is almost always outrageously expensive. I thanked him and said I'd be there in an hour.

The repair was flawless, and after I paid him, Jack offered to show me around his shop. After his earlier abruptness, this sudden openness surprised me, so I took him up on it. He described each machine meticulously and showed me some of the custom work he was capable of doing. I was impressed to see a one-inch diameter stainless-steel bolt with threads precision machined on an enormous lathe, and realized that the repair he had done for me was child's play.

Later I told Dave about the inexpensive repair, and he said, "Well, Jack liked you because you listened so politely to his tirade the other day. The work he did is easily worth twice what you paid, and you agreed to settle up right away. A lot of the cruisers down here try to chisel him or say they haven't got the money. He sees you as a good guy." For my part, I was relieved to have the boat ready for next year's cruise. Susie and I could relax and enjoy our summer and fall in Maine.

When we returned to the boat in January, however, we discovered she needed more than a minor repair. The crew I had hired to varnish the brightwork on the boat's transom had lowered the dinghy from its davits and used it as a floating work platform. Not a problem in and of itself, but one evening, when they hauled it back up into the davits, they neglected to take the plug out. There was a heavy rainstorm that night, and with the plug still inserted, the dinghy filled with water. The weight was too much for the davits to support, and it buckled.

I called Jack and told him that this time I had some real work for him and that it was essential before we could take the boat to sea. He agreed to come to the marina and scope it out, and thus began a design, construction, and installation project that lasted almost three weeks. Because a davits is such a conspicuous contraption, its construction has to fit aesthetically with the lines of a boat, as well as being functional. This meant that Susie would have to be involved, which added another dimension to the job, because after only a couple of conversations with him, she confided to me, "I don't think Jack really 'gets' women." Further, we'd have to coordinate with Dave for the davits installation, since as Jack had told me, he didn't work on boats.

Working through the many details of the project meant spending a lot of time with Jack, and it gave us the opportunity to get to know each other. We began to appreciate different aspects of our lives and personalities, and a friendship developed. He learned to be patient in explaining engineering calculations and characteristics of materials to a liberal-arts major, and I learned how to put up with the rants of a disaffected expatriate and the compulsive need for an engineer to explain how a clock worked when all I really needed to know was the time. It got to the point that we enjoyed sparring with each other, challenging opinions, calling the other guy out, and commenting on personal quirks. These exchanges never got harsh or insulting; they were just the easygoing banter that men fall into when they are comfortable with each other.

As Jack cautiously related parts of his life story to me, I realized he was a very unusual person. Susie and I had been sailing around the Caribbean and up and down the East Coast of the United States for ten years. We had come in contact with a Technicolor cast of characters who contrasted sharply with the black-and-white world of homogeneous, bland, and comfortably affluent folks with whom we associate when on land. The cruising community was different, bound together only by a love of the free-wheeling lifestyle and reliance on one another, where respect was conferred by how good a sailor one was. It included an international collection of retired naval officers, firefighters, musicians (some from well-known bands), electrical engineers, plumbers, emergency-room doctors, lawyers who had gotten sick of the grind, and former corporate executives. There were also those whose pasts were less savory, people running from bad marriages, unpaid tax bills, lawsuits, and even criminal charges. Even up against this mélange, though, Jack was in a class by himself.

The triggering incident that got me started on writing Jack's story happened two years after he built the new davits. Although Susie and I cruised the southwest Caribbean for five or six months every year, we returned in May or June to the river where Jack had his shop to secure the boat for the hurricane season. These were occasions for reunions, and we got together with Jack to see the improvements he was making to his house and shop, have a few beers at a riverside bar, and share some meals. Our relationship had evolved from business dealings to a genuine friendship. He even cooked dinner for us from time to time.

That year, for the 2009 winter cruise, we were sailing between Nicaragua and Panama and stopped at the island of Siguaterra. Fellow cruisers had told us this was not to be missed. A thirty-two-mile-long, one-mile-wide tropical island, Siguaterra is barely visible from the mainland, and then only on days of low humidity. A spine of low mountains runs along its length, and it is covered with palm, pine, oak, lime, mango, cashew, and breadfuit trees, as well as bushes with variegated leaves in shades of green, yellow, and deep red. Hibiscus, bird of paradise, bougainvillea, and bottlebrush abound, attended to by black- and orange-banded honeybees and iridescent emerald hummingbirds.

The west coast of the island is in the lee of the mountains and therefore provides numerous calm anchorages in deeply indented harbors, locally called bights because their shape resembles a loop of line. Just offshore, there is a string of mangrove-covered cays and a reef that rings the whole island. The east coast, exposed to the trade winds, is more rugged, as the sea crashes into the cliff bases and creates rocky promontories. At several places along this coast, the action of the water has pounded the rocks and corals into deep powder-white beaches with sea grape, palm, and almond trees shading the land one hundred meters back from the water.

Susie and I thought Siguaterra might be a good place to buy some investment property, where we could build an island retreat for when we got tired of hauling lines. Overhearing us discussing this at a bar frequented by other cruisers was a fellow who introduced himself as a former sailor. He said he had fallen in love with the island when he anchored there years ago. He also let it "slip" that he kept busy as a buyer's agent for an island real estate company. We rose to the bait, and he agreed to pick us up at our boat the next morning to show us what properties were available.

We were able to keep our perspective until he brought us to a remote section on the north end of the island and showed us a hilltop compound of five buildings overlooking a sheltered harbor. There was a deep-water channel through a break in the reef so boats could safely enter it, and he told us about the interesting naval history of the area, going all the way back to the pirate days of the seventeenth century. We turned our attention to the view and gazed at the sapphire-blue of the Caribbean Sea, which gradually brightened to turquoise as it shallowed to sand patches along the reef. There were two cays about a mile offshore, the larger of which had a small house and dock on its western side and a sandy beach at the south end. In addition to its million-dollar view, our agent explained, the property had a deeded dock at the bottom of the hill with its own dock house and slips for four boats. It was accessed by an easement across a neighbor's property.

The place had been for sale for several years, not only because it was remote—forty-five minutes on a rain-rutted road to the nearest town, only eleven kilometers away—but also off the power grid. Electricity for the buildings and equipment was generated by solar panels, stored in twelve large-capacity batteries and passed through an inverter to produce 120V house current. Water came from an 8000 gallon cistern the main house was constructed on top of, and was distributed around the compound by a high-pressure pump. The cistern was fed by rainwater collected from the roof by a system of gutters and downspouts, and purified by activated charcoal filters impregnated with silver nitrate. There was also a well 109 steps down from the house from which water could be pumped up in the dry season. Gas for cooking came from hundred-pound propane cylinders that had to be hauled "down island" for periodic refills. Maintenance and repairs on all buildings and systems had to be handled by the owners, as did personal security. Although there was a police department in the town, it would take them an hour to get to us, assuming they had a car available—and it had gas in it. The broker explained that there just weren't that many people were willing or able to take all this on.

We, on the other hand, were live-aboard sailors and therefore accustomed to being self-reliant. After years of anchoring in hidden coves where there were often no other boats, we had found we enjoyed the feeling of creating our own little world with nobody else around. It was pleasant to contemplate that if we bought it, the compound couldn't sink. It couldn't drag its anchor in a storm and beach itself on a leeward shore either, as our boat had occasionally done.

We were hooked, and after sleeping on it asked the agent to help us negotiate a purchase price. He did so, but also advised us (he was a buyer's agent, beholden only to us) to stipulate in the contract that closing would be contingent on having clear title to the property and the insurance to prove it. Island property lines and ownership, he told us, were kind of loosey-goosey in Nicaragua. People would pass land to the next generation without any sort of survey. Juan would get the parcel from the old oak tree down to the creek; Maria would get the rest, from the creek to where the church used to be.

He referred us to an attorney specializing in real estate, and it took her nine months to satisfy all thirty-six of the title insurance company's requirements before they would issue the policy. Finally, in February of 2010, we sailed back to Siguaterra and closed on the property. We tied *Mariposa* up to the dock, thinking how great it would be to have her available for short cruises during our winter stays on the island. We could easily take her back to the San Juan River for the hurricane seasons.

Soon after we moved to our new home, we had a problem to resolve with a neighbor. This fellow owned the land that the dock connected to, and although there was an existing easement to cross it, he claimed the easement had been rendered invalid when the property changed hands. He did offer to let us cross his land if we paid him an annual fee of $1,000. To emphasize his point, he had a stone wall built blocking access to the easement.

We went back to our attorney, and she told us our easement was valid because it was included in the deed to the property. What our neighbor had done was illegal, and on our attorney's advice, we filed a complaint with the police. We had to use our own car to bring investigators out to see the wall, and we also provided them with a copy of the deed. After reviewing the evidence they had collected with the town attorney, the chief issued a citation to our neighbor, ordering him to remove the wall. But this fellow had lived and done business on Siguaterra for forty years, selling the large tracts of land he had inherited from his father. He knew how to work the system of payoffs and was able to repeatedly delay compliance with the citation.

In the middle of all this, Jack accepted our invitation and came for a visit. One evening, as we were sitting on the deck having sundowners, we told him about our mounting frustration with getting the easement issue resolved. What had appeared to be a straightforward matter was becoming emotionally upsetting as our neighbor thwarted us at every turn.

Jack said that after twenty years of living in Central America, he knew how to work the system too and offered his help. He said he had an old business colleague and friend who was now a high-ranking officer in the Nicaraguan military. This man could get around the corrupt and ineffectual bureaucracy, and Jack said he could contact him on our behalf. We told him we would be very appreciative.

A few weeks later, Jack called and asked if there had been any progress in resolving our issue. I told him there hadn't been, and he said he would give his friend the go-ahead. He asked for some information about my neighbor — his name, where he lived, his office address, and personal and business phone numbers. I assumed Jack was going to ask his well-connected friend to contact the man and try to persuade him to cooperate.

Two more weeks passed, and Jack checked in one more time. He assured me the matter would soon be resolved: either my neighbor removed the stone wall blocking my easement or he himself would be removed. My name would not be mentioned, and whatever action was taken would be done anonymously. It wasn't until that moment that it dawned on me Jack's friend was prepared to do more than just pressure my neighbor to comply with the citation. He was going to have him killed.

Incredulous, I told Jack that this was a real-estate dispute, not something I wanted a man murdered over. He said he was disappointed that I hadn't realized earlier what was being contemplated, but would contact his friend immediately. He said it was going to be a difficult conversation because he had worked with this fellow before and the wheels were already in motion. Fortunately, Jack reached him in time and my oblivious neighbor was spared.

Susie and I talked a lot about what had almost happened. What kind of person had we befriended, we wondered, willing and capable of arranging a killing? Had I not stopped it, I would have had it on my conscience for the rest of my life. I told Susie that my first instinct would have been be to talk with Rev. Mary, the senior pastor of our church in Maine. But would that have absolved me of my guilt? And what if Jack was mistaken about the man's death not being traceable to me? Nicaraguan prison is no place for a gringo, and although bribery to get people released was common, how much would it cost for a capital offense? Regardless, Susie's and my life would have been unalterably damaged.

On the other hand, we had to admit that it was perversely comforting to have Jack as a friend. And not just any friend, but one willing and able to exact the ultimate retribution should anything serious happen to either of us. We had apparently earned Jack's friendship over the past few years, and based on what he was prepared to do, it was unconditional. How could we reject him in the face of such loyalty?

Jack and I had a lot of conversations about this incident as well, when we took *Mariposa* back to the San Juan River in May. In retrospect, I think this episode encapsulates Jack's life and the code by which he lives. He is a private person, but since he had already revealed such an extraordinary aspect of his personality, apparently he also decided that he could share with me the other details of his sad, strange, and often violent life. I was so astounded by some of the experiences he related, I suggested we collaborate and put them in writing. He took a few days to think about it, then agreed under certain conditions. Given the content and the risks involved, not only to him, but potentially also to me, we would modify names, places, years, events, and any other aspects of his history that could compromise him. He would also have full editorial authority before the fictionalized biography was shown to anyone, even informally. If any monetary gains came from it, we would share them equally.

I agreed with these conditions, and what follows is Jack's remarkable story.

Siguaterra, Nicaragua
June 2014

Childhood

After we made our agreement, I invited Jack to breakfast the following morning at the marina restaurant. He knew the kitchen crew got in at 7:00 and arrived in his skiff at the same time, just as the clouds from a night of heavy rain were breaking up. He motored over to our slip and knocked on the hull.

"Ahoy, *Mariposa!*" he shouted, to make sure I heard him over the rumble of the generator I had running. When I stuck my head out of the companionway, he was already standing in the cockpit. He asked why the gen was on.

"The marina's power was knocked out by the storm last night," I said. "I need to charge up my batteries."

"Can't Susie handle that?" he asked with characteristic bluntness. "I've been up since 5:30. I'm starving."

Susie also stuck her head out the companionway. "Ever the sensitive, guy, Jack. Did it occur to you that I might be hungry too?" Before he could answer, she let him off the hook. "You guys need to talk privately. Go ahead. I'll get a bowl of granola later."

Feeling appropriately chagrined – or at least I was; I'm not so sure about Jack – we walked down the weathered wooden dock toward the restaurant. The sun had come out, and in that yellowy-orange early tropical light, the white hulls of the boats glowed golden. The air was rich with the smells of flowers and damp earth, and the morning chorus of birds surrounded us. A short, wiry fisherman, wrinkled and brown, was on his customary early morning patrol, standing in his cayuco and throwing his twelve-foot-diameter cast net so accurately, it landed right off the transoms of the boats where the fish schooled.

"Is she always like that?" Jack asked.

"Get used to it," I said. "We're going to be spending a lot of time together on this book, and she doesn't think you understand women."

"But I do understand them. When I was married and my wife was being a pain in the ass, I'd go to her dressing table and move everything on it to a different place. Better yet, I'd switch the caps on her lipsticks so the colors wouldn't match the labels. You ever notice that when women put on lipstick, they just check the label and then put it on? They don't look at the color itself, and only realize it's wrong when they see themselves in the mirror."

"Gee, Jack, that really shows great sensitivity and perception. I'll be sure to tell Susie." I knew it was pointless to pursue it further; it would be like trying to explain sound to a deaf person.

The marina's restaurant, bamboo bar, and kitchen were open on three sides, looking up, down, and across the half-mile wide San Juan River. The palm-thatched palapa building was anchored to the shore on one side, but the rest of it was supported by stilts over the water. The floor swayed a bit as we walked across it, looking for a table off to one side of the main dining area where we could be by ourselves.

Cruising sailors are a gregarious bunch, and even at seven in the morning it was entirely possible that a couple of other guys would drag chairs over and want to get into a serious discussion. Anchors were a popular and often contentious subject, because everybody had strongly held opinions about the relative advantages of the different types, based on the fantastic experiences they claimed to be having with their $1200 hooks. These discussions often degenerated into detailed challenges: "Well, *where* in the bay did you drop your hook?" "What kind of *holding ground* did you have?" "How much *scope* did you let out?" (The "dummy" part was always omitted.) Problems with connecting and programming electronics was a good topic too, especially if the equipment had been produced in China. The accompanying one-and-a half-inch-thick instruction manuals might as well have been written in Mandarin for all they help they gave us.

"Let's sit with our backs toward the rest of the restaurant," I said. "I think they'll get the idea."

It worked, but before we could get down to business, breakfast was in order. Jack ate an astounding quantity of food — fried eggs with a spicy green chili sauce, *frijoles refritos,* toasted homemade bread, and a pile of Central American cottage cheese on the side. This he followed with a short stack of pancakes and sausages.

When I asked if he always ate like that, he said, "Look, I won't eat again until dinner, and what the hell, you're paying. There have been times in my life when food wasn't always available. I've learned that when it is, you take advantage of it."

"Remind me not to invite you to breakfast again, okay?" I said as I paid the check. I suspected I'd learn more about the lean times as we got into Jack's life story.

We moved to another table so we wouldn't have to deal with the mountain of dishes, picking one that had been painted with multihued tropical birds, female nudes a la Gauguin, and rain-forest animals. Our view of the river was postcard perfect: a few small huts and uneven wooden docks lined the opposite bank, and the river traffic ranged from fishermen paddling dugouts and tending fish traps to outboard-powered pangas full of schoolchildren—the river version of school buses—and modern thirty- to fifty-foot motor yachts and sailboats. We ordered second cups of dark-roasted Central American highlands coffee, and I pulled out a yellow lined pad so I could take notes about our conversation. I told Jack we could get in maybe two or three interviews like this each week, while Susie and I were readying *Mariposa* to be left at the marina for six months. I estimated she and I had about three weeks of work ahead of us, so we could get a good start on his story before we left.

"So, Jack," I said, "what do you know of your childhood? What's the first memory you have?"

"Well, I know I was born at a Catholic maternity home and orphanage in June of 1945. My father had been killed in the war and my mother—they weren't married—decided to leave me there. She named me after my father, maybe as a remembrance, or maybe to honor his sacrifice. I really don't know. The nuns wouldn't tell us anything about our parents."

"I guess I can understand that," I said, "when I think about how complicated things can get if adopted kids find their biological parents, as they often can in today's world. Back then, everything was kept under wraps. But anyway, what's the first thing you remember from that time?"

"The Looky Loo," he said, and looked at me as if I should understand what that meant. I didn't, so he explained that it was a common term in orphanages. Almost every Saturday morning, prospective parents were invited to come to the orphanage and meet the children. The nuns preselected the kids whose physical appearances most closely matched that week's prospects, knowing that it improved the likelihood of an eventual adoption. They dressed the children up so they would look their best and cutest, and put them together in a large playroom. Once they were engaged with — or fighting over — the toys that had been strewn about, the prospects were brought in. They would observe and mingle with the kids, sometimes sitting on the floor to get involved in their games and have closer contact. At the end of the session, the prospects would inform the nuns if they had found a child they would like to take home for the rest of the weekend. Jack said that even at age three or four, the kids not chosen felt rejected and inadequate, although they couldn't have articulated their feelings. For the older children, it was especially dispiriting, since they had "failed" so many Looky Loos. Everybody came to the events anxiously hopeful, but most had to go back to their rooms dejected. Some cried, and many wet their beds those nights.

This story touched me. My father had been orphaned at age three and must have gone through many of these same rejections. He hardly ever talked about his experiences at the orphanage, but did say that a lack of protein in the diet caused him to develop rickets. His legs were bowed as a result, and he stood only five foot five. He was proud to tell me, though, that he ran away at age eleven in 1917 ("I went over the wall," were his exact words, implying an escape from prison) and had made it on his own ever since.

I also considered my own first memory: as a toddler reaching up and putting my hand on a hot stove. I wondered if most people's first memories were of a sad or painful nature like Jack's, my father's, and mine. In any case, what I found remarkable about Jack's recollection was its thoroughness. This became a hallmark of his stories, and whenever I asked him for clarification or details, he was always able to provide them.

I asked him how many Looky Loos he went through, but he couldn't remember. He did say that even if he was chosen for a weekend visit, it was only the first step in a lengthy process. Sometimes he was returned to the orphanage and learned that the prospective parents didn't care for him, an outcome even more devastating than failing the Looky Loo. Even if the weekend went well, the final phase in the process was a three- to six-month trial period living with the prospective parents, during which time they could decide whether or not to proceed with the adoption. My father had never been adopted. What impact had that had on him?

Jack was legally adopted in 1949 when he was four, but the household he moved into was not the same one he had gone to for his trial period. During the time the adoption paperwork was being completed, his adoptive mother's mother had fallen and broken her hip. His new grandfather was not capable of moving his overweight wife between bed, chair, toilet, and bathtub, so Jack's parents had moved into the grandparents' house. He recalls the atmosphere as being tense, not only from the stress of caring for the injured grandmother, but also the negative attitude the grandfather had about the adoption. He had wanted his daughter to have her own child and took an active dislike to Jack. The old man seemed to look for opportunities to demonstrate his rejection by being deliberately mean.

"I brought a toy with me from the orphanage," Jack told me, "a little rubber dog that squeaked when I squeezed it. A black guy who worked as a janitor there gave it to me. He let me ride on his floor polisher, and whenever I made the dog squeak, he changed the direction he was sweeping. It was great to feel I had some control over an adult, and I really loved that toy. I even named it—Poochie. Dad didn't like it, though. He told my mother that the toy wasn't good for me and that I had to grow up. He took Poochie away and threw it into the fireplace. Can you believe a grown-up would do something like that to a scared little kid? What a miserable bastard. My grandpa was no better. He didn't like the present my parents got me for Christmas. It was a green wind-up car, and I remember running it up and down the upstairs hallway that went by the bedrooms. After a while, Grandpa got sick of it, came out of his room, and crushed the car with his foot."

I didn't know what to say except, "My God, that's terrible. He destroyed your Christmas gift."

"It gets worse," Jack said, and told me about the time he sneaked into his grandfather's wood shop. Every day after breakfast, the old man went into the basement and slammed the door. It was clear he did not want to be disturbed, but Jack said he was intrigued by the sounds of sawing and hammering and the smells of fresh-cut wood, glue, and paint. He wanted to know what Grandpa was doing in there. He waited until a day when Grandpa was out of the house and went down to have a look. What he found fascinated him: a vast array of tools, benches, vises and clamps, drill presses and wood lathes, and shelves filled with brushes and cans of paint and stain. He could only imagine how these things were used to produce the pieces of furniture that ultimately came out of the shop.

He pestered his parents to intercede with Grandpa to let him watch the work — he was too afraid to approach him directly — but they refused and told him not to disturb the old man. "I tried all of a kid's tricks. Complaining, whining, incessant protests, all to no avail. I finally realized that I had to do this on my own, so I waited until Grandpa took one of his frequent bathroom breaks and slipped into the shop. I hid under one of the benches in the back of the room, away from all the ongoing projects."

This trick worked for a while. The bathroom breaks enabled

Jack to sneak in and out, and Grandpa was so focused on his work that he never looked around the shop. Then a sawdust-generated sneeze betrayed Jack's presence. Grandpa swore and threw a piece of wood as Jack ran for the door, and another chunk hit him on the shoulder as he fumbled with the doorknob. He got out and up the basement stairs ahead of Grandpa and ran calling for his mother. He believed the old man was capable of violence, and he was scared. Grandpa came after him, and Jack got behind his mother, hoping she would protect him. Grandpa drew up short, but in a cold and measured tone, he said, "If that little *scheisskopf* comes into my shop again, I will cut off his legs with a handsaw."

Jack remembers this graphic and terrifying threat to this day. To a kid, it was real, and I could only imagine what my feelings would have been. No one, particularly in a parental or official role, had ever said anything like that to me as I was growing up. Kids commonly make gruesome threats to each other, but an adult? I was incredulous.

His mother put Jack in his room for the rest of the day, as much to protect him from her father as to punish him for having disobeyed her. But Jack was so scared of what his grandfather would do the next time he saw him, he climbed out the window and took off down the street. A neighbor, seeing a child running alone, intercepted him and asked what was wrong. He told her in halting, tearful bursts what Grandpa had threatened to do, and his fear was palpable. The woman assured him he would be safe with her and coaxed him into her house so he could calm down. Once he stopped crying, she gave him some ice cream and called his mother, who verified the threat. It was all she could do to get him to come home, and she hurried him back to his room and later gave him dinner there. Another confrontation with her father had to be avoided.

As Jack related these incidents, the only emotion I saw in him was anger. But the events disturbed me, not only because of the psychological cruelties that were inflicted on him, but also because of the matter-of-fact way he talked about them. I had heard interviews with people who had been physically tortured and been amazed by a similar lack of emotion. I wondered how they, and apparently Jack, had been able to put their horrific experiences into perspective. And while he seemed ready to go on with the narrative, I needed a break.

"Why don't we stop at this point?" I suggested. "We've covered a lot of ground, and I need to pull my notes together."

The truth was that I needed time to process what I had just heard, and think about how I was going to structure what I now realized was a major project. It was apparent that after his initial hesitation, Jack had warmed up to the idea of having his life's story told. I would have been flattered too if somebody had found mine so interesting that they felt compelled to write it. And being an engineer, Jack was obsessed with getting every detail right. I wondered what I had gotten myself into.

When I got back to *Mariposa*, Susie wanted to know how it went. I summarized the conversation, and as a mother she said she was disturbed as well by the events of Jack's early life. We had raised two boys, and while neither suffered anything like the trauma Jack had gone through, they had "acted out" (as the school psychologists say) when they were processing sad or difficult experiences. Susie and I lost a baby girl within hours of birth from a chromosomal anomaly, and each boy reacted in his own strange way. T. J. pierced his ear, started smoking, and punched his hand through a window at school. Six stitches. Casey rented a bolt cutter from the hardware store and went out on a bridge over the Ohio River. He cut the chain locking down a hatch leading to the lower level of the bridge, sat on the edge of an I-beam, and started waving to the passing boat traffic. One of the commercial boat captains saw him and radioed the police. We picked him up at the station. So we wondered how Jack had acted out as a result of his mistreatment. I had the feeling it hadn't been good.

We agreed to meet again two days later, but I'd told Jack I wasn't going to be suckered into another gourmand's breakfast, and he should come over to the marina midmorning. We went straight back to the Gauguin table, safe from interruptions since all the other cruisers were now fully engaged in their own preparations for closing up their boats. They wouldn't break for beers until noon, so we had a two- hour window to pick up where we had left off.

Jack explained that the handsaw threat finally convinced his mother that they had to get out of her parents' house. His father, who had never seen the need to stand up for Jack in the family conflicts, gave in to his wife's insistence. They could leave now because Grandma was again mobile, and Jack's father had been able to use his degree in pharmacology to land a well-paying job as a detail man for Hoffmann-LaRoche. He bought a modest house for them in Wichita and used it as a base for servicing the company's Oklahoma territory. Jack remembers the relief he felt when they moved. Not only did he escape his terrifying grandfather, but the tension between his parents also greatly diminished. Within a few months, his mother was pregnant; a year later, Jack had a baby sister, whom they named June. Meanwhile, his father had saved enough working for the drug company that he bought a pharmacy in town.

The money had come, Jack learned later, from the prescription drug samples Hoffmann-LaRoche gave his father to use as promotional items. There were a lot of samples, because his father's territory was the whole state of Oklahoma. Jack still remembers a truck pulling up to the house once a month to off-load cartons of the samples. They were intended for the doctors his father called on. But he didn't hand out everything he had been given, skimming off as many as half of them. He put the pills in bottles he got from pharmacies, and when he had a full course of the prescriptions doctors typically wrote, he sold them to the pharmacies for a lot less than the drug wholesalers charged. This was a common practice at the time among the detail men who represented competing drug companies like Hoffmann-LaRoche, Lilly, Upjohn, and Merck. The men had their own informal fraternity and communicated constantly. If one of them needed, say, six more pills to make up a full course of a given prescription, he'd get it from a "competitor." The man thus supplied would do the same for others in the fraternity, and so over time, everyone was a winner. The pharmacies loved it too. Not only were they assured of the supplies they needed, they also pocketed the difference between the normal price for the drug and the reduced amount they paid.

A special occasion for Jack was accompanying his mother when she brought dinner for his father on the nights the pharmacy stayed open late. She dropped it off in the early evening, and Jack was allowed to stay at the store until the eight o'clock closing. This gave him the opportunity to look at the myriad items lining the shelves, the uses of which — especially those with pictures of women on them — often eluded him. Just what were Norforms, he wondered, and how did they solve "your most intimate marriage problem"? What *was* a woman's most intimate marriage problem? What did *intimate* mean? He also overheard the conversations his father had while waiting on customers or talking on the phone with doctors. He asked for explanations for the words he didn't understand, and sometimes his father would take the time to tell him. As a result, Jack's vocabulary grew beyond that of a normal preschooler.

"I didn't like the guy," Jack said, "and I think the feeling was mutual. But I did learn a lot of new words from him."

This tranquil phase of his life did not last long. The next disruption occurred when Jack started kindergarten at a nearby parochial school. His parents were "nominally Catholic," he said, and his father's income made the modest tuition affordable. "I could have gone to public school, but everybody knew the Catholic schools provided a better education."

I knew he was right, especially in small southern towns in 1950, but I wondered if Jack's rough early-life experiences would impede his adapting to a school environment. How would he handle the normal give and take of childhood play?

The triggering incident occurred after three months. "I was playing in the sandbox, and another kid threw a handful of sand at me. I went ballistic. I filled a tin bucket with sand and hit the kid over the head with it. He ran into the building with blood pouring down the side of his face. I was hauled into the principal's office, and she called my mother to come get me."

She reminded Jack's mother that Jack had had problems before, but this was a lot more serious. He had really hurt the other child. She told Jack's mother not to bring him back, and that he should get some counseling so he could learn to control his anger.

"I don't remember much about the counseling sessions," Jack said, "but I do know the therapist told my father to make more 'quality time' for me, and suggested we go camping together. I had never gone camping before, so when he agreed, I was pretty excited. But I was scared too, because I knew I'd be spending a lot of time alone with a guy who hadn't really been much involved in my life. I didn't know what to expect."

Jack and his father—guided by his mother—shared in

acquiring and assembling all the camping paraphernalia and then packing the bedding, clothes, and food. It was one of the few times he remembers having the feeling of family, everyone working toward a common goal. On a Saturday morning, they loaded up the car and drove to a state-run campground in the woods a couple of hours distant. The campsite consisted of twenty or so dirt plots, each one with a ring of bricks to contain a fire. There was a grill that could be placed on top of the bricks for cooking. The sites were spaced far enough apart to give the campers some privacy, and tents had been pitched on about half of them. The campground had been built with the common bathroom facilities centrally located, but Jack's tent was on the periphery, so it would be a bit of a walk to reach them. Not a problem in good weather, but just as he and his father had finished pitching their tent and setting up two cots inside, it started to rain.

It rained all day, and all of the campers stayed hunkered down on their sites. With no break in the forecast, most gave up and went home on Saturday night, adding to the bleakness of the place. It was impossible to get a fire lighted, and Jack and his father were reduced to opening cans and eating cold food. By Sunday morning, his father had reached the end of his patience with the miserable conditions and a bored, complaining child. Jack remembers his father shouting at him, "This is your fault. They told me I *had* to take you!" and throwing their gear into boxes and suitcases. Jack cut his hand falling on a broken bottle as they were rushing back to the car in a downpour.

"He wouldn't take me to the doctor, though. I think he was too cheap. He just wrapped my hand in a towel and drove back home. Then he sat on me and picked the glass splinters out with tweezers."

I formed an image of this in my mind, and it made me so

uncomfortable that I twisted in my chair. Again, I was reminded of my own father and how he reacted viscerally whenever he heard or read about a child being physically abused. He literally could not stand it, and would shut off the radio or TV, or throw the newspaper he had been reading on the floor. As a kid, I thought his reactions were oddly strong, but that was just the way he was. Now, hearing Jack's story and knowing of his early years in the orphanage, I put two and two together. My father had been abused as well.

"Where was your mother when this was happening?" I asked. "Why didn't she stop him and take you to the doctor?"

"She really couldn't tell him anything. He never hit her, so far as I know, but she was intimidated anyway. But I survived." He said this with the same dispassion he had evidenced in our first interview, but did show me the two inch scar on the meaty part of his right hand under his pinky.

Therapy or not, they still had to get Jack back in school. Fortunately, there was another parochial school on the other side of town, and the sisters running it had more experience with kids like him. The principal told them, "There are no sandboxes here, and we can help your son learn to control himself." It looked promising.

Jack finished kindergarten at the new school with only minor incidents, but he became more disruptive in first grade. He began speaking out in class, and one day would not be quiet even after repeated warnings. His teacher, a lean, stern, thin-lipped older nun in full coif and habit, administered the classic Catholic school punishment of rapping Jack's knuckles with a ruler. She first hit him with the flat side, and when that did not produce the desired apology, she turned the ruler metal edge down. After another smart smack that raised a bloody welt, she asked him what he had to say for himself.

"I said to her, 'Nothing, you black-robed bitch!' I really didn't know what that meant, but I knew it was a bad word. I didn't care. I was just mad that she made my knuckles bleed."

Jack remembered another trip to the principal's office and his mother coming to get him. He got thrown out of that school too. I saw an ominous pattern of anger, defiance, and violence emerging in Jack's behavior, and could only guess what other incidents he would relate as his story progressed.

"We've been at this for over two hours," I said, "and I need to hit the head (sailor talk for go to the bathroom). Then we can take a walk through the marina and see who's around. You might even scare up some new business for your shop."

We did run into several sailors and chatted casually with them about their projects, including a stainless-steel welding job one of them needed Jack for. Then, as if by some prearranged signal, everybody knew it was noon and descended on the bar. Ice-cold beers were served up by Lydia, a shapely, petite, and demure girl of Indian and Spanish heritage with high cheekbones, shining brown eyes, and jet-black hair that fell around her face in ringlets. She was everybody's secret fantasy. When she placed a beer in front of a customer, she invariably lowered her eyes, tilted her head to one side, and quietly asked, *"Algo mas?"* in a way that suggested she might mean something more than just a drink.

After a couple of rounds of sharing frustrations about dropping tools into the water, boat parts being held hostage by customs officials, and bilge pumps that ran intermittently, constantly, or not at all, we shared the observation that most people think the cruising lifestyle is romantic: sailing one's boat over gently rolling, foam-flecked seas to secure anchorages in exotic locations and spending leisurely afternoons in the cockpit sipping piña coladas. The reality is different. "It's a boat" is what sailors say, meaning that they are philosophical about something always breaking, requiring maintenance, or needing improvement. Some of the work is pleasant and rewarding, like being in the open air sanding and varnishing brightwork. Yes, it's being done under the tropical sun, but far better than having one's head down in the bilge groping through the opaque, smelly, oil-slicked water for a loose pump connection. Work at the masthead is nice too, because the view is great. But it can be tricky when a big powerboat goes by and its wake sets you swinging through the air in alarming arcs. But compared to removing the discharge hose from the head and flogging it against the side of the boat to dislodge the accumulated toilet sludge, it's a dream. Jack says that's why he doesn't work on boats anymore. You want something fixed, you bring it to him.

One fellow told us that he was rewiring his whole boat, a fifty-footer of French construction. The savvy sailors rolled their eyes, knowing how quirky, if not bizarre, Gallic wiring could be. We knew this job would require the combined skills of an electrician and a contortionist, coupled with the patience of a saint. Bill was a retired financial consultant who had made a lot of money managing the investments of millionaires. Why didn't he just hire someone to do this hot, tedious, frustrating, and time-consuming project?

"Can't trust 'em," he said. "And I need to know where the wires lead, because sure as hell something will come disconnected on an overnight passage in six-foot seas."

This drew knowing nods of commiseration, and to change the subject we asked him where he thought the markets were headed. We were really asking him for tips, but he was used to that, sort of like doctors getting hit up for free medical advice. He talked about a couple of technical start-ups he had investigated and put some of his own money in. Some of us bought the stock, but Jack didn't. He was still kicking himself around the block a year later.

Two beers into the conversation, the women started to show up for lunch. It was clear Jack and I weren't going to make any more progress on the story that day, and Susie and I needed to get on with decommissioning *Mariposa*. Jack said he had a project near completion in his shop anyway, and he wanted to get paid. We agreed to reconvene the next morning.

Military School

Things were a little chaotic on the river that morning. The electricity on the dock was out again, which was not surprising given what had happened. At about 2:30 in the morning, I was roused from a sound sleep by an unfamiliar motion of the boat. Sailors get to know their vessels intimately, becoming sensitive to deteriorating varnish, loose stays, gaps in deck planking, and anything else that "just doesn't look right." We know how they smell faintly of diesel and mildew after being closed up for months in a marina; the sounds of the engine starting up or the toilet macerator pumping; the feel of the boat as she pauses at the crest of a large wave before deciding whether to plunge to port or starboard down into the trough; and how she rides at anchor or tied to a dock or mooring ball. So I was accustomed to how *Mariposa* rocked in the marina when a passing powerboat threw a big wake, and I didn't react when the first wave hit. But then she rose up several feet and drove back, straining the forward dock lines, which creaked and groaned on the pilings.

I was up as if I'd been launched from a cannon. I was in the cockpit within seconds, with Susie right behind me. It had to be a huge powerboat moving at speed to create that much motion.

But there were no vessels on the river, and no explanation for the low roar I now heard. Then the next big swell hit and lifted *Mariposa* four feet and again thrust her back. These were not any ordinary waves. They stayed high far too long, and when they moved on toward the shore twenty feet behind us, they seemed to suck all the water out from under the boat. *Mariposa*'s keel bumped bottom and she started to heel over, but the water bounced off the shore and came back to lift her upright again. This happened repeatedly until the waves were smaller, and finally there was absolute silence and calm.

As our adrenaline subsided, Susie and I speculated about what could have caused these strange conditions. I checked the lines and cleats to make sure nothing had broken or pulled loose, and the only thing I could come up with was an earthquake generating a minitsunami in the river, as improbable as that seemed. But in the morning, we learned that an earthquake on the sea floor twenty miles offshore had indeed been reported. Still, those waves couldn't have made it all the way up a twisting river, so they must have been generated by shifts in the crust beneath it.

The restaurant was abuzz that morning with sailors comparing notes about the phenomenon and describing how it had affected them. Some boats and docks had sustained minor damage, but nobody was hurt. After people started repeating the same stories only using different words, I said, "We've beat this one to death. I have to get the instruments off the masthead before it gets too hot." The informal meeting adjourned, and everyone went back to their boat projects.

Hurricanes in the Caribbean often come with violent thunder and lightning, and a sailboat mast sticking sixty feet into the air is an obvious target. One strike can cause thousands of dollars in damage, as the lightning runs down the mast, courses through everything electrical on board, and sometimes even blows a hole in the hull — often below the waterline, so the boat fills up with water — as it seeks to ground itself in the river bottom.

The solution, although this can be another subject of heated discussion (if not derision), is to fasten a lightning arrestor at the masthead. This piece of equipment looks like an oversized circular makeup brush, with metal filaments flaring up into the air from the end of a rod. The filaments are supposed to dissipate the lightning bolt so it doesn't come down the mast. Maybe it works, maybe it doesn't, but if a forty-dollar do-hickey may mean lightning hitting someone else's mast, it's worth the cost and effort to put it up.

I had to go up the mast anyway to take all the other stuff *down*. The masthead of a cruising sailboat is festooned with gear: tricolor running lights, an anchor light, a radio antenna, a wind-speed instrument, and an apparent wind indicator. All of them had been exposed to the elements for months, and I never knew what I would find when I got up there. Typical discoveries were seabird guano coating everything, a nest of bees, galled fasteners, seized threads, and heads sheared off bolts.

Getting up a sailboat mast has to be done carefully, and cruising sailors have worked out their own safety protocols. Ours involves a bosun's chair, a stout, rectangular board on which I sit, with lines running from all four corners to a stainless steel ring positioned in front of my chest. This ring is shackled to the halyard normally used to hoist the mainsail. The halyard runs up the aft side of the mast, over the sheave at the masthead, back down to deck level, and is led to the cockpit. There Susie wraps it three times — no more, no less — around a winch from which she can lead the line to a cleat. We are fortunate to have electric winches, so Susie doesn't have to crank it by hand — hard work even given the mechanical advantage of a winch.

Once I have the board positioned securely under my backside so I don't slide off, I give Susie a thumb's up two or three times, and she pushes the button activating the winch. As it hauls me up the mast, she maintains constant tension on the line tailing off the winch. She never takes her eyes off the winch, because a slipup here could mean me plunging to the deck. My life is literally in her hands.

The halyard is marked at the point where it should be stopped when I get to the masthead. When she sees the mark coming closer to the winch, she stops my ascent, cleats the line, and looks up at me. I give her as many thumb's ups as I need additional feet to position myself for the removal of the masthead instruments and to attach the lightning arrestor. I snap one end of my safety harness into the ring of the chair, wrap the strap around the mast, and snap the other end to the ring. I am now secured even if the halyard slips.

The view from sixty feet up is spectacular and completely different from what everything looks like at water level. I can see miles up and down the river, starting with a colonial fort guarding the entrance to Lake Nicaragua, where the Spaniards had stolen the Indians' silver and enslaved them in the mines. In the other direction I have a bird's eye view of the town and the marinas dotting the banks. Beat-up fishing boats are headed to the town dock to off-load their night's catch, men are paddling their cayucos along the shorelines, and pleasure craft of both power and sail are heading for their next adventure. I dismiss the stares of the tourists in the pangas passing below, who must be wondering: *What is that idiot doing up there, flailing around at the top of that mast?* For my part, I feel superior and smug, thinking: *You people have no idea what it's like to be the master of your own boat, knowing how to take care of her, knowing she will take care of us in return, and sailing confidently to places you will never see.*

Using a separate masthead halyard, Susie hoists a bucket to me, filled with every tool I could imagine needing up there. Inevitably, one has been left below in the shop. So, lower the bucket, retrieve the tool, put it in, hoist the bucket back up. Once I have all my tools, I remove or install the gear with one hand. A time-honored sailor's maxim is "One hand for the boat, one hand for you" when working on the mast, and I try to observe it. Everything takes twice as long as a result, and there is a high likelihood of dropping something down to the deck, where it bounces once and goes straight into the drink. I remind myself that is better than *me* dropping sixty feet to the deck, and I get to work.

With all the instruments off, I load the tools and the instruments into the bucket. Susie lowers it with me guiding the line so it doesn't snag on something and dump the contents onto the deck and into the water. When everything is safely on the deck, she goes back to the cockpit to let me down. This is trickier than going up, because she has to uncleat the halyard, take one wrap off the winch, and then let just enough tension off the two remaining wraps so it slips slowly around the winch in the reverse direction, lowering the bosun's chair. This is again the moment when I realize the importance of always treating Susie with honor and respect. She doesn't take her eyes off the winch during this maneuver either until the line goes slack, indicating that I'm standing on the deck. As I free myself of the confines of the safety harness and chair, Susie goes below to the galley. When I get back to the cockpit, she has a cold beer waiting for me, even though it's ten o'clock in the morning. Can't ask for a better crew than that.

I waited around for Jack, enjoying the satisfaction of completing an important task (and the beer). The sun had burned off the morning haze and the wind hadn't come up yet, so it was too hot to work outside anymore. I was looking forward to our next conversation in the shade of the restaurant. He showed up late, explaining that his skiff had been pushed so far up the bank by the minitsunami, he needed two more guys to push it back into the water. We settled back down over coffee at the Gauguin table for the interview.

"So what happened after you were thrown out of school the second time?" I asked. "What did the therapist have to say this time?"

Jack explained that the psychologist began digging deeper into the family's domestic life, looking for clues about the aggressiveness and disrespect Jack had demonstrated. He was reluctant to talk about it with the therapist, and when asked why he had hit the kid with a pail full of sand or insulted the nun, he just mumbled, "I don't know." "I was only six years old," he told me. "I didn't have words to describe how I was feeling. All I could say was that I was mad at them."

Things came to a head when Jack showed up for a therapy session with his father and a bruise on his face. The psychologist asked him what had happened, but he refused to answer. After an awkward silence, his father said, "He just fell off his bike, that's all."

"Any other places you got hurt?" the doctor asked. "Didn't you try to break your fall with your hand, or scrape your knee on the way down?"

Looking at his shoes, Jack only said, "No, I just fell."

"I didn't tell him," Jack said to me, "that at dinner the night before, my father had reached across the table and smacked me in the face. I have no idea why, but it knocked me off my chair."

He now realizes that the therapist had seen and heard these things before, and concluded that Jack was in an abusive environment, with a father who hit him and a mother too scared to do anything about it. He thinks the doctor decided it would be best if he didn't live with his parents, but rather than have him removed and put in foster care, he made it palatable by suggesting that they consider a military boarding school. He said he knew of one in a small farming community 150 miles away that had experience in cases like Jack's. Having run out of parochial school options, and fearful that a public school would be even less able to handle him, Jack's parents accepted the psychologist's recommendation and enrolled him in Pershing Military Academy. He started second grade there, at age seven.

Jack didn't know how to feel. He was attached to his mother and knew that she loved him, but they were both afraid of his father's capricious violence. Even so, he couldn't imagine being separated from the only family he had ever known. Was the new school going to be like the orphanage? Were there soldiers? Would he have his own room?

"I just had to accept it," he told me. "I mean, I was a scared little kid being told what to do by grown-ups. I had no say in the matter."

Founded by a retired army major whose family owned land in the community, the academy was located outside the town, bordered on three sides by woods and farms, and across a river that was no longer used for shipping agricultural products. On the far side of the river was a wooded rise that had been cleared at the top for a public golf course. The town center was a few miles beyond the golf course.

The school itself was self-contained. There were four red-brick two-story classroom buildings, two barracks divided by age groups, a common mess hall/kitchen, athletic fields, and the inevitable parade ground. The instructors and administrative personnel lived on campus, their white clapboard New England-style houses contrasting with the institutional-looking classrooms and offices. A split-rail fence ran along the perimeter of the property, four rails high, the rails eighteen inches apart. Gates through the fence opened onto the one road leading up to the school or onto footpaths into the woods and farms. It was a bucolic setting in which military-school discipline could be maintained without distractions.

Jack turned out to be a handful even for the former military and law-enforcement personnel who ran the school. He continued to act out his aggression against what up to that point had been a life of rejection and abuse. He spoke out in class and refused to accept rules for which no satisfactory explanations could be given. After only two months, the commandant of the school, Major Hill, called Jack's father and told him to come out to the school. When he arrived the next day, the commandant summoned Jack to his office. Hill, who after his military career had been the supervisor of the guards at a federal prison, was a huge-handed man whom the students had nicknamed "turd fingers." Thick-necked and bullet-headed, he had a tremendous ego and a compulsive need to be in control of everything and everyone at the academy. He considered the students inmates and treated them as such.

Hill also ordered Captain Marten, the chief disciplinarian at the school, to be present at the meeting. When everyone was assembled, Hill recounted examples of Jack's lack of self-control and defiance of military-school protocols. Jack's father shook his head in disgust and pronounced him to be "an incorrigible delinquent with no respect for authority." He refused to take him home, saying he had paid tuition, room, and board for the whole school year.

The stalemate was broken when Captain Marten, who was also Jack's English teacher, interceded to give the boy "one more chance" under his direct supervision. To this day, Jack doesn't know what prompted the captain to stand up for him, but it was the first time any adult other than his mother (and she unreliably) had ever done so. Major Hill relented, and thus began the most meaningful and rewarding relationship in the boy's life. Marten took Jack on as a personal project and gradually became his surrogate father during his years at the academy. It was the best thing that ever happened to him, and Jack still considers Captain Marten the best friend he ever had.

From the outset, the captain refused to let Jack slip into self-defeat. When Jack asked him one day how to get the "collar brass" that indicated status in the military, Marten told him, "You follow the rules and get good grades." When Jack said he'd never get it if that were the case, Marten countered, "Sure you will. I'll show you how." He turned it into one of many coaching sessions in which he explained the reasons behind the various regulations and why it was wrong to speak out in class. Jack responded positively to this kind but firm man and began to do better at the academy. Having started his life in an orphanage, he found it relatively easy to accept the structure and rituals of the military environment—once he understood the rationales—and he was grateful to Marten for helping him gain some self-confidence.

There were the usual Thanksgiving, Christmas, and Easter breaks from school for the students to go home and be with their families. When Jack returned for his first Thanksgiving, "Grand Maw" (so named because of her "carnivorous, gaping mouth") was there, and he remembers it only as a miserable time. It was just a prelude to Christmas, however, when his still-hostile grandfather showed up as well. No toys this time, for obvious reasons, just clothes and other utilitarian items. Making it worse, his sister June got the kind of presents the little girl loved. It was no fun for seven-year-old Jack, and from his point of view, being at school was preferable to tolerating, and being tolerated, at home.

Throughout Jack's first year at military school, Marten kept track of his academic progress. He learned from Major Hill, who in addition to being commandant also taught mathematics, that Jack was ahead of his class in arithmetic. As Jack's English teacher, the captain knew he was also good in reading and vocabulary, and now was more careful about the words he used. Oddly, Jack was a catastrophe in spelling. Traditional methods such as flash cards, phonetics, and repetition drills were only sporadically successful. One day he would spell a word correctly, the next day he couldn't.

When Jack told me this, it was a revelation. I had seen his notes when he was designing the dinghy davits for *Mariposa*, and some of the misspellings were so bad that it was hard to keep from laughing. I hadn't known him well enough then to risk embarrassing him over it, but as we got comfortable with each other, it got to be a standing joke between us. Even Susie kids him, though she knows he can't help being dyslexic, and he accepts it good-naturedly. "Send us an e-mail, Jack," she'll tell him. "We need a good laugh." By contrast, Jack's strength in math would prove to be the basis of an interesting and quite unconventional career.

After successfully completing second grade, Jack returned home and his father put him to work in the pharmacy, sweeping floors and carrying boxes of pills and cosmetics to the back of the store. He remembers it as an employer-employee relationship only; there was no emotional warmth. On the plus side, his mother did care for him, even if she was intimidated by his father, and his little sister looked up to him and was fun to be around. Best of all, Grand Maw and Grandpa (especially Grandpa) were blissfully absent. It was an uneventful but ultimately tedious three months, and Jack was happy to get back to school.

But classes could be tedious too when the subject matter wasn't challenging or interesting. There was always the risk that he would become disruptive because of the boredom, but Captain Marten's close supervision helped keep his behavior under control. "I was never bored in arithmetic, though," Jack said. "I liked it so much that I studied lessons in advance. Then I could ask complicated questions that sometimes even stumped the major. It was sort of a payback for his negative attitude toward me. I worked hard at it."

Back home for the following summer, Jack again worked in the pharmacy, doing whatever odd jobs his father assigned him. Home life was pretty routine as well, until the night when he heard June choking in her bedroom. He woke his parents, and his father used the Heimlich maneuver to dislodge a piece of candy the girl had hidden in her room. As June was catching her breath, his father inexplicably turned to Jack and blamed him for the incident. He hit Jack, shouting, "What did you do to your sister? You almost killed her! We should never have brought you home from the orphanage."

Jack was stunned. His quick action had saved June and now he was being punished for it. Incredulous and angry, he vowed to steer clear of his father as much as possible in the future, but had no option other than finishing out the rest of the summer at the pharmacy.

Back at the academy, he told his classmates about his unhappy home life and concocted reasons why he couldn't return there for holidays. He was often successful in getting invitations to spend school breaks with his friends' families, but after a while this wore thin. There were just so many credible excuses he could come up with, and as the invitations became less frequent, Jack spent more and more holidays at the school. Regardless of whether he was visiting with friends or staying in his dorm, arranging to not go home required some ingenuity. Jack had to write to his parents, asking their permission to be elsewhere for the holidays, and if there was no reply after a reasonable amount of time, the school gave Marten the authority to act in loco parentis. Knowing the mistreatment Jack was getting at home, the captain was sympathetic, and also enjoyed having Jack around. The process became so routine — Jack's parents never responded to his letters — that Jack simply ran off the same letter on a mimeograph machine and posted it two weeks before each holiday. It was clear that he didn't want to go home, and just as clear his parents didn't care if he did.

Summer was a different story, though; Jack had to go back. The third year, he worked for his father again, and in addition to the usual odd jobs, he worked at the soda fountain. The regular soda jerk had quit, but rather than paying for a replacement, Jack's father had Jack fill in. Because of this height, he had to stand on upended Coke cases to reach the levers on top of the array of fountains that dispensed the various beverages. But it was a welcome change from sweeping up and stocking shelves, and he got to talk with the customers at eye level.

He could also observe what was going on all over the store, and after a while he noticed the cosmetics manager picking certain items off the shelves and dropping them into her handbag as she left for the night. He watched this for a week to be sure he wasn't mistaken, and then rightly concluded that the woman was shoplifting. Thinking his father would be grateful to know what was going on, he reported what he'd seen. His father's reaction was completely unexpected. He called Jack a liar, told him the cosmetics manager was a trusted employee, and that he should just shut up and do his job. And so Jack did as he was told, but he promised himself he would never work for his father again.

"I didn't even go home for the next two years," he said. "I got permission to stay at the academy for the summers, and they let me attend classes for the dumber kids. I only sat in on things I liked, and it was great. We were finished by noon and there was no marching or required sports. I got way ahead in math." This head start would prove invaluable to Jack's future.

He spent many summer afternoons working at Captain Marten's new house, and during the school year Jack worked off demerits there. From his point of view, it was better than sitting in study hall. On one occasion, the captain had him cut down tall weeds that had grown up all around the property. He got blisters on his hands from swinging the scythe, and when Marten noticed them, he said, "I wish you had told me, I would have given you gloves." Although the work was a form of discipline, it was obvious he cared about Jack. The captain also trained him in construction methods, starting with laying cinder blocks and then advancing to carpentry, plumbing, and even electrical work. It took three years, but by the time they had finished the house, Jack had gained competency in several trades. These skills would prove useful in Jack's adult life as well.

In order to make money, Jack worked at a driving range, walking around in the field in front of the tees collecting the golf balls and dropping them in a bucket for one half cent per ball. When he had enough saved up, he bought himself a single shot .22 rifle, a Stevens Little Scout.

"Wait a minute," I said. "You were, what, eleven or twelve years old and you just walked into a sporting goods store and bought a gun?"

"It wasn't a sporting goods store. They didn't have sporting goods stores in these little farm towns. I bought it in a hardware store." He explained that it was nothing out of the ordinary for a kid his age to buy a firearm at that time in rural Midwestern states. The hardware store owner probably assumed he needed it to help control varmints on the farm.

Jack had another reason for wanting the rifle. Shooting skills were part of the military school curriculum, and although he wasn't yet allowed to participate, he wanted to get ahead of the game. In this activity too, Marten was Jack's mentor, and showed him how to safely handle, fire, and clean the .22. Some afternoons, when the day's work at the house was done, they would go down to the river that bordered one side of the academy's property. Jack developed his marksmanship by firing at an assortment of stationary targets, such as empty tin cans set on posts or different-sized paper plates hanging on strings from tree branches. When he got good at plinking, as this shooting activity is called, the captain had him turn his attention to the rats that were scurrying around the riverbank. At these times, Jack felt closer to the captain than he had ever felt toward another adult male. The two had developed a father and son relationship.

Jack liked having his own money, and having worked in his father's pharmacy, he had learned something about the retail trade. He sensed an opportunity and set up his own informal store at the school. He was thrifty and habitually put away most of the $2.50 weekly allowance the school provided to each student. He added this to the money he had saved from the job at the driving range, and used it to stock the kinds of things he knew the kids wanted. Candy, gum, and cigarettes were always in demand, and he claimed he even supplied beer for the upperclassmen.

"Come on, Jack," I said. "I can't believe that. How in the world did you get beer? You were just a kid. Who would sell it to you?"

Jack told me about Old Sarge, a black man who had lost a leg in World War II and now ran a bait shop by the river. "What do you think it was like trying to make a living as a one-legged nigger in pre-civil-rights Oklahoma?" he asked. "Old Sarge was willing to sell me beer just to make a buck. He put it in a burlap sack and sank it in the minnow tank to keep it cold. I went and got it out after dark and sneaked it back to the barracks."

Jack's operation was like a modern-day convenience store, and he didn't hesitate to charge whatever the traffic would bear. "Five sticks of chewing gum cost me a nickel, and I sold them for double that. Same for candy bars: bought for a nickel, sold for a dime. Cigarettes were even better. Luckies (Lucky Strikes) cost twenty-five cents a pack if I bought a carton, and I could sell them for fifty cents a pack."

Customers were required to pay for their purchases on Wednesdays, he told me, the day they got their allowance. Theft was only a small problem, because the students' code did not tolerate stealing of any kind, and the school provided each kid with a small locker for personal items. Since Jack didn't have anything else of value, he crammed his with merchandise and a strongbox for cash. The little store was the beginning of a long career in entrepreneurship.

"I gambled too," he said, "betting on the rat fights."

"Rat fights? What the hell are rat fights?"

Jack smiled; he knew he had me—again. "We caught the rats in the field. We'd bet on which ones we thought could kill the others and put them two at a time in a shoe box with a screen over the top. But I went them one better. I caught a shrew in the basement and challenged the other guys, betting them that my mouse could take their rats. And it did. Shrews are ferocious and need to eat almost constantly. We'd put the two animals in the shoe box, and the shrew would immediately back itself into a corner. It would huddle there for a while, quivering with energy, and then suddenly shoot across the box and tear up the rat. It worked great for a while, but then the shrew died. They only live about six months after they're fully grown."

After spending two summers at school, Jack did return home for a visit, more out of a desire to see his younger sister than any affection for his parents. There was an unexpected problem, though, when he went to the house and strangers opened the door.

"My parents had moved and hadn't told me. I explained who I was, but the new people didn't know where they had gone. It was pretty awkward."

Not knowing what else to do, Jack went to the office of the Catholic church his parents occasionally attended. They didn't have an address either, but told him to call the Altar Society. The woman who answered gave him the new address. It was equally awkward when Jack showed up, with his mother offering lame excuses about why she hadn't told him — or the academy — about the move. When his father got home, he didn't even try to explain, but told Jack he could stay at the house. He said the only room available was a ten-foot by seven-foot basement closet next to the laundry, which Jack promptly dubbed the Rathole. But it gave him a place to sleep, and he was able to have regular contact with his little sister. June was now a bright six-year-old who reminded him of Shirley Temple with her mop of dark curly hair and inquisitive blue-green eyes. Her home life was acceptable — their father mostly ignored her and wasn't abusive — and Jack enjoyed playing the role of the protective older brother. There was no thought of going back to work at the pharmacy.

Jack was fortunate to find a job caretaking the house and grounds of Dr. Clarence Wilson, their family physician. Dr. Wilson was winding down his practice and needed someone known to him to watch over his property while he and his wife went on an extended European vacation. As part of the deal, and also not to let the car sit idle, Dr. Wilson told Jack he should take his Corvette out for a careful drive from time to time, but just around town.

"Jack, you weren't old enough to drive. Why would the doctor ask you to do that? How did he even know that you knew how to drive a car?"

Jack acknowledged that he was underage for a driver's license, but Oklahoma was a state where special farm-to-market and home-to-school permits were issued starting at age twelve. So seeing a youngster behind the wheel was not unusual, and he had learned to drive when he visited a schoolmate's home over a Christmas holiday.

"Well, Okay," I said. "But how many twelve-year-olds were bombing around in Corvettes?"

He did attract attention. On one of his drives, Jack was spotted and pursued by Officer Wolfe of the town's police department. The chase ended at a railroad crossing. A train was approaching, and not wanting to risk damaging Dr. Wilson's pride and joy, Jack pulled over. The cop was furious because Jack hadn't stopped immediately and accused him of having stolen the car. Jack tried to explain that he was working for the doctor, who had instructed him to drive the car periodically. Wolfe called him a liar, and said he was speeding to try to avoid being caught with a stolen vehicle. He ordered Jack to drive to the police station with him following and hauled him inside to the desk sergeant. When he demanded Jack explain himself, Jack's response was, "Fuck you, I already told you I have Dr. Wilson's permission to drive his car."

Wolfe said, "Well, we're just going to have to hold you until we can verify that. Who are your parents?"

Jack denied having any family he could contact. He knew his

father didn't care where he was, and his mother was helping her aged parents relocate to a retirement home somewhere out of town. She had taken June with her, so Jack was on his own.

Wolfe locked Jack up in a four-by-four foot solitary cell with a three-inch drain in the center to be used as a toilet. "The Hole" was normally used to punish difficult offenders, and inmates wouldn't have contact with anyone for days. The only relief Jack got was when meals were delivered twice a day through a double door at floor level. A guard would open the outer door, place a metal tray down, and close the door. Only then could Jack open the door on his side to retrieve the food, all of it in one mysterious pile in the middle of the tray. No words were exchanged. After a week of this, Officer Wolfe appeared and demanded, "*Now, what have you got to say for yourself?*" Jack's response was again, "Fuck you," and the stalemate continued. I was reminded of the incident with the nun; it was the same pattern of defiance of authority, the same willingness to take the punishment.

Finally, a public health inspector noticed that Jack had been locked up for almost three weeks and demanded that he be charged or immediately released. With really nothing more to go on than a suspicious story by a defiant kid, the police let Jack have a shower and gave him a decent meal. They dropped him off a few blocks from the station, telling him to get lost. Jack, who was a skinny kid to begin with, was emaciated when he was released.

He carefully planned his payback. Making sure he wasn't seen, Jack observed the routes Officer Wolfe typically took on his motor patrols around town. He chose a spot near a derelict four-story apartment building that the cop passed almost every day, and then executed his plan. First, he went to a consignment store and bought a large ladies' handbag. He carried it to the spot he had chosen and waited for Wolfe to show up. As the patrol car approached, Jack dashed out in front of it, clutching the handbag. Wolfe stopped the car and gave chase on foot, doubtless thinking he was about to arrest a purse snatcher. Jack stayed ahead of him, but close enough to be certain he was always in sight. He ran into the apartment building through a door he had left standing open and headed up the stairs. Wolfe followed, shouting at Jack to stop. Jack let the distance between them get shorter so it was a real footrace all the way up to the fourth floor. When he got to the landing, Jack charged down the hallway to the fire door he'd left open, ran through and slammed it behind him. He jumped across the badly rusted fire-escape landing and started down the ladder. Wolfe burst through the door in pursuit, only to find himself standing on disintegrating metal slats. Unable to get a handhold, he fell through and went down all four floors to the ground. He was impaled on a piece of rusty metal that had been dislodged by the fall. Jack climbed back up the ladder, and used the landing's framework to maneuver around the gap and get back to the door. He went down the stairs, left the building, and walked away.

Miraculously, the fall didn't kill the policeman, but it left him with broken bones, internal injuries, and paralyzed from the neck down. He was unable to write or speak, so had no way of communicating to fellow officers what had happened. It was clear he was going to be hospitalized for a long time, and Jack waited a couple of weeks before he went to see the man who had put him in jail. Visiting hours were almost over and most folks had gone home when he asked permission at the nurse's station to go to the cop's room. He went in, approached Wolfe's bed, and stared down at him in silence. Finally, Jack softly said, "Now, what have *you* got to say for *yourself?*" and then walked out of the room.

Wolfe died from complications of his injuries three months

later.

I took a deep breath and tried to gather my thoughts, stunned by what I had just heard. I could buy Jack's explanation about driving the Corvette, but would a policeman, no matter how incensed, really put a twelve-year-old in solitary confinement? I challenged Jack about it.

"Look," he said. "This was small-town Kansas in the fifties. The cops could do pretty much whatever they wanted. There were no civil rights, community relations efforts, or internal review boards like you have today. You would be amazed at the abuses they were able to get away with back then."

"Well, OK," I said. "Maybe I can accept that explanation. I really have no way of knowing. But are you telling me that you actually engineered this cop's death?"

"I didn't know that the fire escape was going to collapse," Jack said. "I just wanted to get back at the guy."

This sounded disingenuous to me, just a little too facile. "I don't buy that. You planned out every detail: Wolfe's route, the handbag, the deserted apartment, the deteriorated fire escape. You deliberately set out to hurt him."

"Yes, I wanted to hurt him, but I didn't intend to kill him. I was a twelve-year-old kid without resources he'd put in solitary and starved and taunted for weeks. There was no way I could let that go. But do I feel bad about the way it turned out? Not really."

I had stopped Jack at the eleventh hour from having a guy killed over the disputed property easement on Siguaterra. I knew his history of violence went back a long time, all the way to the incident with the kid in the sandbox. Now I learned that as a youngster he had exacted the ultimate retribution on a cop, albeit unintentionally. What else was I going to learn about this man's extraordinary — and disturbing — life?

Advanced Pranks

Susie was all ears when I came back to *Mariposa* for lunch, wanting to know what Jack and I had talked about that day. I started by telling her the story about Officer Wolfe arresting him, and she was as incredulous as I had been. In particular, she was skeptical about Jack's three-week absence without his mother getting involved. I told her Jack's excuse, that she had been out of town getting her parents situated in assisted living.

"Yeah," she said, "but that doesn't take three weeks. And a mother wants to know where her kids are."

"Hey, that's what he told me. Maybe she was used to his being away for weeks at a time and didn't think much of it. He was away at school for long stretches, including whole summers, and usually went to friends' houses for holidays. Maybe she was so detached, she didn't care, like when she didn't tell him the family had moved. Maybe she was so intimidated by her husband that she felt powerless. I really have no way of knowing."

Then I told her about how Jack had planned and carried out his payback. "Wow," she said. "You mean he started killing people when he was *twelve*?"

"No, no, you're getting carried away. He didn't set out to kill the guy, he just wanted to get back at him. It was an accident that the cop died."

"Well, just to be on the safe side, let's not piss this guy off. He's been hurt too many times and obviously won't let anyone get away with it. It doesn't seem like he'll let anyone get away with hurting his friends, either. We saw what almost happened to our neighbor."

"Right, and I've never been anything but a straight shooter with Jack. I'm glad he considers us his friends. How about you?"

Susie had to admit that although she was discomfited by Jack's violence (as well as by his apparent obliviousness to all things female), it was good to know he was on our side. We hoped we would never need to call on him.

When Jack and I got back together the next morning, I asked him bluntly, "What did you do for the rest of that summer, after you killed — er, after the cop died?"

He shot me an annoyed look, but shrugged and said, "I kept working at Dr. Wilson's. I never took the Corvette out again, just started it in the garage every week. But that didn't stop me from going out for rides."

"How did you manage that without a car?"

"I didn't have a car, but my father did."

"Yeah, but he wasn't about to let you drive it, right?"

"He never knew about it. I took it out in the middle of the night after he went to bed."

"Okay, tell me," I said, fully expecting another hard-to-believe story.

Jack said having his Rathole in the basement, rather than where the rest of the family slept, gave him his opportunity. He could creep silently up the basement stairs and through the kitchen, where there was a door to the garage. His first challenge was getting the overhead door to open and close without the normal clunking and rattling. He accomplished it by waiting until the house was empty and then heavily greased the door's tracks and joints. He opened and closed it repeatedly until it worked almost soundlessly. Now he just had to wait until everyone else was asleep, raise the garage door, and push the car out and down the street before starting it and going for his ride.

The next challenge was how to get the car back into the garage without being heard. He couldn't drive it in, because the sound of the engine would wake his father. It took some practice, but Jack determined just how far the car would coast with the engine off. He also had to ascertain the decelerating effect of making the ninety-degree turn off the street and into the driveway, but leaving enough momentum to carry the car up into the garage. He took careful measurements of the distances involved, especially between the street and the back of the garage. He practiced the maneuvers repeatedly at a vacant house on the other side of town until he was confident it would work.

It did, and for the rest of the summer, Jack enjoyed a number of midnight drives unbeknownst to his parents. I asked him if he wasn't worried about being caught, since midnight is not exactly the time kids are likely to be driving to school or the farm market. He said the risk was minimal, because there was almost no one out on weeknights in his small town. The residents still adhered to farmers' hours, and even the police stopped their patrols after ten o'clock. His drives were a solitary pleasure, but the exhilaration of getting away with the stunt was reward enough.

When he added that it got boring and he was happy to return to the academy, I realized that what motivated Jack was not just getting back at those who had mistreated him, but doing it in creative ways. It explained why he studied ahead in math to stump the major, why he lured Officer Wolfe into the chase that ended on the fire escape, and why he worked out the details of sneaking his father's car out of and into the garage. The more I learned about Jack, the more I understood why he kept wanting to get the better of those in authority, whether it was school administrators, the police, or even—as I later learned—the federal government. It was a test of his creativity.

When he got back to school that fall, he bought a beat-up 1949 Ford using the money he had saved from his summer jobs. When I asked who would sell a car to a twelve-year-old, he just said that the guy needed the money.

"I understand that," I said, "but what about getting the title and registering the vehicle?"

"You still don't understand how things were in the '50s in rural Kansas. There wasn't the kind of regulation we have now. I didn't care about title or registration, and neither did the guy who sold it to me."

He kept the car in an abandoned salt mine, and when I asked why he needed a car in the first place, he began another of his outrageous stories.

Jack had learned from selling beer to upperclassmen that alcohol was very profitable. Since Oklahoma was "dry" at the time, he saw an opportunity to capitalize on the restriction by making whiskey runs into Arkansas to buy moonshine. He discussed the idea with Old Sarge, who told him how to make contact with the bootleggers he bought from. The one-legged black man gave Jack directions, telling him where to turn off the highway onto a dirt road and how far to proceed before he reached a pickup truck blocking access to an even more rugged track. He would be challenged, Old Sarge said, and he warned Jack to be straightforward. It would be obvious from Jack's age that he wasn't a government agent, and the cash and empty one-gallon Coke syrup bottles he brought along would indicate he was serious.

One moonless night, Jack went down the downspout outside his room and picked up his car at the salt mine. He followed Old Sarge's directions, and an hour and a half later was stopped by the pickup across the road. A gaunt hillbilly with tobacco juice in his beard got out of the truck and approached Jack's Ford, holding a .12 gauge double-barreled shotgun at hip level, pointing it at the open driver's window.

"Wha'choo doin' down here, boy?" the man asked, and spat.

"Old Sarge told me how to find you. I want to buy some 'shine."

"Who's you talkin' 'bout? I don't know no Old Sarge."

"Sure you do. He's the one-legged nigger sometimes comes by here. Look, he told me to bring empty bottles and cash. You want to see? Let me open my trunk."

"Git out real slow and lemme see your hands th' whole time."

Jack did as he was told and showed the man his empty Coke syrup bottles and a roll of bills, realizing he could easily be robbed. But after a few more exchanges, the hillbilly seemed satisfied and moved his pickup to the side of the road.

"Jes' drive down a couple hunnert yards. Park yer car at the wood bridge goes over the crick and walk on down 'til ya sees a fahr. Tell the boys Caleb said it was okay."

Jack had never seen a moonshine still, and what he found, while crude, appeared well thought out. First of all, it was located in a "holler," as the locals called it, a hollow with a creek at the bottom. This meant that not only was there water, but that the smell of wood smoke and the fermenting process was somewhat contained in the windless space. Being Jack, he asked how the process worked, but the backwoodsmen were suspicious. They just filled his bottles from a large tank of the distilled moonshine, took his money, and sent him on his way. After several more visits, though, their apparent leader accepted Jack as who he said he was and showed him the equipment.

The still consisted of a vessel that looked like a hot water heater and had coils of copper spiraling inside it. This was placed over a vat of fermented grain mash. The mash had the consistency of rice pudding and was being slowly boiled over a hickory wood fire. It produced the sweet-sour odor of decaying vegetation, similar to the smell of wet compost. The steam rising from the vat was captured by the flared base of the vessel, and it condensed on the outside of the coils, which were being cooled by creek water. The resulting liquid dripped into a copper kettle that resembled a cement mixer, and which had a second set of copper coils. Another fire burned under this kettle to further purify the first distillate. About three-quarters of the way up the kettle, at the point where the condensate was almost pure alcohol, there was a tap in the coil where the clear liquid was collected. Any that wasn't tapped off was captured by the top of the coil to the base to be reheated and condensed again. The man explained that while boiling and condensing the liquid was a simple process, the trick to getting high-quality "dew" was the intensity of the second fire.

"A little smoke comin' out the tap is whatcha want," he told Jack.

As Jack became a regular customer, the reticent backwoodsmen got comfortable enough with him to share some of their lifestyle. They introduced Jack to the practice of "barking" squirrels for food. The trick was to wait until a squirrel hesitated for a moment in the middle of a stout tree branch and aim a .22 to hit just under the animal. The bullet would splinter the bark beneath it, knocking the squirrel unconscious without damaging any of its flesh. As soon as it hit the ground, the men would quickly decapitate it, explaining that some squirrels recovered fast and ran away with their dinner. The skinned and gutted carcass was then cooked on a spit alongside the fire, not directly over it, so as not to char the meat. Jack said squirrel roasted this way tasted similar to a turkey thigh.

At the end of each run into Arkansas, Jack came back to the salt mine with his gallon bottles filled with moonshine. He poured it all into a clean metal washtub, cut it fifty-fifty with spring water, and added food coloring so it looked like bourbon. He ladled the mixture through a funnel into whiskey bottles he had scavenged from the golf club trash bin. He locked them in the car and left everything in the salt mine until the weekend.

Jack knew from overhearing conversations at the driving range that around 10:00 on Saturday and Sunday mornings, the first round of thirsty golfers would be playing the eighth hole. This was the time when many of the golfers (the men, anyway) would need to relieve themselves of their morning coffee and slip into the woods adjacent to the fairway. During this pause, Jack would walk out onto the green carrying a bottle. He knew club rules only allowed drinking in the clubhouse, so the golfers couldn't carry their own bottles on the course. Jack would make a show of cracking open his "bourbon" as if it were still sealed and offer the men a slug. Inevitably, at least one of the golfers would want more, and Jack would invite the foursome to his refreshment stand in the woods. He had set up a card table and a few folding chairs in a small clearing, everything lightweight and easy to transport. It was good business. He had purchased the moonshine for $1.25 a gallon, cut and colored it, and rebottled it into five fifths that he sold for $3.00. The scheme worked beautifully until 1959, when the state of Oklahoma went from being "dry" to "wet" and the golfers didn't need him anymore.

But the older kids at school liked to drink too, so for the next two winters Jack made what he called Pruno. This was a mildly alcoholic beverage cooked up from canned fruits that Jack stole from the academy's mess-hall pantry. He had figured out how to access the pantry through a storm drain in the basement, and used this route to carry off commercial-sized cans of peaches, pears, apricots, and pineapple. He stockpiled them in an unused storage area until it was time to make some Pruno. The production process consisted of opening the cans, adding yeast and sugar, and then placing the mix on top of a radiator in the dorm basement for several days. Then he ran the fermented liquid through a strainer and into flask-sized bottles that he sold to the upperclassmen. The apricot variety was the most popular, but they all sold well, and Jack's expanded offering made him even more money. At one point, he thought about making his own moonshine from the juice he could collect from the bottom of nearby grain silos, but the still would have been too complicated. Fermented Pruno was much easier to make.

Beer was a regular seller too, but by this time the school authorities had realized from his apparent prosperity that Jack was into a lot more than the candy and chewing gum they had tolerated. And so began a game of cat and mouse, with the goal of intercepting Jack on one of his beer runs. The closest call came one night when Jack was carrying two cases that he had bought from Old Sarge. The veteran had rigged a canvas tarp around the base of the minnow tank, where he regularly left these larger quantities. The challenge was getting the beer across the golf course, over the bridge, and back to the academy, where he stowed it near the trash dumpsters.

Major Baker, one of the commandant's assistants, spotted Jack leaving the campus one evening and seized the opportunity. He positioned himself along the return route and surprised Jack when he was partway across the golf course, out in the open. Jack ran the rest of the way across the course, into the woods, and down to the that ran along the golf course, where he shoved the beer under an overhang on the bank. With Baker behind him, he doubled back to the bridge and ran as fast as he could to his barracks, climbed up the drain pipe, and got in through a second-floor window. He sprinted straight to the bathroom, stripped off everything but his skivvies, got his hair and upper body wet, and arrived back at his room just ahead of his pursuer. When the major burst into the room and demanded to know where Jack had been, he answered, "Well, sir, I just got back from taking a shower." It was another gratifying success at thwarting authority.

During these years and through his experiences at military school, Jack would develop and internalize a personal code of behavior that would guide—or justify—his actions going forward. The cultural environment of the southern Midwest in the 1950s was the context within which his values evolved. Life then was strikingly different from what Jack saw taking place a generation later. For one thing, 90 percent of the people didn't lock their houses or cars. They were also generous. If he was late getting back to school at night, he could go to any farmhouse and ask to sleep in the barn. Half the time, he would be invited to sleep in the house and be given a snack too. Jack didn't abuse this goodwill. If he was out with his .22 and looking for a place to do some plinking, he would ask permission of the landowner and was almost always told to go ahead. "Just don't shoot any of my cows!" If he offered to do an hour's work in exchange for the privilege, he would do it even if the farmer wasn't around. If he opened a gate to get into a field, he closed it; if he found a gate open, he left it open. If he borrowed someone's truck, he returned it with a full tank of gas. Honesty, consideration, and mutual respect were the unspoken watchwords.

Jack also had a clear sense of what was right and wrong that began in his abusive childhood. Grandpa stamping on his toy car was obviously wrong. His father smacking him off his chair at dinner for no apparent reason was too. Later, being locked up in a solitary jail cell for weeks went beyond being simply wrong, and from that he learned the satisfaction of exacting retribution. Now, in his interactions with schoolmates, authority figures, and people in the community, his code evolved. Reasons had to be given before he'd follow a rule, regardless of consequences. Ratting out a fellow student, even if he did not know him, was never acceptable. If staying silent meant assuming a painful position with his knees bent and his back pressed against a wall until his thighs gave out (called "Sitting on a Wall"), so be it. The code would not be broken. Stealing from fellow students or local farmers and shop owners was unacceptable, as these people had individual faces. But it was okay to steal from an amorphous organization, government entity, or major corporation. If money was owed, it had to be paid back promptly. If you borrowed a tool from a farmer, you cleaned it before taking it back. If you accidentally damaged someone's property, you owned up to it and repaired it if you could. Loyalty to friends was absolute. And if you were wronged, payback would be in spades.

Another element of the code was kindness to animals, and Jack and his friends felt strongly that it was wrong to mistreat them. An extreme example of violating this element of the code involved a kid who was found torturing a ground squirrel. Relaxing one afternoon after class, some of the students in Jack's barracks heard surprisingly loud and odd screams coming from the boiler room. When they went down to investigate, they found this boy performing a live dissection of one of the little creatures, its paws thumbtacked to a board. When they challenged him, he tried to shrug it off by claiming it was only an animal and could not really feel pain like people did. Outraged by the kid's cruelty and cavalier attitude, they took away the severely injured squirrel and dispatched it quickly. Then they planned how to impress upon the boy how unacceptable they considered his actions to be.

They knew this kid had a deathly fear of spiders, and decided to use it to teach him a lesson. One evening, they went outside and captured a couple dozen lawn spiders in a jar. Back inside, they emptied one of the large footlockers each student had to store his clothing and personal effects and punched a hole in the top. Then they overpowered the cruel kid, crammed him into the locker, and latched it shut. The jar of spiders was brought in, a piece of cardboard over the top, and overturned over the hole in the locker. When the cardboard was slid out of the way, the spiders dropped through the hole in the locker. The reaction was immediate. The kid began screaming, thrashing wildly, and finally crying. After about twenty minutes, he fell silent. They waited a while longer to be sure he wasn't playing possum, then unlatched the top. What they saw stunned them: the kid was curled in a fetal position, eyes wide open and arms pressed to his chest, fists clenched. His face was contorted in a grimace, and he did not move. They lifted him out of the locker and carried him, still rigid, to his bunk. They were so scared, they put a mirror under his nose to be sure he wasn't dead. When it fogged, they left him there.

The next day, when the kid didn't show up for morning formation, the officer in charge went to his room. He found the boy in bed, still rigid and eyes unblinking. An ambulance was called, and he was taken to the hospital. A month later he returned to the academy, but was so psychologically traumatized that he was unable to function. He was institutionalized, and Jack didn't know if he ever recovered.

Bill Goodwin

Looking back on it, Jack remembered the conversations his friends had in the aftermath of the incident. Some had regrets, but these were tempered by the knowledge that the kid would never hurt another animal. As adults when they talked about it, they recognized what they didn't know at the time: that people who torture animals as children often end up brutalizing humans as adults. The consequences of the boy having broken their code may have been severe, but they rationalized that what they did might have saved others from suffering or being killed.

Another violation of the code involved a kid who tried to cheat Jack by shorting him on purchases and running up debts he did his best not to pay. This kid was not terribly bright, but was a chocolate junkie who ran up a big tab of Baby Ruths, Reese's Cups, and Milk Duds. He was so remiss in paying, Jack finally got tired of waiting and hearing his lame excuses. He made up a batch of what he called Smartenin' Pills and sold them to the gullible kid, telling him they would help his grades. The kid also liked them because they tasted — at first — like chocolate. What he didn't know was that the pills were actually rabbit droppings that Jack had coated with Ex-Lax he had melted on the radiator in his room. When the kid finally figured out what the odd taste and smell were, he told his older brother, also a student at the school. The guy was a senior on the football team and he came after Jack, bursting into his room with the clear intent of beating him up. Having no other escape, Jack dove out his window and landed on a thick juniper bush that cushioned his fall. He ran away before the guy could get down the stairs and out the door to find him. Jack was careful to avoid the boy for a couple of weeks after the prank, giving him a chance to cool down. On reflection, he now thinks it might have been better to take the beating than to spend the next several days picking juniper thorns out of his arms and legs.

There were fun times too. Jack had a rat pack of a dozen or so friends, and they enjoyed some typical boyhood pursuits. After classes ended at noon on Saturdays, the boys often went down to the river to catch catfish. First they threw rocks into the slew to chase away the water moccasins. Once this hazard was cleared, the boys got into the water to go swimming. Later they went to the river to practice *noodling*.

The way a river's current flows around bends causes one side to be shallow and the opposite shore to be undercut, with water about three feet deep. That was where the current flowed fastest, and the catfish lay in holes on the bottom, letting the water flow into their mouths and over their gills. Not only did this allow the fish to breathe without having to move, it also delivered edible bits of debris that were being washed down the river.

In order to catch the fish, the boys walked slowly along the undercut areas, extending their hands below the banks and down into the water. The catfish regularly closed their mouths to swallow or pump more water over their gills, and the kids were able to feel the pressure of the water jetting out. They could even tell the approximate size of the fish by judging the width and strength of the pressure wave. When a boy figured he had zeroed in on one of the desired size, he would wait for the pressure wave to subside — meaning that the fish had reopened its mouth — and thrust a hand into it. This was the trickiest part, because catfish have teeth in both upper and lower jaws. The object was to snag a back inside corner of the mouth, which was soft. The fish swam from its hole, trying to shake the foreign object out of its mouth, and the boy used the momentum to fling the fish up onto the bank. Once they had a dozen or so, they took them back to the mess hall and gave them to the cooks. There was fresh catfish for dinner those nights.

Sometimes, if it was early enough in the day, they cooked the fish themselves. Their method was to decapitate and gut the fish, and then coat them in glutinous, sticky mud from the river bottom. They placed these packages directly on top of a bed of coals from a fire started an hour earlier. More coals were laid on top, and the fish were left to bake for three or four hours. The mud hardened as the water in it steamed off, and the packages had to be broken open to get at the fish inside. The skin—catfish have skin, not scales, Jack pointed out—adhered to the mud, and all the boys had to do was lift out the backbone before digging in to the clean flesh inside.

Jack had been on a roll telling these stories, with me frantically taking notes, and I hadn't wanted to interrupt him. But I finally needed to give my cramped hand a rest and to check on Susie back at the boat. We agreed to get back together in a half hour. As I walked to *Mariposa,* I found myself thinking that hard as some of his stories were to believe, the relaxed and matter-of-fact way he told them was convincing. After I told Susie about the conversation, I added, "You can't make this stuff up. I can't imagine anyone being able to invent story after incredible story like this. Either they're true, or the guy is the most accomplished liar in the world."

"I agree a lot of it sounds far-fetched," she said, "but Jack has lived a completely different life than we have. And why would he lie? What's in it for him?"

"I don't know, but I'm going to challenge him more when he tells me these crazy things. Starting with this noodling business."

Back at the Gauguin table, I said to Jack, "I'm having a hard time believing that story about noodling for catfish. It just sounds preposterous that kids would wade into a river and shove their hands into a fish's mouth to catch it."

"But it's true," he said. "You never lived in rural Oklahoma, so how would you know? People there are still catching catfish the same way, even today. I just read an article describing it in the *Sooner Gazette* because a kid died while doing it. They said he misjudged the size of the fish and screwed up snagging it. His arm went right down its throat, and the fish clamped down before rushing out of its hole, dragging the kid with it. Two miles downstream, they found a sixty-pound catfish caught in a logjam with the boy's arm still lodged in its gills. Both were dead. They even used the word noodling in the article. I'll e-mail it to you when I get back to the shop."

What could I say? Jack had made the story plausible and was ready to prove it. Over the course of our interviews, which took months to complete, I frequently challenged him when his stories seemed illogical or didn't ring true to me. He never failed to verify them with background, detailed explanations, or independent confirmation.

"You found that one about catfish hard to believe?" Jack went on. "Wait 'til I tell you about the annual rattlesnake hunt."

Oh, brother, I thought, but told him to continue.

"Rattlers are valuable. The docs need antivenom to treat snakebites, and the only way to make it is from the rattlers' poison. But to get the poison, you first have to catch the snake. Sometimes it's easy, because if it's out in the open, it will let you know when you're too close. It's an unmistakable sound. Then you have to maneuver around until you can get a forked stick behind its head and hold it to the ground. You pick the snake up with your hand around its neck so it can't bite you. But if you hold a glass with chamois stretched over the top of it near the rattler's head, he will bite down on it. His fangs go through the chamois, and you can see the venom running in two streams down the inside of the glass. Then you throw the snake into a sack. At the end of the day, a lab rep will buy whatever venom you've collected, and local restaurants will buy the snakes. They pay you by how much your sack weighs.

"Sometimes, though, a big snake will start down a hole, and you have to grab him by the tail. You pull him out and swing his body like a whip, and if he's long enough, his head flies off. That's why you want a big snake, so he's long enough for the whip action to work. But you have to run and pick his head up fast, before the venom runs out. Then you can milk it into the glass by squeezing the poison glands."

"You actually did this, right? I mean, it sounds kind of dangerous. Were you ever bitten?"

"Couple of times. Other guys too. But they have a doc out there to give shots of antivenom, so nobody dies. But the bite heals slowly, because the venom is hemotoxic. It attacks the circulatory system, so your arm or wherever you were bitten is discolored and hurts for months."

"That's one hell of a tale, Jack. Does this still go on? Maybe you have another newspaper article you can send me?"

"Well, no. But if you Google 'Okeene Oklahoma rattlesnake hunt,' you can read all about it."

Checking my watch, I told Jack I had another hour before I had to get back to the boat to continue the decommissioning. He offered to tell me a nice story about squirrels, to cancel the earlier grotesque incident involving the live dissection.

"We helped the squirrels get through the winter. They only semihibernate, so they always need to eat. We'd wait until the peanut harvest was over, then go into the fields to collect the ground fall. Those are the nuts that didn't get picked up by the harvesting machinery, and there were typically enough of them to fill three or four big sacks. We kept the nuts warm near the boiler in the barracks basement, and periodically brought smaller quantities up to the TV room. During commercial breaks, we'd grab a handful, go outside to the area where the squirrels' burrows were, throw them on the ground, and stamp our feet. The squirrels learned that when they came up to investigate the vibration, they'd find peanuts."

Another example of kindness to animals happened one spring when two great horned owlets fell from their nest. The boys found them sitting on the ground and chittering for their parents' attention, demanding to be fed. But they realized the owlets wouldn't survive for long down there, so they lined a stout cardboard box with grass and weeds, simulating a nest, and placed the chicks in it. They watched as they grew, first feeding them hamburger mixed with Hoffmann-LaRoche's Vipenta Pearl liquid vitamins, and later with rabbits Jack shot, until they were big enough to be an attraction at the zoo in town. Eventually, the birds had five-foot wingspans. The boys went to see them often, justifiably proud of their achievement. They had learned the satisfaction derived from caring for creatures entirely dependent on them.

There were other creatures in the neighborhood that attracted the adolescent boys' attention as well. The American Legion had a coed home for war orphans several hundred yards away from the academy. The schools were rivals in sports, but the competition didn't stop on the playing fields. The academy boys were always trying to date the girls who lived there, and this infuriated the American Legion boys, who considered these females their personal property. So once every year, in a rite of passage, the academy boys would stage the high school equivalent of a college panty raid. They climbed over the fence separating the two campuses and snuck into one end of the girls' dormitory. As a group, they streaked (clothed) down the bedroom corridor, whooping and shouting for items of underwear. The girls' shrieks drew the Legion boys at a run, and the game was on: get out the opposite end of the corridor and make it back over the fence or get caught and be thrashed. Those who were caught staggered back bloodied, but they bragged anyway about how many punches they had landed. Everyone, beat up or not, got credit for having gone on the raid.

The year before he left the academy, Jack was invited by one of his classmates to join his family in Cuba for Christmas. Never having been anywhere but the neighboring state, Jack was intrigued to know what this exotic-sounding tropical island nation would be like. He readily accepted and flew with his friend to Havana, all expenses paid.

His friend's father was the manager of the famous Copacabana Club, known for its elaborate shows and big-name Latin bands. So, in addition to spending a holiday with a large, boisterous, and happy family — something new in Jack's experience — the father made sure that the trip would be memorable in a way that tracked straight into a teenage boy's fantasies. The showgirls at the club were accustomed to being escorts for customers, and Jack got set up with a dancer named Teresa. At six feet two inches, she was big even by showgirl standards and half a head taller than Jack. Her father's Scandinavian heritage accounted for her height, and combined with her mother's mix of Lebanese and Latin blood, they had produced a truly exotic female. With her large, smoky Middle Eastern eyes, thick blonde hair, and perfectly proportioned figure, Teresa literally stopped conversation when she walked into a room. She was experienced with men and told Jack she thought it would be fun to introduce a naïve youngster like him to some adult pleasures. He lost his virginity to her, and learned for the first time how to appreciate the soft feeling of a woman's unclothed body, her earthy musk and warm slick wetness, the way her breasts swayed as she sat astride him, and the sight of her taking him into her mouth. It was a Christmas present that more than made up for Poochie and his stomped-on car so many years before.

In 1958, when Jack was fourteen, he had amassed enough credits from regular classes and the summer sessions to be able to graduate early. He took his leave with mixed emotions. Graduation meant separating himself not only from a world in which he felt at home, but also from Captain Marten, his life coach, friend, and mentor.

He really had no option but to leave school after graduation, so Jack went back to the Rathole at his parents', took odd jobs, and just hung around town. He was at a loss as to what would come next, but his father in effect made the decision for him. He demanded that Jack be back at home by 10:00 every evening, and one night after he had violated this curfew one too many times, his father was waiting for him. A huge argument erupted, which ended when Jack's father hit him on the head with a walking stick loaded with lead shot and left him unconscious on the floor. When Jack came to, his anger was intensified by his reckless spirit and ramped-up teenage hormones. Feeling he had nothing left to lose, he packed up the next morning and took off in the 1952 Studebaker Champion parked in front of the house, which he'd bought just a casually as the Ford, with earnings from his store at school. He had no plans other than to get away from an intolerable environment.

When Jack's father discovered he was gone, he called the police. Jack was driving on a farm-to-market permit, and his father wanted it known that he wasn't responsible for the boy's actions. At Jack's age, it wasn't legal for him to own a car, and his father told the police they should pick him up. They stopped

Jack at the start of the Turner Turnpike that runs between Oklahoma City and Tulsa and told him he could not drive that car. Jack remembers the cop's words: "Take your shit and git. There'll be a warrant out for you next." He took the one suitcase that had everything he owned in it, stuck his thumb out, and got into the first truck that stopped.

Drifter Days

In the latter half of 1958, Jack hitchhiked all the way from Oklahoma to Maine. He made stops in St. Louis, Chicago, Erie, Albany, Concord (New Hampshire), Bangor, Eastport, and finally Calais, Maine, picking up enough odd jobs to feed himself and find a place to sleep. He had become a drifter.

The job he found near Calais was in a pressboard factory across the border in Canada. It cost him ten cents each way to walk across the bridge to get to and from work, but he needed the job. He was assigned to one of the finishing machines, but it functioned poorly and damaged many of the boards that came out of it. Even then, Jack had an instinctive feel for mechanical things and was able to see what was causing the problem. He pointed out the malfunction to the foreman, who told him if he could fix it, he'd give him $500. Jack did, but rather than paying, the foreman told him he was fired. Jack went straight to the supervisor and told him what had happened. The supervisor listened and, grateful the machine had been fixed, respected the deal and gave Jack his $500. With this cash in his pocket, Jack hit the road again, heading back to Bangor, hoping that a larger city might have better job prospects.

It was winter by this time, and Jack's clothes and shoes were not at all adequate for the conditions. One night, despite the stench, he took shelter in a chicken barn at a farm about thirty miles short of his destination. He was suffering from the cold, and while shivering through the night in the unheated barn, he came up with an idea that would prove critical to his survival. In the morning, he gathered up chicken feathers and used them to create insulation for his clothes. He put on his two pairs of jeans and stuffed a layer of feathers between them, learning quickly that the process was a lot easier if he inserted the feathers quill-ends down. He insulated two pairs of socks in the same way, and finished the job by putting his feet, encased in socks, feathers, and unlaced shoes, into four layers of wax paper bags he found in the barn, securing them with string. To keep his upper body warm, he made up two feather layers, one between his long-sleeved undershirt and top shirt, and another between his shirt and jacket. It smelled awful but probably saved his life.

Feeling and looking like a stuffed scarecrow, Jack started to walk the last thirty miles to Bangor. It soon began snowing, a steady downpour of small, icy flakes. He was from the southern part of the Midwest, and this windless Maine snowfall was a new experience. As he walked, the snow quickly piled up to six or seven inches, forming white cones on the tops of the fence posts. Walking became increasingly difficult. He hoped to hitch a ride, but there weren't many cars to begin with on rural Maine roads and now there were none. Chicken feathers or not, this was a dangerous situation with temperatures in the low twenties rapidly pulling the heat away from his body. Shivering, he plodded on, not having any other option. He hadn't passed a farmhouse for miles, and even if there was one, he wouldn't have been able to see it.

It was pure luck that a snowplow pulled up just when he

started to feel sleepy. He didn't know it at the time, but had he fallen asleep, he would have died, as drowsiness is the next to last phase in the process of freezing to death. The driver told him the road had been closed and that was why there wasn't any traffic. He detoured at the next exit and drove Jack to the police station in a northern suburb of Bangor. Seeing his outlandish boots and chicken feathers sprouting out of his jacket, the officer on duty asked Jack what in the world he was doing out in those conditions. Satisfied he wasn't dangerous, just a kid trying to get to Bangor because he had nowhere else to go, the cop told Jack he could stay at the station until he warmed up. An hour later, when the cop's wife brought him his lunch, she took pity on the boy and brought him a hot meal too. She prevailed on her husband to let Jack sleep in the station's only cell, and took his smelly outerwear and washed it. Jack had a blissfully warm evening and a good night's sleep as the snow silently piled up outside.

The next morning, as the snow-savvy Mainers cleared the streets, the cop gave Jack a ride to a crossroads outside of town where he knew the boy could flag down the next bus leaving Bangor. He explained to Jack that he could not afford, as a police officer, to be seen dropping an obviously underage kid at the bus station, when he really should have taken him to juvenile hall. He gave Jack enough money for a ticket to Portland — he didn't want him staying in Bangor — and a meal. This was a far cry from the rough treatment he had gotten at the hands of Officer Wolfe, or for that matter, most adults he had known in his life. For a change, Jack was genuinely grateful to a person of authority.

In Portland, he found a job bussing tables and doing side work at Re Rah, an Irish pub along the waterfront. He befriended one of the regulars at the pub, also a Midwest transplant, who told Jack about a job working at Sportsman's Park just outside

Chicago. He said the trotting horse racetrack there always needed what he called pony boys, and they would probably let Jack sleep in the tack room. He told Jack to use his name if he applied, since one of the track staff there was a friend from his army days. Jack began saving up his money for a bus ticket to Chicago, and left Portland in the spring.

Jack got the job at the track, but left as soon as he had some money in his pocket. I asked him why, and he said he couldn't stand the way the trotters were mistreated.

"What do you mean, mistreated?" I asked.

"Do you know anything about horse racing?"

"Not really. My father took me to watch the trotters at Yonkers Raceway in New York a couple of times. I was just a kid and I really didn't get it. Why was everybody so excited to watch a bunch of horses running in a funny way with little guys in shiny clothes riding in carts behind them? I do remember the betting windows and people pushing and shoving to get to the rail around the track, but that's about it."

"So you know it's all about the betting and winning money, right?" Jack asked, and gave me a quick tutorial. "First of all, the horses are restrained so they can't break out of a trot, and their race performance is rigged."

He spoke as if I should understand what that meant, but I didn't, so I had to ask how you rigged a horse race. Exchanges like this happened regularly in our conversations, and always pointed up the fundamental differences in Jack's and my respective realities. I was never abused. My parents cared about me and raised me in an affluent New York suburb. My father bought me an MG as soon as I was legal to drive. We had a summer place on a lake in the Kittatinny Mountains area of northwestern New Jersey. I had my own sailboat. They paid for an Ivy League education. I ended my career as an executive officer in a multibillion-dollar multinational corporation. I retired and sailed for ten years on a fifty-foot ketch. Sure, I studied and worked hard, but I was generally able to skim comfortably across the surface of life's lake, essentially oblivious to and certainly untouched by all the gritty reality, rough individuals, and difficult circumstances that characterized Jack's experience. Compared to Jack, I was largely naïve to the ways of the world, even after sixty-seven years of living.

Jack told me that rigging races was nothing unusual at this track, which had gotten its start racing dogs in the Capone era. "Let's say the track wanted a horse to run slower," he explained. "They would cinch it so tightly around its chest that it couldn't breathe properly. Another way to slow down a horse was to cinch too loosely." At my obvious confusion, he added, "The poles of the sulky — that's the cart the little guys in the shiny clothes ride in — jab into its flanks if they're cinched loosely, and the horse doesn't trot as fast because it hurts."

Jack resigned because of the cruelty, but since he was a good worker — and reliable because he didn't drink — the track manager was willing to recommend him as a pony boy to a man he knew at Aqueduct Racetrack in New York. Jack took a bus to the city. As soon as it arrived at the Port Authority Bus Terminal in midtown Manhattan, he took the IND subway as instructed, which got him to South Ozone Park in Queens. Relying on his former manager's name, he was hired on and again given a place to sleep in the tack room.

The atmosphere at Aqueduct was a stark contrast to Sportsman's Park. The horses weren't trotters but true Thoroughbreds, and Jack enjoyed being around and tending to the handsome and generally well-treated animals. He was a quick study and soon learned the ins and outs of a big-time racetrack. One practice he tried his hand at was touting. On race days, Jack would mingle with the bettors and confidentially offer bits of information about the horses. He was believable because he had been seen walking the horses to the paddock, he looked and smelled like a stable boy, and he knew horse-racing terminology. So Jack was able to convince some bettors that he had better insight into the condition of the animals than they could get from the Daily Racing Form, and would share it for $2.00. He worked his way around the crowd, eventually touting all of the horses with a reasonable chance of winning one of the upcoming races. Then he asked the bettors to buy him $2.00 win tickets for all of them, one of which was likely to pay off. Occasionally, it was a long shot and paid handsomely, but Jack made money on almost every race he touted.

He also learned about claiming races. This was a practice only with purses under $10,000, which did not attract much attention from the track officials. Sadly, it was also reminiscent of the mistreatment he had witnessed at Sportsman's Park. Jack learned that an owner would starve one of his horses so it looked weak and ran poorly. He would do this long enough for the horse to have a poor record and for the odds against it to lengthen, and then begin feeding and exercising the animal again to build up its strength and stamina. On race day, the owner would place win, place, and show bets against the long odds, and the now healthy horse would do much better than expected, often earning the owner some real money. Jack could not bring himself to take advantage of this practice, even though he knew how it worked. The cruelty it entailed violated his code.

After four months of regular income, and with the money he made from touting, Jack was able to rent a studio apartment in Greenwich Village. It was an easy commute to Aqueduct, but more importantly it put him in the middle of a magnet for young people. Not only was it the home of NYU's Washington Square campus, the Village was also a haven for artists, writers, and musicians of all genres. There were dozens of inexpensive restaurants offering cuisine from around the world, smoky coffee shops and bars, chess games played on permanent concrete tables with the boards embedded, readings and soapbox speeches by anti-establishment activists or angry poets, and avant-garde off-Broadway theater. It was a throbbing, twenty-four-hours-a-day libertarian scene that attracted people who enjoyed the Bohemian world, including the sort of modern, easygoing young women Jack hooked up with for informal and uncommitted relationships.

One of his girlfriends invited Jack to a shooting gallery one day. This sounded like fun to him, because he enjoyed shooting and had become a pretty good marksman under Captain Marten's coaching. On the day of the outing, Jack brought along his French-made Unique .22 semi-automatic pistol, thinking he would impress his date with his skills. But he soon learned this was not to be a shooting gallery as he understood the term. Instead, the girl led him through a warren of brownstone apartment basements to a dimly lit room where a number of illegal substances were being smoked, snorted, injected, or otherwise consumed. A very different sort of shooting gallery indeed. Jack didn't even drink, but he didn't want to appear uncool in front of his girlfriend, so he decided to try some heroin. He had a head cold at the time, so when he took a snort of the powder, his nose was so stuffed up that it didn't have any effect. He tried another with the same result, but the third snort broke through and went straight to his brain. He doesn't remember anything that happened after that, but two days later he awoke to find himself on a railroad trestle in Elwood City, Pennsylvania. With no idea how he got there and missing his wallet and wristwatch, he decided it made no sense to try to get back to his little apartment in the Village, which had likely been cleaned out by the druggies.

"That was the first and last time I ever used drugs," he told me, but now he was thrown back to his earlier drifter days.

"This seems like a good stopping point," I said. "I've still got a million things to do on the boat before we can leave. How about we pick the story up again late tomorrow morning? That will give me the cool morning hours to get things done. I should be ready for a beer by about 10:30. Why don't you come over then?"

Jack agreed, saying he had plenty of projects going on in his shop and, since he started work at 6:00, he'd be ready for a break around that time anyway.

Decommissioning a sailboat and buttoning her up for the six months of the Caribbean hurricane season was no small undertaking. I had already put up the lightning arrestor and brought down the gear from the masthead, but now had to turn my attention to projects below deck. For one thing, I had to pickle the watermaker, which meant flushing it out for thirty minutes and filling it with an antibacterial solution. It was a complicated process, and I always had to consult the manual to make sure I did everything in the proper sequence. First, I mixed up the three-part solution, taking care to use the correct proportions of chemicals and clean water from the boat's tanks. Then I attached hoses to the front of the unit and led them into a five-gallon bucket filled with the solution. Next, I opened a set of valves to bypass the seawater intake and water tanks and ran the watermaker for twenty minutes, constantly circulating the solution through its plumbing. Finally, I reversed the valves and ran it again to suck all of the solution into the system, where it would prevent bacteria and algae from clogging everything up. It had to be done right, or we'd come back to find a watermaker needing an $1100 membrane replacement. It was also worth the effort because we never ran out of the best-tasting water we had ever drunk, when so many other cruisers were forever going into port to refill their tanks from questionable sources, catching rainwater, taking Navy showers, and otherwise skimping on water usage.

For Susie's part, the boat's interior needed a thorough cleaning, and cockroach poison had to be prepared and set out. Coming home to a boat infested with cockroaches is not only disgusting, it also means washing every dish, pot, and piece of flatware in the galley. The cruisers' solution is to not leave the repulsive creatures anything to eat but a special mixture of honey and baking soda, put in bottle caps placed around the galley and heads. The honey attracts the roaches, but after they eat it the baking soda expands in their stomachs. It is grimly satisfying to come back to the boat and find their little exploded carcasses lying around.

"So you came out of your drug-induced coma in Pennsylvania," I said to Jack the next morning as we wrapped our hands around steaming cups of Central American mountain coffee that the lovely Lydia brought to the Gauguin table, now our accustomed interview site. "You had nothing but the clothes on your back. What did you do?"

"I walked south along the tracks toward Pittsburgh. It was an industrial city, and I figured there would be sidings leading into plants. I was lucky and found a part-time job bagging unhydrated lime. It was tricky, though, because if the lime got on your skin it would cause burns. I wore a burlap sack over my clothes and it filtered out the powder before it could get to me."

This at least enabled Jack to eat and get shelter, but the work was meaningless, and as soon as he had a little cash, he hit the road again. His next job was moving wooden wheelbarrows full of gunpowder sludge from a storage area to the production line of an Olin Mathieson ammunition plant in Ohio. It paid good money for unskilled labor in 1960 — $5 an hour — because the work was so dangerous. Then he hitchhiked to California and began making the rounds of the racetracks there. Santa Anita needed pony boys too, and Jack's prior experience at Sportsman's Park and Aqueduct got him hired. To make even more money, he took a second job washing dishes at the Brown Derby restaurant a few nights a week, and they allowed him to eat for free. He rented a studio apartment in the Bunker Hill area of Los Angeles for $25 per month.

Jack's day started at 4:00 a.m., when a Mexican coworker picked him up and they drove to the track. After work, he got a couple of hours sleep before taking the bus up Wilshire Boulevard for his night shift at the restaurant. The money was piling up, but Jack was exhausted after a few months. His resistance down, he fell sick and went to the emergency room at LA General with chest pain, difficulty breathing, and a high fever. He had contracted pleurisy.

Since he was a minor, the hospital was reluctant to treat Jack without a parent or guardian taking responsibility. They called Jack's father, who denied he had a son. An intern took pity on the young man and instructed him how to care for himself. He gave Jack a course of Gantrisin antibiotic and showed him how to use a syringe to get the fluid out of his chest cavity. He told Jack to count up three ribs from the bottom of his ribcage on the infected side, insert the syringe to a specified depth, and draw out the opaque liquid. He said to do this twice a day until a spot of blood appeared, which would indicate that the infection was clearing up. He sent Jack away with the pills, the syringe, a bottle of alcohol, and some cotton swabs, emphasizing how important it was to clean the needle and syringe after each use. He made Jack promise that he would never say anything to anybody about the help he had been given. "It could cost me my career," he told him, and Jack assured the young doctor not to worry.

"Wait a minute," I said. "Are you telling me that you could stick a needle in your own chest? And that an MD would take that kind of risk and just send you on your way? "

"You'd be amazed at the things some doctors do that could cost them their licenses. Read the paper for a week and I guarantee you'll find a story just as hard to believe."

"Well, okay, maybe I would. But that still doesn't explain how you could stick a needle into your chest two times a day. It must have hurt like hell."

"It wasn't as bad as it sounds," he said. "Once I had to stitch up my own hand after I cut it pretty badly in the shop in Nicaragua." He showed me the scar, an inch-and-a-half long. "It was Friday night and there were no docs around, wouldn't be until Monday. So I boiled a sewing needle and some thread for fifteen minutes and then went to find Dave. When he saw the cut and the needle and thread, he almost passed out. I had no choice but to do it myself. I showed it to the doc on Monday, and he complimented me on my fine stitching."

Being squeamish like Dave, I couldn't quite believe this story at first. But then I remembered reading about an around-the-world solo sailor who had a prostate problem. He had to thread a catheter up his own penis to relieve his bladder. Jack's experience didn't seem so bad in comparison.

After a week flat on his back in the apartment, taking the antibiotic and using the syringe, Jack began to feel better. But it was deadly boring being alone in the apartment, and because it was next door to a restaurant, the place was infested with roaches.

"It was disgusting. I had to find a way to keep them from crawling all over me while was sleeping."

I asked him what he did about it, knowing I was going to hear something creative and probably also hard to believe.

"I went to the store and bought four cans of tuna. Then I stopped at a gas station and bought a quart of motor oil. First I ate the tuna, and then I put the legs of my bed into the cans, filled them halfway with the oil, and smeared some on the legs. The roaches wouldn't come near it."

I was about to ask how he knew this would work, but then I remembered a guide Susie and I had hired when we were anchored in Dominica years earlier. In addition to taking us up one of the supposed 360 rivers on the island — one for each day of the year, he claimed — and into the cloud forest, Lawrence offered to dispose of our garbage and pick up odds and ends for us so we didn't have to keep running into town in the dinghy.

One morning after breakfast, while attending to the seemingly endless number of chores living on a boat entails, I checked the hour meter on *Mariposa*'s engine. It had logged one hundred hours since the last oil change, so I took advantage of being in sheltered water to do another one. When I was finished, I had six quarts of stinky black diesel oil to get rid of. I asked Lawrence if he could dispose of it for me, and he said he could sell it.

"Sell it? Why would anyone want it?"

"People paint it on the posts holding up their houses," he explained. "Bugs won't climb up the oily posts and get inside."

I understood that Jack had used this same trick.

"After I figured out how to keep the roaches off my bed," he continued, smiling, "I still had to look at them crawling across the floor and up the walls."

I knew he wanted to tell me more, so I just sighed and said, "Okay, what did you do?"

He laughed. "I used them for target practice."

"What? You shot them inside your apartment?"

"Well, no, not with a gun. I used a rubber band and paper clips."

Since I'd once been a boy myself, I knew exactly what Jack did: he fully opened two of the three bends in the clips, but opened the third and shortest bend only halfway. Then he stretched a rubber band between the thumb and forefinger of his left hand and hooked the bend of the opened clip over it. He could now draw back the straightened shank of the clip, take aim, and shoot his mini-slingshot at the roaches.

"The clips just bounced off the little bastards," he said, "but at least it gave me something to do."

After another week, Jack felt well enough to go back to work. First, he went down the street to the local blood collection agency and sold a pint so he had some cash, and then went back to the Brown Derby. He decided to limit himself to just working at the Brown Derby this time, and not take on Santa Anita again. Bussing tables wasn't interesting work, but at least the restaurant attracted celebrities, and it was fun to watch the reactions of the other diners when they came in. One evening, his otherwise tedious chores were relieved when Frank Sinatra and Sammy Davis Jr. made an appearance. After Jack cleared their table after dinner, they followed him into the kitchen and gave him a $15 tip. He was stunned, because tipping a busboy or dishwasher was unheard of. He has never forgotten their unexpected kindness.

He soon became bored, though, and found a more engaging job at Whittaker Corporation in Duarte. The company had a contract to produce helicopter blades for the military, and the pay was good at $2.10 an hour. A workmate's mother gave Jack a room in her house for $15 a week, $20 if he wanted dinners. He stayed with the company for six months, as much for the money as for the girl he was seeing, who happened to be his landlady's daughter. Flippy, as she was nicknamed, was a do anything, anytime, anywhere kind of girl who showed Jack her trick for getting a free meal at a good restaurant. He remembers going to Castaways in Burbank, a fancy place that didn't have prices on the menu, and enjoying a first-class dinner. At the end, she filled her mouth with peas, carrots, and coffee and feigned vomiting, spewing the chewed-up mixture on the floor as she ran for the ladies' room. "Must have been something in the food!" she exclaimed loudly when she came back to the table. The maître d' hustled them out of the dining room pronto. He told them dinner was on the house if they would just leave immediately.

Jack became a student of this kind of stunt and has developed a variety of them that he uses as circumstances warrant. He has mastered the gait and speech of a cerebral palsy victim, and will use it to get wheelchair rides through airports when his sciatica is bothering him. His trick for keeping the seat next to him empty on an airplane, or at least to discourage a seatmate from talking to him, is to have a piece of string hanging out of the corner of his mouth. People don't know what to make of it and keep their distance.

The romance with Flippy faded when she began to experiment with lesbianism, and Jack was ready to move on anyway. He bought a beat-up Hudson Hornet and hit the road. He told me the car looked like an upside-down bathtub, sported a batwing-shaped windshield, and for every tank of gas he put in it, he needed to add a gallon of oil to the crankcase. He ended up in Texas and found work in the oil patch, but bailed out after a month and a half. The work was cold and dangerous, and the hazing the old hands subjected him to was intolerable.

He drove to Colorado and looked for a job working inside. He found one on an assembly line, assisting in a metal-cutting operation at a Gardner-Denver compressor plant. At his work station, two-foot diameter solid steel rods were fashioned from a continuous casting being fed onto a lathe. Jack was assigned with breaking off the spiral chip that resulted from the rod being turned to the specified diameter. This chip was about a quarter inch thick and one inch wide, and had sharp, ragged edges. Every foot of it weighed five pounds. As it came off the lathe, the chip would snake along the shop floor if not broken off at the lengths indicated by the production procedures. One day, when the lathe operator was called away, Jack thought it would be interesting to see what would happen if he didn't break off the chip but just let it run. The tightly wound steel spiral worked its way across the shop floor, got between the railroad tracks that ran into the plant, and was channeled out the door. A car crossing the tracks ran over the spiral, causing it to flog around and damage the underside of the vehicle. Jack was summarily fired for this prank, and once again had to move on.

"Why do you do things like that?" I asked. "It's almost as if you're daring people to do something about your pranks."

"I just don't like being pushed around and told what to do," was the only answer he offered, and I made a note to myself to press him for more details about this aspect of his personality when I had more time.

By now, it was springtime in Denver, and Jack saw a Help Wanted sign in the window of the Blue Onion Bar and Grill. He had done restaurant work before, he told the owners, so he knew the routines. Also, he didn't drink (just as desirable a trait in restaurant work as at racetracks) and was hired on to bus tables and do side work, just as he had at the Brown Derby. Soon after Jack started, the sous chef resigned, and the head chef offered to train him for this much more desirable job. The hours were midday and evening, which meant Jack had his mornings free to enjoy the city and the nearby mountains. He especially liked the chance to drive out to the foothills and do some shooting. Other advantages were the good meals he got at the restaurant and the inexpensive lodging at the owners' other business, a small motel.

One of the regulars at the Blue Onion was Dottie, a petite blonde in her early forties with upswept hair and wide-set light brown eyes, a Kim Novak lookalike. She had recently lost her husband from a heart attack and was trying to drink her way through the grief. The owners and other patrons, especially the men, sympathized with her for a while, but the drinking got out of hand. Dottie's behavior, alternatively belligerent or maudlin, eventually became an annoyance to everyone. The owners convinced her that a change of scenery might do her good, and offered to help her make some travel plans. If she would put up $10 a day, they told her they would match it, and the next thing Jack knew he was hired to drive the woman anywhere she wanted to go, "so long as it's away from here." He was offered only five dollars a day, but Dottie had her own car and would pay for his food and lodging. It looked like a pretty cushy job.

Her first destination choice was Mexico, because it promised to be such a completely different experience. Perhaps the Blue Onion's owners were right, and the change would help her get over the loss of her husband. A twelve-hour drive was all it took to get to the border, and Dottie and Jack had dinner at a touristy restaurant with the obligatory mariachi band in Ciudad Juarez. The next day, they continued south in the direction of Mexico City, stopping in Chihuahua. The city had reasonable accommodations, and they even found a place with a pool, restaurant, and bar. Things had been looking good up to this point, but after dinner Dottie headed for the bar and proceeded to get belligerently drunk. It got so ugly, the bartender had to insist she go back to her room. Fortunately, Jack was able to convince her to do so, even in her inebriated state. The evening ended without further complications, but Jack worried about what would happen on the rest of the trip.

They arrived in Mexico City after two more days of travel with no more idea of where they would stay than the names of a couple of hotels in the Zona Rosa that some American businessmen at the bar in Chihuahua had told them about. Plenty of gringos went there, they said, because of the modern accommodations, prevalence of English, relative safety of the streets, and food that wouldn't give them Montezuma's revenge. They were drawn to the Reforma Hotel, located on the broad avenue of the same name. This major thoroughfare with multiple lanes of two-way traffic had a wide center island full of trees, flowering shrubs, and gardens. At each major intersection, *Avenida de la Reforma* became a traffic circle going around heroic statuary or spraying fountains. The hotel itself had a canopied entrance attended by formally attired doormen and red-uniformed bellhops. It turned out to be a great place, although somewhat expensive, and Jack and Dottie stayed there for a week while they visited the tourist sites. They went to the *Museo Nacional de Antropología*, took a day trip out to the archeological site of Teotihuacan, and even attended an evening folkloric presentation at the *Palacio de Bellas Artes*. Dottie's drinking stayed under control, although she did end every evening with a nightcap or two and ran up a sizeable bar bill.

At week's end, when the front desk asked Dottie to bring her account up to date, she offered to pay with a check. They refused and asked for cash, and she had to admit she did not have enough money. She tried to explain that she hadn't realized the Reforma Hotel was really beyond her budget. The hotel manager threatened to call the police if she didn't make good on her bill, but Dottie assured him that she would be able get some cash in the morning. Her late husband, she explained, had been a thirty-second-degree Mason, and she could contact the temple in Mexico City to arrange a loan. The manager reluctantly agreed to let them stay one more night.

The Masons did cash her check, which still had her husband's name on it, but Dottie inexplicably decided to skip out on their bill. She insisted they stay away from the hotel all day, and had Jack park the car in a nearby alley. In the evening, when the lobby was crowded with new check-ins and businessmen returning from work, Jack went in alone to get their luggage. He brought it down on the fire escape, met Dottie in the alley, and they slipped away. Stopping only for bathroom breaks, they drove all night and half the next day until they reached a border checkpoint twenty miles south of Brownsville, Texas. The officials there had been alerted by the Mexico City police and were waiting for them.

Dottie was obliged to get in an official's car, and Jack was told to follow them in hers. They were taken to the police station at the border town of Matamoros. The room was full of people waiting to be processed for their respective infractions, and Jack found himself seated next to a hooker who had failed to keep up with her payoffs. She said to him, "They're so disorganized in here, why don't you just walk back out to your car and drive across the border?" He was suspicious. Was she trying to set them up in exchange for leniency? But he decided to risk it and asked her where the border crossing was.

"It's only a couple of hundred yards away," she told him. "Just walk out the door and get in your car. Go down the street two blocks, look to your right, and you'll see the bridge."

And that is what they did, driving right through the Mexican checkpoint—there were no barriers at that time—and over the

Rio Grande to the American side.

The US immigration officer, having seen them speeding across the bridge, asked why they were in such a hurry. Dottie tearfully explained that they had been tricked by their hotel telling them one price and then insisting on another significantly higher one, and then threatening them with police action if they didn't pay. She said she had panicked and fled because she had heard how women were sexually abused in Mexican jails. The officer, having heard pretty much every story returning tourists could come up with, rolled his eyes and let them through.

Dottie needed to get some more money to continue the adventure, so she had Jack drive to Oklahoma City, where she was able to cash another check at the Masonic Temple there. Then they drove to St. Louis to see one of Dottie's aunts, but she quickly tired of the older woman, and one morning told Jack that she wanted to go to New York City, a place she had never seen. It took two days to get to Philadelphia, where they picked up the New Jersey Turnpike. As they drove north, they were passed by several groups of motorcyclists, many wearing their club colors, also headed north on their Harleys. At a rest stop, Jack asked one of the less fearsome-looking bikers why there were so many of them out on the road in the middle of the week. He told Jack about the annual motorcycle rally at Laconia, New Hampshire, which culminated with Father's Day weekend. On learning this, Dottie was excited about the prospect of seeing what actually went on at these rallies, and told Jack to drive to her straight to New Hampshire.

By this time, Jack had grown weary of Dottie's drinking and abrupt changes of mind and mood. She had also run out of money again and stopped paying him, saying she would cash a check right after the rally. Having seen what happened at the Mexico City hotel, he didn't believe her. In Laconia, he waited until the second evening and, when Dottie had passed out in the car, drove to one of the biker bars. He offered the keys to anyone who would give him $500, but said they would have to take Dottie along with the car. It was a tempting offer because even unconscious, she was good-looking. A stoned biker took the deal.

Changes for the Better

After the fiasco with Dottie, Jack returned to the Southwest where he felt more comfortable than he did on the East Coast. He found work with a general contractor happy to find a guy familiar with foundations, carpentry, plumbing, and electricity whom he could use in so many ways. Jack enjoyed the variety of the projects, but after a while the old wanderlust kicked in and it was time to move on. He went back to Oklahoma to see his mother and sister, and asked a friend from school if he could put him up while he looked for work. He wouldn't go to his parents' house because he wanted to steer clear of his father.

Jack contacted Dr. Wilson and asked if he had any work for him. The doctor knew about the run-in Jack had had with the police while driving his Corvette and its fatal aftermath for Officer Wolfe. As a result, he was reluctant to hire Jack directly, but did use his medical contacts to find him work. Nursing and convalescent homes, because of their high turnover, always needed staff, and Jack was hired by one to assist elderly or otherwise incapacitated people manage their daily activities. He was able to put up with the tedious and sometimes disgusting chores for a while, working for a few different homes, but the patients and the work depressed him, so he asked Dr. Wilson if there was anything else. This time, the doctor sent Jack to the Oklahoma Medical Research Foundation, where the work, while not exactly disgusting, was certainly ghastly. He was assigned to the morgue, where he helped take care of the cadavers — or pieces of them — that were used to train medical students. He didn't last long there either, but what he learned from both of these experiences would prove useful in unexpected ways.

Because he couldn't find decent work, Jack volunteered for the draft in 1962. His army experience was cut short, however, when he was arrested by the MPs for being involved in a bar robbery on his first leave after basic training. He didn't actually participate in it, but when he refused to divulge the names of the men who committed it — shades of military school — the army gave him undesirable discharge. He had almost certainly dodged a bullet, since at that time many draftees were being sent to Vietnam.

Jack went back to looking for a job, and this time had the good fortune of finding one with Aero Commander in Bethany, Oklahoma, which hired him because of his prior military-aircraft experience with Whittaker. He was assigned to fair out dings in the surface panels of airplane wings to tolerances of one hundredths of an inch. Jack's meticulousness and precise work was noticed, as was his aptitude for things mechanical and mathematical. Because the war in Vietnam was heating up, business for defense contractors was booming. Thinking Jack's innate abilities might signal wider potential, his supervisor sent him to personnel for a thorough evaluation. In addition to work-related skills testing, Jack also took psychological assessments, including the Stanford-Binet IQ test and the well-regarded Minnesota Multiphasic Personality Inventory. The results, combined with his job performance, were encouraging. Not only was Jack a precision technical worker, he was also intelligent (so intelligent, in fact, that he later joined Mensa) and demonstrated personality characteristics that correlated highly with successful engineers. The company sent Jack to some of their advanced technical training, and then offered him the opportunity to attend engineering school at the University of Oklahoma.

This was an extraordinary break for a kid who had randomly knocked around, and been knocked around, for most of his life. The exception to this sad history was his success in military school, and Jack contacted Captain Marten to tell him, rather proudly, about this opportunity. The man who had believed in Jack since he was seven strongly encouraged him to pursue it. He wrote a letter of recommendation and had Jack's transcript sent to the university, where Aero had put together a program to educate young men like Jack they wanted to invest in. Jack was accepted, and he moved into a basement apartment in Norman to get ready to attend classes. It was cheaper to live there than in Bethany, and it was within commuting distance so he could continue working. The company transferred Jack to the four-to-midnight shift so he could follow the normal daytime schedule of classes.

It was a grind going to school full-time and working full-time, and there wasn't much time for a social life. But Jack got help with his dyslexia from the coeds in exchange for helping them in math, and he found the arrangement a much more efficient way to meet girls than the usual party scene.

The first summer when school wasn't in session and Jack had time on his hands, he looked for ways to make money beyond his pay at Aero. He and a friend, whose father was an out-of-work preacher—he'd gotten a little too deep into the sacramental wine—came up with the idea of organizing a weekend revival meeting in rural Oklahoma. They rented a tent and two hundred folding chairs, then advertised the revival with fliers they put up in the small town's store windows.

Rev. Harwood preached on Friday and Saturday nights and on Sunday morning, inviting people to "Come to Jesus!" and "Be saved!" Admission was $1.00, so from this alone they took in almost $600 over the course of the weekend. Regular collections "for the work of the church" were also received. Another way they boosted the take was to have Rev. Harwood call out to anyone having a birthday. By simple probability, there was one about two out of three times, and the plate was passed for a birthday donation. Then there were special collections for "Brother Jim who needs an operation" and for "polio-stricken Jimmy's new braces." The people being recognized had no way of knowing how much was contributed, so Jack and his friend skimmed off a portion before giving the recipient his or her gift from the congregation. Unfortunately, one of the attendees at the final Sunday service was the county sheriff. He approached Rev. Harwood and asked if he had a permit to hold the revival. His son and Jack saw what was happening and slipped out of the tent, taking the money with them. They called the tent and chair rental company Monday morning, informing them of the location of their items and telling them to keep the deposits. They split the remaining money three ways.

Following that summer's misadventure, Jack just stayed at school so he could graduate early. He was awarded his BS in mechanical engineering in 1965 after only three years. Four months later, Aero Commander was sold to Rockwell International, and the newly-minted engineer was relieved of the contract requiring him to work five years in exchange for his education. Jack quit rather than being assigned to a different, less interesting job with Rockwell in Texas, and instead found a job with Gates Rubber Company in Denver. He designed hangers for V-belts that were sold to garages and shops as a way to keep their fan, alternator, and AC belts organized. The design department at Gates was housed in a building one block long and half a block wide, filled with drafting tables. Jack's station was in the back row, where newcomers typically worked, and where he had a view over the rows of tables stretching toward the supervisor's area in the front. What he saw dismayed him. The rows closest to him had young men with full heads of hair, but in front of them were thinning or receding hairlines, and then heads with gray hair (or no hair) populating the rows farthest away. The prospect of moving up one desk at a time as people retired or died seemed to Jack like a forty-year jail sentence. The defining moment came when he observed an old man in the front row drop dead at his drafting table from a heart attack. Even before the ambulance arrived, Jack saw the man at the adjacent table begin collecting his drafting tools, preparing to move over.

By this time in his life, Jack had been in restaurants, racetracks, oil-patch outfits, and manufacturing companies, always working for somebody else. He had to acknowledge the extraordinary good fortune of having his engineering degree paid for, but if all that got him was a job at a drafting table, he concluded he would be better off going into business for himself. He stayed on with Gates in order to keep the income stream going while he networked his contacts to find work as an independent engineering contractor. His break came when a sympathetic colleague at Aero who knew about Jack's abilities — and how they were being wasted at Gates — put him in touch with a friend at United Controls in Seattle. The company was looking to extend its medical products offerings and wanted to develop a controlled heating chamber for premature infants. They did not have the R & D manpower to pursue it in a timely fashion, and Jack was brought in to provide the engineering for its design and manufacturing. He worked with company personnel to come up with a product they jokingly referred to as Crispy Critters.

The boss's secretary, Norma, objected to such flippant and unprofessional language being used in reference to an important and emotionally sensitive matter as that of saving newborns' lives. Being a manipulator, she leveraged her position to give Jack and his team a hard time by imposing delays, demanding rewrites, blocking access to the boss, and generally being an obstacle any way she could. Jack was in danger of being at least late, if not entirely unable to meet the terms of his contract.

Norma's boss seemed powerless, having been completely taken in by the woman. She was sexually attractive, knew it, and used her sexiness to keep him off balance. She habitually wore no panties, and when she sat down at her desk, she would flip up the back of her skirt. Her solid oak chair had a gap between the seat and the back so her boss, whose desk was behind hers, got regular flashes of bare buttocks.

This control trick would prove to be her undoing, however, because Jack came up with a way to get back at her. Crazy Glue was used in the production process to keep electrical components in place on their circuit boards. The word went out to alert Jack when Norma was coming back from lunch, which gave him a couple of minutes to perform his mischief. He squeezed a U-shaped bead of Crazy Glue around the edge of Norma's chair, just inside the part of the seat that had been contoured for a person's backside. Without pressure on it, the glue remained in gel form for a few minutes, but once Norma sat down on it (first flipping her skirt up) the glue set instantly. An odd expression crossed her face as she settled on the chair seat, but when she tried to stand, the chair was firmly cemented to her bottom. It took the fire department fifteen minutes to get there, and when they first arrived they were at a loss as to how to assist her. They decided on trying solvents to unstick Norma, and tipped her forward on her desk, lifting the back of her skirt to have access to the problem area. They tried a number of chemicals over the next half hour to melt the glue, much to the enjoyment of the crowd of men — and to a number of women Norma had mistreated as well. The firemen finally succeeded, but along with melting the glue, they burned some of Norma's skin. She was taken to the emergency room for medical attention, and she did not return to United Controls.

The incident with Norma confirmed an aspect of Jack's personality I had seen before and would again, repeatedly. It was so ingrained as part of his code, he never gave it a thought. If hurt, deceived, taken advantage of, or otherwise wronged, he would have his revenge. It could be as brutal as it was in Officer Wolfe's case, or as mischievous as it was in Norma's. But no one could cross him and get away with it. Retribution would be swift if possible. If not, Jack would take his time, do his research, and work out a plan. He never forgot, let alone forgave, and would wait years if necessary to deliver a payback. It didn't even matter to him if the person never knew it was Jack behind his misfortune. In some cases, that was preferable. It was satisfaction enough just to know the debt had been paid. Conversely, as Susie and I had found out, if he was treated with kindness, respect, and honesty, friendship was as much a part of Jack's code as revenge.

"You know, Sus," I said to her after one of Jack's annual visits to Siguaterra, "if anyone harmed you physically, I could ask Jack to do whatever I wanted to the guy, and he would make it happen."

"Let's hope it never comes to that," she said.

"Right, right. But knowing a price would be paid is strangely comforting. I can't explain why, but something inside me relaxes when I think of it."

"How would you feel about it, though? I mean, being responsible for someone getting badly hurt, or worse. Remember how you felt when you realized that Jack was going to have our neighbor killed for blocking the easement?"

"That was just a real estate dispute," I said. "You are my life."

Jack and I had to suspend our interviews for a few days, since Susie needed my help in constructing a cover for *Mariposa*. We had seen the effects on other boats when they were left exposed to both the tropical sun and the heavy rains that came during hurricane season. The ultraviolet rays would deteriorate the varnish on the boat's extensive brightwork and leave it a peeling mess, and we could sacrifice weeks of the next cruising season while we sanded and laid down five or six new coats to bring it back to Bristol condition. Also, not having salt water splashing on the teak deck would allow mold to form, and the dry and separated planks could leak when the rains came. Allowing this moisture to accumulate in the hot and stagnant air below the decks of a buttoned-up sailboat generates a riot of mildew. We had seen boats after the rainy season where every surface was coated in black spores, necessitating days of scrubbing. It was worth several day's effort to build a cover and prevent these problems.

We had built these covers twice before, but it was still a challenge. The hardest part was figuring out where to cut the tarps so the masts, stays, and shrouds could go through them, leaving enough spare material for wrapping and overlapping to make an effective rain barrier. Susie is a wizard with a sewing machine, and can visualize and accurately measure what needs to be done before cutting and stitching. Since my spatial relations intelligence is so limited as to be nonexistent in any practical sense, my part of the project was wrestling the tarps around and feeding them smoothly into the sewing machine as Susie stitched. I also constructed the ribs over which the tarps would be stretched, which entailed cutting and joining lengths of PVC tubing and then lashing them to lifeline stanchions and over booms. This was tedious and straightforward work that required no visualization, so was a task I could handle.

Successful cruising couples have figured out this division of labor. Each partner acknowledges and respects the other's competencies, and there is no ego involved. Susie would no more try to rig and sail the boat than I would try to make a cover for it. In the intricate art of living on a boat, complementary sets of abilities are necessary, and this explains why being in company with other cruisers is such a pleasure. Fractiousness is almost nonexistent, because the partners know they must be able to count on each other. It doesn't happen often, but sometimes their lives depend on it. So people are companionable, relationships are positive, humor is high, and help is willingly given and gratefully received. Whether as individual couples or in the community as a whole, we all keep each other afloat.

More challenging for me than the cover or the ribs, I had to finish disconnecting and stowing the electronics mounted in the cockpit and below decks. Lightning arrestor or not, a bolt could still come down the mast, and anything wired to anything else could get fried. The navigation instruments had twenty-odd interconnections; the single sideband radio alone had seven. I labeled each wire, because I had learned the hard way how much I could forget in six months. The uh-oh moment of trying to remember where to connect each strand of the multicolored spaghetti had to be avoided.

The final step in the process was shielding the disconnected instruments from any charges of electricity that got inside the boat, whatever their source. My solution was to stow as much of the equipment as I could in the galley oven, and the rest inside *Mariposa's* wood burning stove (a real lifesaver when coming down the East Coast after the Annapolis Boat Show in mid-October). In effect, the metal oven and cast iron stove were small-scale Faraday cages, like the seven-foot-diameter hollow globes covered in thick wire often seen at science and technology museums. The docent demonstrating the Faraday cage enters the globe and sits on a wooden chair in the middle, while an associate cranks up the voltage in two large metal spheres on opposite sides of the cage. The machinery whines steadily louder until, in a fraction of a second, a hundred million volts of artificial lightning explode across the room, apparently shooting straight through the Faraday cage. The wires on its surface, however, conduct the electricity away from the person inside. I used the same physics to protect my electronics.

These big projects completed, I finally had some time available to get back to Jack. Susie and I would be leaving in a few more days, and there was still a lot of his story to tell. We picked it up right after the Crispy Critters incident.

Still gleeful about gluing Norma to her chair, Jack was driving distractedly through the ever-puddled streets of Seattle in 1966 and failed to notice a young woman standing at a corner, waiting to cross the street. He cut his right turn too hard, putting his rear wheel in the gutter, and splashed water all over the front of her dress. Her response was a string of expletives worthy of a stevedore, and hearing such language from such a well-turned-out lady piqued Jack's curiosity. He circled the block, hoping to overtake her on the return lap. By that time, she was halfway down the other side of the street, but he spotted her, pulled over, and attempted an apology. This was met by another salvo of four-letter words, but Jack persisted. She finally agreed to a cup of coffee, but only if he agreed to pay for the dry cleaning.

Jack continued to apologize for what an inconsiderate jerk he had been for not paying attention to the puddles, and the woman—whose name was Lillie—finally softened. He learned that she was finishing up a liberal arts degree at the University of Washington, and he told her he was an engineer on a medical-products contract for United Controls. Lillie at first seemed dismayed, telling Jack that the engineering students she knew were narrowly focused on their technical areas and not given to socializing except with their nerdy friends. Jack related his tutelage under Captain Marten, saying it had included reading some of Shakespeare's plays, learning chess, and studying philosophy. Lillie brightened noticeably at this apparent paradox. She said she liked being able to carry on an intelligent, wide-ranging conversation with a no-BS guy, unlike so many of her affected liberal arts acquaintances. Jack was encouraged.

For his part, Jack was glad Lillie wasn't a liberal arts cultural snob, but rather a tough, direct, independent-minded young woman who wouldn't accept shabby treatment from anybody. She told him she had fought her way through high school, describing herself as an outcast, a small and wiry 105 pound girl with a plain face, who wore pants and combat boots, the complete antithesis of the popular cheerleader type. Home life was rough too. Her father was a highway maintenance man who frequently got drunk, sometimes hit her mother, and occasionally grabbed her sexually. Her mother had defended the kids and made a home for them as best she could while coping with an abusive husband, but she had been killed in an auto accident when Lillie was fifteen. She moved with an aunt rather than stay in the same house with him. Her only brother shot himself and died at age twelve, her older sister OD'd on speed and heroin at nineteen, and her younger sister ran away from home at seventeen. Lillie hadn't heard from her since.

After graduating from high school, Lillie was accepted at the University of Washington but had to work her way through. She had held jobs waiting tables, as a secretary, in a bookstore, and finally landed a production-line job at Boeing. It lasted until a new male supervisor began hitting on her, sidling up and making suggestive comments, and eventually grabbing her backside. She'd had enough of that with her father, so one day when the guy again invaded her personal space, she threw hot coffee on him, kicked him between the legs, and walked out of the plant.

Hearing this story, Jack admired her spunk and sensed a kindred spirit. He wanted to get to know her better and invited her to dinner. She accepted, characteristically telling him that they would go to a place she knew. Jack respected this take-charge lady, understanding she was not to be trifled with. When he picked her up for dinner, Lillie said she wanted to get something straight. She bluntly asked Jack what his intentions were, and he, just as bluntly, said, "To be completely honest, I want to get into your pants."

"Not until after dinner," she said.

Later, they went to a play, and good night was a peck on the cheek in front of Lillie's apartment. Jack said he'd try to get in touch. She seemed taken aback by the unusual comment but said, "Okay, you do that." Two nights later, he slipped a note under her door that said, "I'd like to invite you to dinner again, this time I pick the place. Please call me if you are interested." He wrote his phone number at the bottom of the page. Lillie called and told Jack she had been pleasantly surprised by this novel approach, and would be glad to have another date with him.

The venue turned out to be the Seattle Sportsmen's Club, and as they pulled up in front and a valet took Jack's old Hornet, Lillie said, "What do you think you're doing? This is the most exclusive club in Seattle. They'll never let us in."

"Relax," Jack said. "I'm friends with a member here, and he said I could come as his guest. He said I could bring you too."

Apparently not ready to accept Jack's blithe explanation, Lillie asked him how he'd become friends with a member of the club. "I mean, no offense, but you're just a contract engineer at United Controls."

Jack told her the story of being in the company parking lot one evening after work. The lot was almost empty, but there was still plenty of daylight. The lot bordered on a wooded area, and he decided to do a little plinking to relax. He was confronted by an older gentleman in a suit who informed him that what he was doing was against the law.

"Whose law?" Jack asked. "Yours, the government's, or God's?" There was a pause, and then Jack added, "Would you like to take a few shots?"

Another pause, and the fellow reached for Jack's .22. They took turns firing shots, setting up targets, and finally just leaning on Jack's truck talking.

It turned out that this gentleman was on United Controls' board of directors, but a common interest in shooting sports trumped the vast differences in their roles in the company. They became friends. Jack – ever the engineer – helped the executive with gunsmithing projects and got invited to the Sportsmen's Club in return. Jack's military school training had included what utensils to use in a formal dinner setting, so he was comfortable at the club. As they were leaving one evening, the exec introduced Jack to the doorman, put him on the guest list, and told him he could go there whenever he liked.

"Use my membership number when you sign for drinks and dinner," he told Jack, "but keep a record of the charges and be sure you've paid me back within a week."

"I've never been in a place like this before," Lillie confided, and Jack was concerned about how she would handle herself in such a setting. But she mimicked what he did, and the dinner went off without a hitch. Later, after a tour of the impressive premises, Jack showed her the rudiments of chess in the club's smoking room. Their game got interrupted when Jack was called back to the office to deal with a technical issue, and he paid for a cab to take Lillie home.

The next week, Jack asked Lillie if she would like to try plinking herself, and she said she thought it might be fun. They went off to the woods, and Jack taught her how to aim his rifle, take half a breath and hold it before firing, and to squeeze, not pull, the trigger. When the ammunition was gone, they waded in a creek, had a picnic lunch, and talked the day away.

A month later, after a few more dates, Jack drove Lillie home and risked it. "Are you going to invite me up?" he asked. Her response, typically direct, was, "Why not right here in the car?" It was cramped, furtive, and fun in the backseat of Jack's car, and it set a pattern of adventurous behavior that would become one of the foundations of their partnership.

They decided soon thereafter that it made sense to move in together, and so flipped a coin to decide whose place they would cohabit. Lillie won, so Jack moved his stuff into her alley-view apartment. At that stage of their relationship, fueled by natural amphetamines, it really didn't matter where they lived, just so they could spend time together. After work, they would have a few drinks, talk about their day, make dinner, maybe go to a movie, or just stay home and watch TV. More often than not, they concluded the evening making love. It was the first long-term relationship for both of them, and as the months went by, the amphetamines were gradually replaced by comforting endorphins. They relaxed into the glow.

One night, to celebrate their six-month anniversary of living together, they decided to go out to dinner. For the first time in her life, Lillie wanted to put on false eyelashes. She said all the girls were wearing them, and that at least for this special night she wanted to feel glamorous. Never having applied them before, she made a mess of it. After several unsuccessful and even comical tries, she got frustrated and threw them out a window into the alley. She said she didn't care if they went to dinner, but Jack didn't buy it. He spent the next half hour crawling around the alley in the twilight, and finally found both sets of eyelashes. Triumphantly, he went back to the apartment and announced, "Our evening is saved!" This time, Lillie got them on right. Their lovemaking after dinner wasn't especially passionate, but deeply satisfying to both of them at a level that transcended sex. They had found their soul mates, and six months later, they got married.

Vietnam

Susie and I were headed home and we wouldn't be back for six months. Jack and I had a farewell beer the afternoon before we left and tried to figure out how to continue the interviews long distance. We decided to have monthly conversations via Skype or over the phone. I told Jack Skype would be better, because calls from the States to Nicaragua were expensive. He said that if Skype didn't work, he'd call me. Inexplicably, calls from Nicaragua to the United States cost just a few cents a minute. The telephone people apparently hadn't thought this through yet, and we wanted to take advantage of their inattentiveness while it lasted. We arbitrarily picked the second Sunday of each month for the contact, and agreed that 1:30 p.m. Maine time made sense for both of us. He wouldn't be working in the shop on Sundays, and would be refreshed after his nap; I would have finished the Sunday paper and have had lunch.

It was good timing for another reason as well: our place in Maine was lakefront, and the weekenders would be zooming up and down the lake on WaveRunners or towing groups of screaming children on tubes behind their boats. The early afternoon was no time for serenity-seeking sailors like us to be out on the water, so it was a good time for me to talk with Jack. Later, when everyone had headed back to Boston for work on Monday, Susie and I could go out on the deserted lake in our pontoon boat to enjoy sundowners in the peace and quiet.

Like many Maine lakes, ours was cold and crystal clear because the water in it came from the White Mountain snowpack, and the streambeds leading to it all had rock bottoms. Also, months of being covered by foot-thick ice kept algae growth to a minimum. The water was so clean that some of the long-timers used it for drinking. Surrounded by thickly forested dark green hills, it had a more intimate feel than larger, open bodies of water because of its many islands, coves, and inlets. The lakeshore was covered in pine, oak, maple, and white birch, sheltering everything from hummingbirds to eagles. In the mornings and evenings, the thrushes serenaded us with their double-throated trills and kingfishers dived for minnows. We almost always saw loons, a protected species but common on our lake because the fishing was so good. These are large, handsome birds with a contrasting pattern of black and white plumage topped by a white-collared black head and glowing red eyes. A loon can dive and travel underwater for a hundred or more yards, often popping back up on the opposite side of the boat from where we first spotted it. If we were lucky, chicks would have hatched in the spring and we would see them being ferried around on the backs of the adults. The call of the loon (think *On Golden Pond*) varies depending on circumstances of danger, courting, or territory, but is always mournful and haunting. It's loud too, and many first-time guests, never having heard it, often stop in midsentence to listen.

On the first appointed Sunday, Jack and I tried our Skype interview. Initially, the connection was good, but after about fifteen minutes we started getting echoes, faded audio, and voices that were a combination of Elmer Fudd and Donald Duck. When the video started looking like one of Picasso's cubist paintings, we shut the video off and proceeded with audio only. Neither Jack nor I are male-model material, so not seeing each other was no great loss.

Jack told me that after finishing the Crispy Critters incubator project with United Controls, he began networking with the defense contractors the US military was relying on to support the Vietnam War effort. One of these companies was Dynalectron, and Jack's prior experience working on helicopter blades and airplane wings fit nicely with a project they had. The primary fighter aircraft being used in Southeast Asia was the F-4, and these planes were being outfitted with ground-traversing radar. Jack was offered an assignment to inspect, and remove and replace if necessary, this equipment. But because of its proximity to Vietnam and the diplomatic relationship between the United States and Japan, he would be stationed at Misawa Air Base, where the F-4s were routinely serviced.

Jack discussed the opportunity with Lillie. He didn't want to be separated from his new love, no matter how good the job sounded. She didn't like the idea either, but as they talked it through, they reluctantly came to the conclusion that it would be good for Jack's career and their future. They told each other it would only be for a short time, and that they would keep in touch as best they could. Rationalized in this way, Jack accepted the assignment.

Upon arrival in Japan, he was given the responsibility of writing quality-deficiency reports, describing which aspects of the radar were not performing properly. The first such report Jack wrote was about one and a half pages long. When he presented it, he was told to flesh it out, to go into more detail and put more words on the paper in order to make the report longer.

Jack dutifully presented a report of five pages, but that wasn't enough either. He asked his boss, the Dynalectron project manager, just how long the report needed to be, and was told that twenty pages would be about right. Jack realized what the game was: produce enough material to justify more spending – or at least not less – in the military's budget. This seemed absurd to him. There was no way he could fill twenty pages with anything meaningful, so he began to insert nursery rhymes like "Mary Had a Little Lamb" in the body of his reports. The now appropriately long QDRs were sent to the Pentagon to be printed and were incorporated into the technical manuals for the planes. Eventually, his prank was discovered by an enlisted airman in Germany, and the military told Dynalectron to cancel Jack's contract.

Canceling the old contract did not mean the company couldn't give him another one, however. Given his intelligence, technical aptitude, and willingness to take risks – as evidenced by some of his drifter jobs – Jack was sent with a select group of other contract employees for special training at Fort Benning, Georgia. Over the next seven months, the military trained him in a wide range of firearms and explosives, explained logistics and tactics, and gave him language and map-reading skills. The chemistry and mechanics of explosives particularly intrigued him, and he was singled out for specialization in this area. The training was intense; sunup to sundown plus two hours homework every day except Sunday. He finished the program with field experience, training alongside Green Beret personnel, and then was sent with a contingent of these elite fighters to the central highlands of South Vietnam, near the border with Cambodia. He was to serve as an advisor to the Montagnard tribesmen.

The indigenous Montagnards are ethnically akin to South Pacific islanders and had originally been coastal fishermen. They were displaced in the ninth century by the more aggressive Vietnamese people, who came from the north and drove the Montagnards inland. There they adapted and learned to be farmers, but the Vietnamese took the farmland too and forced the natives into the mountains. Because of this history, the Montagnards were susceptible to American recruiting, welcoming the chance to settle age-old scores.

In July of 1967, Jack was deployed as an advisor to Phong Hoangan, a unit of the South Vietnamese Intelligence Coordination and Exploitation Program (ICEX). He made it as far as his assigned location, but before he had time to establish himself with the locals, his camp was overrun by the Vietcong. In the fighting, he was bayonetted in the stomach as he struggled to get out of his tent. He was evacuated to the hospital at Tan Son Nhut Air Base near Saigon and spent the next several weeks healing from the wound. Then it was back to the bush.

This time, Jack looked for ways not to be trapped in a tent. One day on a patrol, he happened upon an almost completely overgrown trail that disappeared into a thicket of thorny bushes. He got down on his stomach and slithered along underneath the branches, discovering that there were no thorns at the base of the plants. Taking the chance that this trail was not being used by the VC, he cut out a sleeping area for himself in the middle of the thicket.

"Just a minute," I said. "You mean they let you sleep in the bush and not in the camp? That doesn't sound like any military regulations I've ever heard of. How did they know where you were?"

"Remember," he said. "I was not in the army, I was a contractor. I didn't have to follow their rules. All they cared about was if I showed up for work in the morning."

I had to take Jack at his word, but promised myself that I

would verify this independently at a later date, which I did. I was, however, compiling a long list of things Jack told me about that would require future research.

Jack's specific assignment was to work with the Green Berets helping the Montagnard tribesmen and the Phong Hoangan learn how to defend themselves from incursions of the VC, and to slow the VC's advance south. He discovered that just finding the locals could be difficult. The intelligence they were given was often so poor, Jack and his crew were sometimes sent to villages that didn't exist. When they finally did find a populated settlement, their first challenge was to gain the trust of the villagers. Once they were accepted, Jack and the Green Berets familiarized the tribesmen with the weapons and tactics of modern warfare. Jack's special training in explosives now came into play. He had learned at Fort Benning how to assemble various types of charges and what purposes they served, and how to detonate them from a distance using hard-wired detonators or timed fuses. Conveying this expertise to the tribesmen, some of whom still conceived of war as raids on neighboring villages while armed with bows and arrows, was painstaking.

One particular method of ambush still stands out in Jack's mind because it was so effective. The Ho Chi Minh Trail wound through the mountains, and the VC used it to move troops, equipment, and supplies to the southern part of the country, where most of the fighting was going on. The objective was to disrupt these movements, and the tactic was to place explosive charges on a heavily trafficked stretch of the trail, usually "over the fence" —that is, in Cambodia or Laos. It was tedious and dangerous work, not only because of the nature of the explosives, but also because it had to be done under the constant threat that evidence of their work, or of them, would be discovered.

After a nerve-wracking week and a half, everything was ready. Two series of charges were strung, the first made from light blasting cord along one side of the trail, and another with heavier charges on the opposite side. When lookouts signaled the approach of a VC column, Jack took cover in a ditch with a detonation control box in hand. Once the soldiers were in the killing zone, he detonated the lighter charges, which went off in random but closely spaced order to simulate small-arms fire. The soldiers, thinking they were being attacked from that side of the trail, scrambled to take cover on the other side. When they were hunkered down, Jack set off the bigger charges, which all exploded at the same time. The effects were devastating.

Jack was also proud of a device he invented. "I called it the tin can grenade," he told me, and then paused, waiting for me to ask him about it.

"Okay, I'll bite," I said. "How did you make a tin can grenade?"

"First you drink a beer and cut off the top of the can. Then you remove the top of a grenade and take out the delay fuse. You fill the space with gunpowder and put the top back on."

"It sounds pretty dangerous to be fooling around with a hand grenade like this. Couldn't it go off?"

"Well, you do have to be careful, but if you know what you're doing, it's no big deal."

Jack went on to describe the rest of the procedure: With the top of the grenade back in place, remove the pin; hold the "spoon" tightly against the side of the grenade so it can't spring out and detonate; slide the whole affair into the beer can; tie clear monofilament line to the neck of the spoon and hang the can on a tree behind some foliage; and finally, string the line across the trail at about five feet off the ground.

Jack explained that the VC's practice was to send one soldier twenty feet out ahead of the main column. His job was to walk bent over, sweeping a reed over the ground in front of him, looking for trip wires. He almost always passed underneath the monofilament, but the first man in the column, walking erect, ran into the almost invisible chest-high line. The line pulled the grenade out of the can, allowing the spoon to spring out. The grenade detonated instantly since there was no delay fuse. And because the soldiers in the column walked only two arms' length distance from each other, the explosion killed or injured several of them. Cases of grenades with delay fuses removed were also left behind when American forces pulled back from an area they had been occupying, typically under VC pressure. Enemy soldiers, feeling fortunate to have captured a quantity of US grenades, carried them into their next firefight. When a soldier pulled the pin to throw a grenade that was missing its delay fuse, it would explode the moment it left his hand.

In addition to the grenade tricks, Jack was also excited to tell me about what he called the jumping barbed wire. This tactic called for burying a single strand of barbed wire down the center of a thirty or forty foot stretch of trail, with one end tied to a softball-sized stone concealed off to one side. The other end was attached to a large rock held in place by a wedge thirty feet up a tree. When VC soldiers traversed the area, they tripped a line attached to the wedge, pulling the wedge out and causing the rock to fall to the ground. As it fell, the barbed wire was lifted from the ground and caught the VC troops around—and sometimes between—their legs. The injuries were compounded by the wire continuing to move as the smaller stone was dragged along the ground, pulled by the falling rock.

Never having served in the military, I was taken aback by the deviousness of these tactics. Up to this point, my vision of combat was the typical one: opposing armies maneuvering in the battlefield with tanks and artillery and shooting at one another. I knew conceptually that Vietnam was a guerrilla war, not like WWII or even Korea, but had no idea about the details. Jack was quick to assure me that the VC were equally devious, even cruel. He asked me if I had read some of the returning soldiers' accounts or seen the movie *The Deer Hunter,* and I had to acknowledge I was repulsed by the enemy's treatment of captured American servicemen.

The Vietnam War was a dirty affair in ways that the American military could not admit to, and that was why contractors were used. For example, perforated canisters of odorless, colorless chemicals were put into creeks upstream of VC camps. The chemicals, which were lethal at full concentration, were still potent enough even when diluted in creek water to make the VC soldiers so debilitated they could barely stand up, let alone fight. Occasionally, US soldiers would dip porous bags of these same chemicals into the drinking water of obnoxious officers as a way of settling scores.

Jack's role as an adviser was goals oriented, meaning that the military or the CIA could tell him, "Here is what we want you to accomplish, and we don't care how you do it." These were the circumstances that engendered the most disturbing thing Jack had to do while in Vietnam. He was assigned to advise the Montagnard villagers in interrogating captured enemy soldiers. As guidance, Jack was allowed to read, but could not have a copy of, a manual titled "Field Expedient Methods of Interrogation." Produced by the military's secretive ICEX program (later renamed Phoenix), it was only twenty-five pages long but detailed methods whose cruelty equaled that of the Vietcong.

Jack told me about one of the more grotesque methods, which was used not only to get information, but to intimidate other VC prisoners. In this interrogation technique, the unfortunate captive was placed in a chair with his ankles tied to the legs and his forearms tied to the arms, facing an audience of other prisoners. The interrogator made an incision on one side of his lower back, inserted a hand inside the man's body, and squeezed the kidney. The results were predictable. Not only did the interrogator get the desired information from the captive, it also encouraged the voluntary cooperation of the other prisoners. Jack recalled that the field manual cautioned interrogators to avoid puncturing the peritoneum. Not only would this result in the almost inevitable death of a now good source of information, it also released an extraordinarily disgusting odor. The Phoenix program was discontinued in 1975, and the military has since outsourced this sort of activity. If confronted with incidents of indiscriminate killing or mistreatment of prisoners, the Pentagon can now claim plausible deniability.

"Are you telling me you cut into people's bodies and squeezed their kidneys to get information from them?" I asked. I understood Jack's pranks were part of a personal code, and I even accepted the retribution he exacted on Officer Wolfe. But was he also capable of torture?

"No, no, you don't understand," he said. "I never touched a prisoner. But I did tell the Montagnards how to do it, and they had seen what the VC had done to their own people. You don't want to know what those bastards were capable of. So the tribesmen had no problem brutalizing them."

"You're right, I don't want to hear anything more about this. Let's take a break, okay? I need some time to process what you just told me."

I was profoundly disturbed. Not only could I not stand to hear, read, or see depictions of torture, I now had to try to reconcile my friendship with Jack with what he had done in Vietnam. I knew torture had been used throughout the history of warfare—was still being used—but to be face-to-face with a man who had coached others in inflicting it was unnerving. I still wanted to tell Jack's story, but I was recoiling from him. I feared what I had heard would not only color our interviews but fundamentally alter our relationship.

I discussed the interview with Susie. As always, she wanted to know what Jack had told me, and this time, I *really* needed a sounding board.

"War makes men do brutal things they wouldn't do under normal circumstances," she said. "It's no wonder our young soldiers come back so damaged."

"But doesn't this make you afraid of him?"

"Not now. It was a long time ago under extraordinary circumstances, and he was paid to do what he did. We know Jack is capable of violence, so I guess I'm really not surprised."

In the final analysis, I had to accept that Jack was just another cog in the mutual depravity of Vietnam. The VC mistreated prisoners with equally grotesque methods, as when pairs of captured soldiers were sent back to their lines, one blinded and the other with his larynx cut out. Since the sighted one could see but couldn't speak, and the blinded one could speak but couldn't see, their grisly interdependence was not only cruel and permanently disabling, it was intended to instill terror among their comrades.

When we got back together, I told Jack I'd heard enough about killing and torture, and wanted to hear about some of his other Vietnam experiences. Jack agreed and began telling me stories that didn't involve combat operations. Not all of his time was spent in the bush. There were periods of R & R in Saigon, and reports and debriefings at Tan Son Nhut. It was during one of these breaks, he told me, that he figured out how to take advantage of his contractor status and make some additional money.

"US troops were paid in military pay certificates – MPC – but private contractors had the option of receiving their pay either on base in MPC or in dollars deposited to their bank accounts in the States. Contractors could also get any MPC they got on the base credited in dollars to their US accounts, since MPC and dollars were of equivalent value."

The MPC currency could be spent on the base or in town, where the locals gladly accepted it for the kinds of services in demand by soldiers, such as transportation, restaurant meals, drinks, and sex. The locals involved in these transactions tried to ingratiate themselves with the men, so they could ask them to buy things at the PX using some of the MPC they had accepted in payment. They sold the items they acquired this way for a huge profit on the black market. The locals weren't the only ones taking advantage of this system, and so the military periodically – and without warning – changed the appearance of the MPC bills, making the old ones worthless. The intent was to keep anything of value out of the hands of the VC, and it had the additional benefit of disrupting the black market in goods from the PX. But there was an unintended consequence of changing the MPC: it created a money-making opportunity for anyone who had advance knowledge that the change was coming.

Some of the contractors on the base, and Jack was one of them, had friends who let them know when the new MPC was about to arrive. Once alerted, Jack went out into the community and informed the locals of the impending change, then offered them 10 percent of the value of their old MPC, paid in US dollars. Everyone accepted the deal because dollars were extremely valuable, and also because they knew it was either accept the 10 percent or be left with worthless currency. With the old MPC in hand and a few days in which to exchange it for new bills, Jack could make a 90 percent gain on the transaction.

It took me some time to grasp all this. For Jack, seeing a way to work the system to his advantage was instinctive, but I was naïve to such machinations. As he described the MPC exchange game, I had to interrupt him repeatedly to be sure I understood how it worked. He became exasperated with me for not being able to see what was obvious to him, and again I had to tell him my reality was so different from his that such things just didn't occur to me.

Jack went on to tell me that he needed to employ his scheme carefully, because too many or very large exchanges could arouse suspicion. What he was doing, in essence, was manipulating US currency, and if caught, he could have gotten himself a long stay at the federal facility in Leavenworth, Kansas. So Jack wasn't greedy, but over the course of several MPC changes he was able to accumulate the equivalent of about $30,000. He had it all credited to his US bank account.

By now I thought myself pretty savvy, so I narrowed my eyes and challenged him: "So how did you get the dollars to give the locals? I thought you told me that you only got MPC on the base." I thought I had him on that one, but once again Jack was able to trump me.

"You're right," he said. "Dollars were really hard to come by. The military would do anything to keep them out of the hands of the North Vietnamese government."

"Why did they want dollars?" I asked, suddenly feeling not quite so savvy.

"Hanoi needed hard currency so it could buy weapons and medical supplies from Russia. The Russians wouldn't accept local currency. Didn't you know that arms deals are always denominated in dollars?"

"Well, yeah, now that you mention it, I do recall that the last time I bought a tank, I had to pay for it in US currency."

This drew a wry smile from Jack. I think he was finally seeing that we did indeed come from different worlds.

"Okay, I understand why dollars were so important," I said. "But you still haven't told me how you got what you needed to buy the old MPC from the locals."

He explained that the key was getting the American currency into Tan Son Nhut. Although he normally took some of his pay in dollars, they were credited to his US bank account and could not be transferred to Vietnam. Jack overcame this obstacle by transferring funds from his US account to a trusted friend's US account at another bank. This fellow was a former Dynalectron contract employee Jack had worked with in Japan. He had appreciated Jack's prank of inserting nursery rhymes in his QDRs, and they often had a few Kirin beers after work, commiserating over the wasteful money games the military was playing. No longer a military contractor but with a lot of local knowledge, Jack's friend had established a small consulting firm advising US companies looking to do business in Southeast Asia. He had set up a US dollar bank account in Bangkok to support his business, and he could transfer dollars there from his US bank. So Jack transferred the amount he needed to his friend's stateside bank, and his friend transferred it to Bangkok and then withdrew the cash. He put it in an official-looking Dynalectron envelope marked *Confidential* and addressed it to Jack. He asked an Air America crew member to deliver it to Jack in Tan Son Nhut. In this way, Jack was able to accumulate the dollars he used to buy old MPC from the locals.

Jack's final assignment in Vietnam was burial detail. He was chosen for it because his employer knew he had worked one summer in the cadaver room of the Oklahoma Medical Research

Foundation, where Dr. Wilson had gotten him a job. The instructors there routinely requested limbs, organs, and sometimes intact cadavers for work they were doing or classes they were teaching. Jack retrieved the needed items from their tanks of formaldehyde and delivered them to the instructors.

In comparison to the sanitized conditions at the Research Foundation, doing this sort of work in a war zone was ghastly. When a firefight was over and the dead and wounded had been evacuated, the men on burial detail patrolled the combat area looking for body parts, which they would bag and tag to be sent to the morgue. Labels like "hand, complete" and "lower leg, incomplete" were typical. Still, except for the smell – awful in the tropical conditions – the work of handling remains was similar to what Jack had done in Oklahoma and he was okay with it.

But it was brutally hot and humid work, and the men often developed fungus infections, especially in the groin. It was so common they even had a name for it: the creeping crud. Jack's answer to the problem was to sew his fatigue shirt to his trousers, and not wear a belt or underwear. The result was a better flow of air under his clothes and no chafing. It worked perfectly until the day, while Jack was working in his altered uniform, a new commanding officer spotted him. The just commissioned 2nd Lieutenant Willis was a stickler for military protocol and was offended when he saw Jack's modified fatigues. He ordered Jack to wear the uniform of the day. He refused, characteristically, as the man could not give him a good reason beyond "rules and regulations." That hadn't been acceptable when he was in military school, and it certainly made no sense out here, especially for a contract employee.

So Jack continued to wear his special outfit and was reprimanded a second time. It was beginning to sound ominously like his standoff with Officer Wolfe. By the third time, when Willis said he had no choice but to report Jack's insubordination to his superiors, Jack capitulated rather than risk losing his contract with Dynalectron. He was forced to give up what was a practical solution to a common problem, but by this time in his life, Jack was good at getting even.

He waited until one of the celebrated army meals, creamed chipped beef on toast (what the men called shit on a shingle) was served at breakfast. Jack spooned part of his serving into one of his empty collection bags, put it in his pocket, and carried it out to the graves registration point. He tossed it into a bin that already had a number of other collection bags with body parts in them. When Lieutenant Willis came by to check his uniform, Jack made an obvious show of taking his bag out of the bin. He opened it, scooped out a handful of the gross-looking stuff, and ate it, looking Willis straight in the eye.

"Wow, the maggots sure are soft today!" he exclaimed, and the lieutenant vomited. He went straight to the Division CO and accused Jack of cannibalism. Fortunately, Jack's assignment to burial detail was the last one on his contract, and he was moved out before the charge could be pursued. He was heading home.

Reunited

In contrast to Jack's convoluted tale, Susie and I were having an idyllic summer at the lake. The days were long, the bass fishing was good, and we were surrounded by friends. There were always projects to keep us busy, me splitting and stacking wood for our autumn fires, she composing and arranging music for our 250-year-old New England Congregational church. One project stands out, though, as it resulted from Susie's annual physical exam. The doctor told her that at her stage in life, she needed to be doing weight-bearing exercise if she wanted to avoid osteoporosis. Aerobic swimming in the lake and energetic hikes up nearby mountains were fine, he said, but it just wasn't enough. She needed to lift.

I began researching home gyms, and was amazed by the number and variety of these devices, all of them apparently designed by fiends intent on inflicting mild torture. Free weights would have been the simplest solution, but Susie had never done any weight training and was concerned about getting hurt. So I focused on controlled-motion machines, where the weights were safely stacked and confined in racks. There were hundreds of them for sale on Internet sites, most having been used only a year or two before their owners became disillusioned that they didn't look like Jane Fonda or Arnold Schwarzenegger.

I read the reviews on home gyms too, and found the predictable range of praise and complaint reflected in the prices. The machine I settled on was not found in the used equipment listings, which on reflection made sense: if it was really that good, nobody would want to sell it. Having no other choice than to spend four times what I intended, I ordered a new one. Because of its weight, only certain carriers would deliver it, and the one I chose—shortsightedly on the basis of price, it turned out—refused to bring it down our steep, curving driveway. It took me over an hour to shuttle the twenty-odd cartons down to the house in the trunk of my car. Since the thing literally weighed a ton, moving it was a workout in itself. *Wait a minute,* I thought, *Susie's the one who is supposed to be performing this weight-bearing exercise!* But she had conveniently arranged to be practicing the organ at church while I was struggling with the cartons.

Once I had everything in the basement, I had a look at the 143-page owner's manual. It was immediately apparent why the machine's manufacturer had counseled professional assistance for its assembly. There were hundreds of parts: the weights themselves, of course, but also angled frames, adjustable seats and backrests, cables, clamps, pulleys, and guides, plus a two-pound bag of assorted nuts, bolts, and washers. When I saw that some of the contraption's components were so intricate that they required subassembly, I knew I was in trouble.

I called my friend Paul, a retired General Electric machinist, and asked him to take a look at the manual and tell me if I should call in the cavalry. Paul is a wizard with a front-end loader/backhoe, maintains all of his vehicles, boats, trailers, and power equipment, and has more tools in his shop than I knew existed. I would take his expert advice about seeking assistance.

He asked me to leave the manual with him for the evening and call him in the morning. I went home, poured a glass of merlot, and told Susie what I had gotten myself into — all for her benefit, of course. Susie was raised Catholic, so I figured I'd play into her ingrained guilt. It didn't work.

"Don't give me that," she said. "You really bought the damn thing for yourself."

I went over to Paul's after his midday breakfast, eaten at that time because even years into retirement, he had never gotten over being a second-shift guy. "Well, doctor," I said, "what's the diagnosis? Do I need a specialist?"

"Nope. I can show you how to put this thing together, but you'll have to do the work. I don't have much strength in my hands these days."

I knew this admission bothered Paul, but he suffered from a degenerative nerve disorder, and it was getting harder and harder for him to perform manual tasks.

"No problem," I said. "You just tell me what to do, and if I screw something up." I didn't care if he couldn't tighten a wrench, I was just happy to have the help. "But this looks really complicated. Are you sure you want to take it on?"

"Look, Bill, you don't know this, but one of my jobs at GE was working on jet engines. I even wrote the maintenance manuals for a couple of them. Trust me, your weight machine will *not* be a problem."

He was right, but even so it took us over sixteen hours and I forget how many cold beers — I had stocked up with Paul's favorite — to get the job done. We proudly called Susie and Linda, Paul's wife, away from their quilting project so we could show them what we had accomplished. Linda, ever the direct New Englander, said to Susie, "You actually think you're going to get on this thing?"

"After sixteen hours and $1800, she better," I said.

I may have succeeded in getting her to use it eight or ten times over the next two years, but it wasn't a total loss. I worked out on it pretty regularly when we were in Maine, since I didn't have the sailboat to beat me up. I had to admit Susie was right; I did buy it for myself.

After Jack and I exchanged pleasantries on our next Skype call, I picked up where we had left off, at the end of Jack's contract in Vietnam. "I've heard that coming back to the States after being over there was pretty rough for a lot of guys," I said. "Especially with all the antiwar protests going on."

"It was May of 1969 when I landed in San Francisco. Do you have any idea what hippie central was like in California back then?"

"I do, actually. I was a graduate student at Berkeley. But what was your experience like?"

"I was three days out of the bush and found myself with an army haircut in Haight-Ashbury. I guess I looked like what I was, and the stoned locals pegged me right away. I also spoke like I was still in the service. You do know the military has its own way of talking, right?"

"Yes, I do. You can hear it today if you go to the airport and listen to their conversations. Kind of abrupt and clipped, with a peculiar intonation."

"Whatever it was, they hassled me for having been involved in the war. I mean, I'd just be walking down the street and would hear the comments and insults. None of them had the guts to confront me directly, and that was a good thing. After two years of constantly being in danger, I would have reacted without thinking. But the atmosphere was so strange and hostile, I had to get out of there. I called my buddy John and asked him if I could come up to his house in the New Mexico mountains. He said he wasn't going to be there, but I should feel free. He told me where the key was hidden and said I could use his guns if I wanted to do some shooting, just to clean them when I was done."

Jack was delighted to hole up in his friend's house and begin to relax after the constant stress of being in a war zone. Just as important, it got him away from the noise and attitude of the people in the city. After three months of solitude and catching up on sleep, he felt well enough adjusted to think about civilian life again. He decided to take a leisurely walk north through the Sierra Nevada mountains and back to civilization.

"I was used to packing and hiking," he said with a wry look. "It was kind of like Crocodile Dundee going on walkabout in that movie, and the best part was I didn't have to worry about getting shot. I ended up in Wyoming and called Lillie. She cursed me out for not calling sooner, but said she realized that most guys coming back from Vietnam needed some time to get their heads straight. 'I'd rather wait a few months than have you strangle me if I accidentally kicked you in bed,' she told me. She agreed to come down and meet me in Wyoming."

Jack still had a lot of cash from his military pay and MPC schemes, so on a lark the two of them went to Woodstock to hear music, lie in the mud and rain, and (he admitted) sample some of the substances that were so readily available at the festival. Then it was back to Seattle, where they had met and where Lillie had been working on a military contractor's production line while he was away. Now Jack had to find work.

He started by calling around to the places he had worked before going to Vietnam, and a friend from the Blue Onion in Denver suggested they join forces and start a machine shop building molds and making tools.

"He said he had figured out a way to get started and would provide the financing for a share in the profits if I would run the shop," Jack said. "I asked him how he was going to raise the money for the building and equipment, and he told me, 'We'll use a modified title deed.'"

"What's that?'" I asked him. "I've bought and sold a lot of houses and boats in my life, but I've never heard of a modified title deed. Was this guy a lawyer or something?"

"No, but let me tell you how it worked. We dug out the title document to Ed's house, carefully whited out his name and substituted it with mine. I made a copy and took it to a bank in town and told them I wanted to use the property as collateral for $100,000 in financing so I could set up my shop."

This sounded fishy to me. "You mean they gave you a $100,000 loan on the strength of a dummied-up document?"

"Noooo," he explained patiently. "They didn't actually give me any money. What they did was, set up an account for that amount that I could use to buy the equipment and materials I needed."

"So when you found a lathe or drill press or whatever else a machine shop needs, they would let you take out the cash to pay for it?"

"No again. They disbursed the funds directly to the vendors. The money never came into my hands."

"But Jack," I said, "didn't the modified title look funny to the bank? I mean, it wasn't an original, and the typing of your name must have looked different from the printing on the rest of the document."

"Well, yeah, it did, but we had Ed's attorney initial and certify it as part of the business arrangement he drew up between Ed and me. You have to realize this was a small-town bank, where Ed and his attorney were known to the manager. They understood what we were trying to accomplish."

Jack was able to pay off the loan in two years, but then they hit a slump. He needed $5000 a month to run the business and support his family, but was only taking in $2000. By this time, Lillie was at home with their three-year-old daughter Shelly — born in 1970, following the "Summer of Love" in Woodstock — and they didn't consider daycare an option. "My break came in 1974, when a company affiliated with Dynelectron contacted me about a contract they had to help Robert Mugabe's resistance moverment in Rhodesia. He was in prison at the time, but his supporters in ZANU had amassed a war chest over the years since the movement started in 1963, and they were hiring foreign mercenaries."

Knowing what a bad actor Mugabe turned out to be, I asked why we wanted to help *that* guy. "I mean, he appropriated people's property, wrecked a perfectly good economy, and brutalized his people."

"You really don't know much about history, do you? Back then he was seen as a good guy, trying to liberate his country from British colonial rule."

Jack tried to tell me that the local black population wanted free elections, but I said, "Not all of them. Susie and I met a former Rhodesian couple when we were out cruising, and the guy, who was white, said he had fought alongside the blacks who opposed Mugabe. It wasn't as simple as blacks vs. whites, he said. It was a tribal power struggle among the locals about who would run the country after the white-minority government fell."

"Look," Jack said, "I didn't care one way or the other about the political machinations. They offered me a six-month contract at $10,000 a month to go to Rhodesia and train the Mugabe people in Vietnam-style tactics. I accepted."

After Jack got back from Rhodesia, he used the money he had

earned to pay off some overdue pediatric bills, and had enough left over to keep the business going. Orders stayed reasonably strong for the next few years, and then in 1977 he got a major contract offer from an aircraft company in the Pacific Northwest. It meant they would have to relocate the business, but Lillie didn't argue. Seattle was familiar turf, and she had friends there who could help her and Shelly get settled. They moved to Redland, a suburb on the opposite side of Lake Washington from Seattle, an easy commute to the company's main plant.

The project was building a mold for the main cabin windows in one of the company's midsized jets. Jack had signed a contract with them, and when he delivered the mold they claimed that "first article inspection" approval had not been received and refused to pay him. They offered a second contract, promising to pay off the first one at the same time they made the down payment for another mold.

"At this point," Jack said to me, "I was wary. When they said they needed my quote in three days, I said to them, 'How do I know you'll pay me if I do this job?' and pointed out the delay on the first mold's inspection. They gave me a verbal guarantee that they would do the first article inspection within a week of my delivering it to them. So I said okay and wrote up the quote. They accepted it, and I guess in an attempt at good faith after what had gone down, they gave me a deposit to start work. I waited until the check cleared, then I made the mold. I ran three window parts with it and delivered them to the company. They said the parts looked good and asked me to give them the mold. I said, 'I'll give you the mold after I've seen a third party's inspection approval on it and you've paid me for my work on both molds.' Three days later the approval came in and they showed up at my shop with a bank draft. I said, 'I won't accept anything but cash,' because I didn't trust them not to cancel the draft as soon as they had the mold in their hands. The next day, they appeared with $24,000 and I gave the mold to them. They told me they would never give me another job, and that saved me from having to tell them I wouldn't work for them anyway."

Soon after that, Jack got a contract to make molds for Hewlett-Packard computers. He moved his shop to Portland to be closer to the company, thinking he might get similar work from the other high-tech companies in the area. He switched his emphasis to designing rather than physically making molds because the money was better.

"I could get a 50 percent profit on the designs I came up with, and when I made the parts as well, I got another 25 percent."

Jack ran his shop profitably and the business grew steadily, but he was getting bored with only domestic assignments. Once Shelly was in school, he gradually brought Lillie on board and trained her. He was confident that she, along with their long-time secretary Phoebe, could run things if he was away. He began seeking out contracts with satisfied repeat customers who had operations outside the US, where his expertise was uncommon and therefore would be well compensated.

Jack accepted assignments in several countries during the late '70s, and in some cases he was even asked to use his expertise in explosives. These projects were extremely lucrative for someone willing and able to execute them, and Jack was inventive. He was vague when I pressed him for details, saying it wasn't wartime and these were private contracts with organizations who would not appreciate being revealed. But he couldn't resist telling me about a flashlight he fabricated to conclude one assignment.

"It's human nature," he said. "A person finding a flashlight on the ground next to their car will pick it up and try to turn it on. It's automatic. Nobody thinks the thing might blow up."

Jack's abilities with explosives were not only applied in

offshore settings. He was willing to help friends in the States as well, and one incident stands out for how badly it went. He was contacted in 1979 by a Vietnam buddy who'd had a tree fall on his house in an Oklahoma tornado. He'd spent the past year and a half fighting with his insurance company. Their position was that since the house was not a total loss, they would not honor his claim. When his friend told him about this, Jack offered to help. The house in question was heated by a gas furnace in the basement, and this gave Jack an idea. If the basement could be filled with gas and detonated remotely, the house would indeed be a total loss. So Jack built a radio-controlled sparking device and placed it—with his friend's knowledge, so he could make sure his family was absent and get his valuables out—on the wall opposite the furnace.

As his friend was checking his mail on the appointed day, he found a notice from the insurance company stating that they would honor some of the claim after all. He called Jack and told him there was no need to blow up the house. He removed the device from the basement, but before he could get it back to Jack to disarm it, his seventeen-year-old son found it.

"It looked menacing enough," Jack told me, "and the stupid kid took it to a bank, put in on the counter in front of a teller's window, told him it was a bomb, and demanded money."

The teller later told the police he figured that even if it was a bomb, the kid wouldn't be dumb enough to set it off and blow himself up along with everything else. He pushed the silent alarm button under his side of the counter, but hesitated long enough that the kid spooked and ran, leaving the device behind. Jack's problem now was that the police had it. They ran a photograph in the newspapers, asking for information. The owner of the electronics shop where Jack had assembled the device recognized the photo, called the cops, and told them he knew the man they were looking for.

"They caught up with me and I was charged with conspiracy, which could have put me in prison for ten to twenty years. I didn't want to risk that, so I took a plea bargain and pled guilty to 'actions that would effect, delay, or impede commerce.' It was still a felony but it carried a lesser sentence of nine months to seven years."

I was incredulous. "Are you telling me that you're a convicted felon?"

"Yes, I am," he said. "Spent three years in prison."

In my sheltered life, I had never known anyone who had gone to prison, although I did know some who probably should have. During my business career I had seen examples of intellectual property infringement, restraint of trade, and bribery. The perpetrators of these white-collar crimes were defended by corporate lawyers who negotiated fines, not imprisonment. The companies meted out their own punishments for the costs involved, typically involving reassignment to lesser jobs or banishment to remote locations. Rehabilitation after a few years of obscurity was frequently possible, but some people never recovered. I knew one officer-level executive who was apparently so stressed by his lower-level job that he suffered a stroke and was confined to his bed. His mind was unimpaired, and for such a brilliant and driven man, his suffering must have been extraordinary. I told Jack about this fellow and asked him which he would choose: this man's fate or his three years in prison.

"Prison," he said without hesitation.

I wanted to hear more about Jack's experience, so I asked where he was sent. What had happened next?

"They couldn't figure out where to put me. It was my first offense, at least as far as they knew, so a level one out-custody facility was possible."

"What does that mean? Is it a minimum security prison, like a camp you can't leave?" I realized I was about to learn a lot more about how the criminal justice system operated.

"Unfortunately not," Jack said. "They discovered my history with explosives and considered me too dangerous for minimum security. The parole commission was ordered to prepare a presentencing report to give to the judge."

"What's a presentencing report?"

"Before they could decide on where to send me, the judge said he needed a lot more information."

In working up the report, it came out that Jack had a BS in mechanical engineering, his IQ was 147, and he belonged to Mensa. He didn't have any longstanding social ties to his community, and had done contract work as a mercenary in several countries. They also found that years earlier, on a lark, he and Lillie had moved a friend's sailboat from Portland to San Francisco without notifying the lien holder. He was therefore implicated in interstate transportation of a stolen vessel.

"You have to understand," he told me. "Once these people get their hooks into you, they never let go. You're part of the system. They will always find something to hang on you."

The parole commission's report concluded that Jack represented a threat to society. On this basis, the judge increased the minimum of Jack's sentence to one year, which was the threshold for being sent to a real prison, not an out-custody facility. Further, his case was remanded to the commission to determine when he could be released. Their preference was for the maximum sentence of seven years, but because Jack had no prior arrests, they were constrained to giving him a mandatory release after forty-eight months.

"They were pissed because they couldn't lock me up longer,

so they sent me to a level-five maximum-security prison, put me into six-foot by nine-foot cell, and allowed me out in the yard for only an hour a day."

Under these restrictive conditions and with the lack of exercise, Jack developed a swelling in his chest due to a blocked lymph gland and was moved to a prison hospital in Missouri. When he recovered, he was sent to a medium-security facility, the first time during his incarceration that he was in company with other prisoners.

He was assigned a bunk in a two-man cubicle with chest-high partitions. Each contained upper and lower bunk beds, two lockers, and a table. The cubicles were arrayed along the two long walls and down the middle of a rectangular room. Bathrooms were at the ends. The guards' office was against one long wall and was flanked by a TV area on one side and a pool table on the other. An airlock-style double-door sally port for entering and leaving the room was located directly across from the office. A holding area, referred to as The Bullpen, could be accessed from the sally port and was used when prisoners were going outside the walls. It was also a rectangular room, but contained only rows of benches that ran the length of it, four feet from the walls and five feet apart. There was a toilet and a sink in one corner, open to the rest of the room. No privacy.

The most common reason for going through the Bullpen was for court appearances, but regardless of their destination, the men were always put in restraints. They were handcuffed, and the handcuffs were shackled to a chain going around the midsection. A second chain ran from the belly chain to leg irons attached to the ankles. The leg irons were shackled together by a twelve-inch chain. The end result was that the men were unable to use their hands and could only take mincing steps.

"See, they try to make going to court as uncomfortable as

possible so guys won't file complaints. If you do send up a kite — that's what filing a complaint is called — they try to resolve it in-house with an overseer team of counselors. If that fails, you have a right to take it to court. The process typically requires ten appearances over six months, and each time you have to get up so early you miss breakfast. Then you get chained up in the Bullpen, marched to the bus, chained into the bus, and taken to the courthouse by ten o'clock. Then you wait. Maybe the judge will call you, maybe not. In any case, you miss lunch because there's no kitchen there. By the time you get back to the Bullpen and they take the chains off, dinner is over. So you've spent the whole day in restraints and missed all three meals. They do give you a banana and a sandwich with one slice of ham and cheese, but the whole experience is so bad, most guys avoid it."

"Let's go back to when you started at the new facility," I said. "Tell me what it was like."

"On my first day there, a nigger stopped by and tossed a bag on my bunk. He said he was the welcoming committee and told me the bag had candy, cigarettes, soap, and a toothbrush in it. He told me it would be three days before I got my commissary privileges and I could probably use the stuff. Then he walked away. My cubicle mate, Big Bob, said to me, 'If you touch that bag, you're his bitch,' and I understood what that meant. I thanked Bob for the insight. Then I asked him if he could use his commissary privileges to get me a G string for a guitar.

"'You don't have a guitar,' he said. 'What do you want a G string for?' I told him he was right, I didn't have a guitar, but that I'd appreciate it if he would get it for me just the same, and he did."

"I'm with Bob," I said. "Why did you want a G string?"

"You know what a G string is, right? It's the one that plays the higher middle notes, and it's made of thin but very strong single-strand wire."

I had a feeling I knew where this was going.

"See, if you break off two six- or seven-inch lengths of a broom handle, you can tie the ends of the G string around the middle of each piece, leaving about two feet of wire in between. I waited until after the eleven o'clock headcount and then went around to the back of the nigger's bunk and looped the wire over his head. I pulled it tight enough across his throat that he knew what it was and he shouldn't try to sit up. I could have pulled that wire straight through his neck. I said to him, 'You come near me again, I'll cut your head off and put it where it can only see my boots.' You can't do that now, though. They make the broomsticks out of stiffened paper."

"I can see how that takes the fun out of it," I said, intending to be witty. He gave me a crooked, knowing smile.

Jack's history also helped him get squared away in his new surroundings. It got around that he had fought as a mercenary, had advised Green Beret teams in Vietnam and had killed a lot of people. His absolute refusal to cooperate with anyone in authority was respected too.

"You know what goes on in prison, right? Especially to the new guys? You have to make it clear from the get-go that you are not to be messed around with. After I scared off the nigger, the bad guys left me alone. I made friends with some of the other convicts and I learned a lot from them, stuff I was able to use later. That's what they say prison is, you know. Graduate school for criminals. But they're wrong. It's Wall Street that awards the advanced degrees."

Jack was probably right about making the first move, I thought, remembering what he had said when he got me a .357 magnum revolver for Susie's and my protection at our place on Siguaterra.

"There are no police out there," he said. "If someone breaks in, you shoot first. The guy who shoots first wins."

"Should I shoot through the door when I hear the guy trying to get in?"

"Naaa, don't ruin your door. Wait 'til he's in the house, then shoot him. If you're using a flashlight, hold it out to one side. No sense giving *him* a target."

I asked Jack if he'd had any other kind of problem in prison, and he told me about the time he took the place of another guy in the prison's machine shop. The warden knew about Jack's education and experience as a machinist, and reassigned the less capable man.

"He was pissed and let me know he was going to get back at me. But before he could do anything, I got him moved to another facility."

"How the hell did you manage that?"

"You have to understand how these people operate," he said, and explained how he pulled it off. "I took an empty tin can and put a couple of tomatoes in it. Left it under my bunk for a week until a green mold formed on the surface. Then I scooped the stuff into my hands and went to the guy's bunk. One night, I waited until he was snoring with his mouth open, and when he was about to take a breath, I blew the mold into his face. Two days later, he had a lung infection and was shipped out to the prison hospital. When he recovered, they moved him to another location. In incidents like this, it was their practice not to send the guy back to where he was before."

After years of silence, Jack was finally opening up about his experiences in prison, and it was clear he wanted to keep talking. "You know the difference between an inmate and a convict, don't you?" he asked, his tone indicating he was sure I didn't. I think Jack liked regaling me with his tales about the underbelly of life, and this subject would give him another chance to educate me. In fact, I welcomed it. I had seen the TV shows, read *In the Belly of the Beast,* and taken college and graduate courses in abnormal sociology, including one that dealt with prison communities. But that was conceptual book learning. Jack had lived it.

"Well," he began, "inmates call the guards Correction Officers or COs. Convicts call them hacks, like when you hack up phlegm. An inmate will talk cooperatively to a CO one-on-one, with no witnesses. A convict will not cooperate in any way with a hack, and if they do talk it's with a silent 'cosigner' present. If there's an incident, an inmate will report what he has seen (although not who was involved), while a convict will have seen nothing.

"Also, convicts often walk alone in the compound, but inmates always walk in groups. And in the housing units, 75 percent of the guys are inmates."

"It sounds like the inmates are seeking safety in numbers, am I right?" I asked.

"Yes, but it doesn't always work. The convicts don't respect the inmates because they cooperate with the COs. More important, they don't trust the inmates. There's no way of knowing what they're saying to the COs. So if the convicts believe an inmate has ratted someone out, there are ways to get back at him. Like the light bulb trick."

Shades of Vietnam, I thought. "Go ahead. Tell me about the light bulb trick."

"First, you remove the light bulb over the inmate's bunk. You tape a straw to the glass at the base of the bulb, take a nail, and shoot it down the straw using a rubber band. The nail punches a hole in the glass but doesn't shatter it. Then you pour acetone or some other flammable liquid into the bulb and screw it back in. When the hack comes in to do a bed check after dark, he switches on the lights. The bulb over the inmate's bunk explodes and sprays flaming liquid all over the guy. This doesn't work anymore, though. They've replaced all the incandescent bulbs with LEDs."

"Took the fun right out of that trick too, didn't they," I said.

Jack didn't miss a beat. "But the convicts are trustworthy, and that's why they get the higher echelon jobs in the prison industries. They're the chefs in the kitchen and the supervisors in the manufacturing shops. The inmates aren't allowed to serve meals, because they'll steal food or short the guys' rations. In the shops, they'll walk away with supplies and even tools. So, they're assigned to clearing tables or sweeping up. The convicts, on the other hand, are meticulous. They keep track of every item that comes in, account for how it's used, and put every utensil or tool back in its place at the end of the day. If you ask a hack who he'd rather work with, he'll say the convicts. He may need the inmates for information, but he respects the convicts."

"How is it determined which you are, an inmate or a convict?"

"It's up to the individual. You can be weak and be an inmate, or a hard-ass and be a convict. How you behave lets everybody know. Are you going to be nice to the COs and let them mess with you, or be a convict who refuses to cooperate with the hacks in any way? In my case, the way I handled the nigger let people know I was a convict from Day One.

"Convicts play it straight with each other too, just as they walk the straight and narrow in their prison jobs. I'll give you an example. Most guys have a hustle or two to make money, like getting drugs or other contraband in and distributed. My main hustle was getting money *out*."

"How in the world did you manage that?"

"Remember, I was working in the machine shop. We made stuff to be sent outside to supply other shops, so I had access to the shipments. When guys needed to get money to their wives or whatever, they'd give me rolls of quarters."

"Rolls of quarters? Why rolls of quarters? And how did the guys get them?"

"We all had commissary accounts where we put the money we made in the prison industries, or it got deposited from the outside. We could make withdrawals once a week, but they only gave it to us in rolls of quarters."

"Okay, so the guys gave you rolls of quarters. What did you do with them?"

"I packaged them in a box like the ones we used to ship things outside. When I was making up the shipping labels, I put a nonexistent address on the box with the quarters. There were usually a couple of dozen boxes in each shipment, so one label with a dummy address wasn't noticed. When the shipper couldn't deliver the box with the quarters, they put it in their warehouse as a 'Will Call.' A friend of one of the guys inside picked it up and distributed the money like he'd been told to."

"How did the guys know they could trust this friend not to just steal the money or skim some of it off?"

"Look, I told you that convicts were trustworthy. They wouldn't steal from each other, it was against their code. If someone betrayed that trust, the consequences were serious."

Jack would have continued in this vein, but I stopped him. "I think I've absorbed about all I can about this for now." The insider information about the two parallel cultures was certainly fascinating, but regardless of the spin he put on it, the fact remained that Jack was in federal prison from 1980 to 1983.

Fleeing South

Autumn had come to Maine. The loons were still around, but would soon be heading back to the sea, where they would be able to catch fish during the winter. Somewhere back in their evolution, loons had learned that fishing in a lake frozen over with a foot of ice was not possible. Now, in preparation for the flight and responding to some hard-wired signal in their brains, they were practicing takeoffs. For a creature so graceful in the water, getting airborne was awkward. Loons' legs are positioned so far back on their bodies that they can't walk on land, but if their wings can lift up the front end of their bodies, the legs can paddle rapidly enough in the water to achieve liftoff at the rear. They literally run a hundred yards or more along the surface, feet and wingtips slapping down until they have gained enough momentum to take off. A couple of circles to exercise wings not used to flying all summer, and then they splash down, rest a while, and take off again. After a week or so, Susie and I would realize that we weren't hearing the loons' calls anymore. It would be a melancholy sign that the seasons indeed were changing.

Fortunately, we had one more harvest moon to enjoy before

taking the pontoon boat out of the water and lifting the dock up far enough that the ice couldn't reach it. We knew from high school physics that water expands as it freezes, while most other fluids in nature contract as they cool. Docks left in the water during a Maine winter are twisted and splintered by the pressure of the expanding ice.

We had set things up with Linda and Paul weeks before, planning for the September full moon that we knew would rise at the same time as the sun was setting. It would be a dramatic sight, with the skies to the west glowing and turning the water golden, while in the east the moon rose and cast its silver shimmer on the lake's surface. All we needed was clear skies, uncertain at this time of year, but Providence favored us.

The previous season, I had mounted a propane grill on the rail of our pontoon boat. Susie and I still derived great satisfaction from being able to prepare and enjoy an alfresco dinner on board, even if it was only on a lake and not some Caribbean anchorage. The important thing was to be on the water. One evening earlier that summer, Paul and Linda were out on their pontoon boat for sundowners and saw us setting up our boat's folding table, salmon steaks smoking on the grill and a bottle of pinot grigio in the ice bucket. Paul asked me if I could set up his boat the same way, and I was glad to be able to return the favor of his guiding me through the assembly of my home gym.

As soon as I had mounted his grill, we planned the sunset/moonrise dinner party. We were fortunate that the two boats could be rafted together so their side gates lined up, with the grills extending out from the rails on the opposite sides. It was like having a square two-piece dining room floating on the lake. As we sat enjoying snacks and cocktails while the claret breathed and the rib eyes grilled, other boaters came by and asked good-naturedly if they could make dinner reservations for the next night. Unlike seafarers, lake people might barbeque on their docks, but wouldn't go to the trouble of setting up for a meal afloat. I'm sure we were seen as oddballs, but maybe a little envied too.

On our next Skype call, Jack told me he had been let out on parole six months before his mandatory release date. I couldn't resist it. "Why? Because of good behavior?"

"Ha-ha, very funny. They did it so they could send me to a halfway house."

"That must have been a big improvement over being locked up in prison, right?"

"You'd think so, but it's actually risky. Half of the guys in those places screw up in some way. The house management can set whatever rules they like, and if you break one, it's a parole violation. Could be something as minor as showing up a minute late for dinner. Then they can send you back to prison. I knew a guy who was in his last few weeks when he broke a rule, and back he went. No credit for the five months he had put in. They just tacked another six months onto his sentence."

The practice was to send people to halfway houses in their home states, so Jack was assigned to one in Oregon. "They took me to the bus terminal in handcuffs and a belly chain. As we approached, the people at the ticket window backed away from us in a wave, like you see when you drop a stone in the water. The hacks gave the agent written authorization to issue me a ticket, and only after the agent passed it to me did they take off the restraints. But I had to wait half an hour for them to finish their coffee and donuts and leave. Then I sold the ticket, went to the airport, and took a flight to Portland that Lillie had paid for. Since they had allowed me two and a half days to get there by bus, I had some unsupervised time with her and with Shelly. She was thirteen by then."

Jack had been locked up for a total of almost four years, so the sense of freedom was exhilarating. He took his family to a small resort in the mountains of western Oregon that had walking trails through the pine and aspen forest. There was a clear, cool stream running through the property, with rainbow trout feeding where the water cascaded over the rocks. The air at night was so crisp, it seemed to crackle. The stars were brilliant, blue-white points that reminded him of diamonds. It was paradise, the experience heightened by knowing it would be so short.

But there was no escaping the halfway house, and Jack reported there as ordered. In his initial interview, he was told that as part of his reintroduction to society, he was required to work. They were surprised to learn that he already had a job. He had contacted a former associate from the Colorado machine shop who now had his own business in Portland, and he had offered to take Jack on as a contract employee. The arrangement was that each time he completed a project, he would be paid; he was not salaried. The first project netted him $9700, and after two and a half months he had earned nearly $22,000. As a condition of his halfway-house status, Jack had to inform his parole officer about the job and how much he was making, and she was incensed. He was making more than she was. She told Jack that the system didn't work that way, and that rehabilitation meant that he was supposed to "start at the bottom." But because he already had the job, she could not force him to resign. Frustrated, she began harassing Jack's boss with endless bureaucratic questions and demanding documentation of working hours, FICA payments, and tax withholdings. It became so onerous that he had to ask Jack if he would leave, just to get rid of her.

After the machine-shop job, Jack was sent to Freightliner for an interview. The personnel man there saw his CV, and realizing that he had a technical degree, offered him a position as a liaison between the engineering department and tooling. Again, this was not "starting at the bottom," but Freightliner was a big company, and as part of their normal business practices they had all the information the PO could ask for. This time, she was unable to get Jack fired, and he stayed with them until his six months at the halfway house were completed. But her frustration had turned her against Jack, and she went out of her way to cause problems for him during that time.

"I was only allowed to leave for work one hour before my shift started, and I had to be back within an hour after it ended. They wouldn't let me have a car or take out enough money for a cab, so I had to take the bus to work. The problem was, there were no buses running when I got off and I had to jog back in order to make it on time. There were other rules. I could only use the house phone if I told them in advance who I wanted to call. I couldn't receive calls, except from family members who had been cleared. If I wanted to buy something, I had to get prior approval and let my PO know where and when I spent the money. When I got paid, I had to show her a copy of the bank deposit. I could only withdraw small amounts from the account. Fortunately, Lillie could access the money."

There was a rare bright spot in this restricted existence. The halfway house had some Japanese residents, and these men were given a two-hour leave every week to go to a bathhouse. In fairness, non-Japanese got the same leave, and Jack took advantage of this privilege. "I went into the bathhouse with my Japanese friends but walked right out the back door. Lillie picked me up and we had our weekly conjugal visit."

This opportunity to get away became especially important when Shelly suffered a seizure while on her way back from a visit to Lillie's mother in Los Angeles. The seizure was the result of an aneurism in her brain, and Shelly underwent surgery. The operation was successful, but while in the hospital she contracted meningitis.

"I wanted to see her, but my PO refused to let me go. She said I was still considered a security risk and wouldn't be supervised while I was away. I was turned down three times by that heartless bitch. I found out later that she didn't even record my requests."

He went anyway, using his Japanese bathhouse privilege to manage it without being caught. He could spend a few hours with his daughter and return about the same time the bathers did. Sadly, Shelly's condition deteriorated and ultimately she died. Jack was devastated, but his PO even denied his request to go to the funeral. No record of this request was made, either. The woman was obviously out to make Jack's life as miserable as possible, and he finally lodged a number of complaints about her. She was demoted, but vowed to get back at him for it.

The hospital bill was another blow. Shelly had been in intensive care at Portland General Hospital for almost a month, and the final bill was $1,422,000. Jack's shop insurance paid $680,000 of it, and he paid $742,000 by emptying all of his business accounts, holding back just enough to cover Shelly's funeral. Technically, he still owes Portland General $65,000.

After grieving his daughter's loss, Jack pulled himself together and eventually found a job in another machine shop. But his new PO had been coached by her predecessor and found out about it before Jack started work. She prevented him from taking the job, saying she would not allow him to be in a business similar to the one he had previously owned, where he would have the possibility of fashioning explosives. She told him that so long as he was on parole, even after he was released from the halfway house, he couldn't go back to his own shop, either. In frustration, he told Lillie to sell the business.

Jack was angered and dejected by this turn of events. He was, after all, finding work and believed that was the idea behind the halfway house and parole concept, so that offenders didn't end back in prison. But being repeatedly stopped by the system from accepting or holding decent jobs made him cynical. "I came to the conclusion," he told me, "that the prison, halfway house, and parole arrangement were set up so that those employed in it could keep their jobs. If they could make the ex-cons so angry they returned to crime, the cycle would repeat itself. And it worked: the majority of halfway-house residents are back in jail within a year."

"I need to ask you something," I said to Jack, "and I hope you won't be offended. How much do you think your attitude may have contributed to all the mistreatment in your life? I've been writing your story for months now, and ever since your run-in with the nun who rapped your knuckles, I've seen a pattern of defiance and even revenge. Sometimes it was just getting around the rules, like your shady enterprises in military school, but sometimes it was directed specifically at one person, like the lieutenant in Vietnam or Officer Wolfe. Now you've got the prison and parole people against you. What's going on?"

Jack didn't hesitate. "You're right. I can be my own worst enemy. Do you remember what I told you shortly after we met? I described something nasty I had done and I said to you, 'I'm really not a nice person.' You thought I was joking at the time, but now you know better. I'm not a nice person. I'll do whatever I have to do to make my way, and to profit from it if I can. If you cross me, I'll pay you back as harshly as I need to in order to feel better about it." He paused for a moment. "On the flip side, if you are my friend and need my help, I will do anything for you.

That guy who blocked the way to your dock in Siguaterra was a dead man if you hadn't called me off at the last minute. If he gives you a hard time again, or if anybody hurts Susie, just call me. But realize what will happen."

Susie and I had intuited what Jack's code of friendship might mean for us, but this was the first time he had laid it out explicitly. It was akin to his revelation about being a felon; both had taken him years to get comfortable enough with me to talk about. I told him again how unusual a person I thought he was, that I had never known anyone else like him, and was glad to have him as a friend.

When Jack was released from the halfway house on parole, he told me that he and Lillie found a print shop for sale in Tacoma, Washington. He was allowed to buy it—"I guess they figured it was unlikely that I could build bombs in a print shop"—and he was transferred to a PO there. Unfortunately, the man was a relative of Jack's first PO in Portland. This fellow made a habit of visiting the print shop during business hours. One day when there were a lot of people around, he announced that he was the parole officer for the shop's owner. The word spread, and all but the most understanding customers stopped frequenting the shop. The business suffered. To make matters even more difficult, the PO demanded an audit. The auditor found that the way quarterly taxes were being handled was open to fraud, and Jack had to divest himself of ownership in the shop.

He went back to Denver at his old business partner's suggestion to see if he could restart the machine shop they had set up there years before. In this new location, Jack was fortunate to get a decent PO who allowed him to run the business. Finally having someone on his side would soon prove critical. Lillie had stayed behind in Washington to sell the print shop, and she was still grieving Shelly's loss. Her anguish was made worse by a thoughtless seventeen-year-old girl in the apartment above her, who played loud music and had frequent late-night parties.

"Lillie finally had it one night and went upstairs to confront the girl. She told Lillie to mind her own business and pushed her away from the door. I told you that nobody pushed Lillie around, didn't I? Well, Lillie punched the girl in the face and threw her down the stairs. She went after her and bashed her head on the floor a bunch of times. Somebody called the police, and they warned Lillie she could be charged with assaulting a minor. They told her that the girl was the mayor's daughter, and if Lillie was arrested, it wouldn't look good."

When Lillie told Jack about the incident, he confided in his parole officer and requested to go to Washington to pick up his wife. The PO said yes, but warned him, "We never had this conversation." He added that Jack's former PO in Washington had not yet transferred his file to Colorado, so technically he wasn't responsible for Jack's actions. Jack left immediately, even though he knew that if he helped Lillie, he risked being charged with "aiding and abetting flight to avoid prosecution." He didn't care; he had to get her out of there as fast as possible. He borrowed his former partner's car, called Lillie, and told her to pack only one suitcase. "Be ready to walk out when I get there. Have everything you're taking just inside the door. No last minute items. I want to be pulling away within a minute of getting there."

They drove straight back to Colorado. The assault charges against Lillie were indeed filed, and Jack's former PO in Washington was informed about it, because it was known that Lillie was his wife. The man told his counterpart in Colorado that he was going to charge Jack with violating his parole and see to it that the aiding and abetting charge was also lodged against him.

"My PO in Denver told me to prepare myself for more jail time."

But Jack had learned from a buddy in prison—a jailhouse lawyer—that it typically took a week for charge sheets to be sent to and from DC, which they had to be since he'd been convicted of a federal offense. This gave him enough time to finish a mold project for a customer in Utah and put some money in his pocket before making his next move. He called his friend Brad, a former Green Beret he had worked with in the Vietnam highlands who now also lived in Colorado. Jack explained the situation and asked Brad if he could borrow his truck to drive to Utah and finish the project. His friend agreed and Jack took off, leaving Lillie with Brad. I found it odd that he would leave his wife with another man, no matter how honorable, and asked why she couldn't just stay at his place.

"If anybody came snooping around, I didn't want to take the chance of them finding her at my place." Jack was already operating in flight mode.

"The guy in Utah paid me $7500 for the mold, and I used some of the money to buy a twenty-eight-foot Airstream trailer. I hooked it up to Brad's truck and drove back to our place in Colorado. We packed our things into the trailer and then towed it over to Brad's. I had him drive me to the biggest used truck dealer in the area, and used the rest of the money I had to buy us our own truck. I told the dealer I would pay cash if he would agree to an open title."

"What's an open title?" I asked. "Why did you want it?" I was thinking back to the modified deed Jack had used to finance the shop in Denver. He sighed, and I knew I had asked another naïve question.

"Because it wouldn't have my name on it, and I could fill in whatever name I needed, depending on the situation."

It dawned on me that Jack was doing everything he could to make himself hard to find. He drove the truck back to Brad's, hooked up the trailer, and he and Lillie headed south.

When they got to Arizona, Jack approached a former client for whom he had done one of his more unsavory overseas projects. Because of the nature of the project, the guy owed Jack a favor. "I told him it was payback time, and that I had to get out of the country. I needed a new identity to cross into Mexico."

Jack admitted it was an implicit threat, but he felt he had no choice since Lillie was facing charges and he would go back to prison. He asked for the man's driver's license number, a copy of his birth certificate, and some rent and utility receipts. Jack saw that the man was reluctant, but he must have realized the risk of getting caught up in this temporary identity switch was small in comparison to the consequences of his overseas actions being exposed. He agreed and gave Jack the documents he needed.

"We drove to Phoenix, and I took the documents to the department of motor vehicles. An hour later, I walked out with an Arizona driver's license with my client's name on it, but my picture. I put his name on the truck's open title too."

Although at that time they could get into Mexico on their driver's licenses, Jack knew they would eventually need passports. As they went through Albuquerque, he went to see a pawnbroker with whom he had done business during his lean drifter days and who was savvy — as pawnbrokers usually are — in the ways of the world. The pawnbroker referred him to an attorney who worked on immigration matters and could handle the details in absentia. Jack paid him with the money he had gotten from pawning a 9mm Luger and asked to have the passports sent via DHL to the American Express office in Cancun. With those wheels in motion, and Jack's "valid" driver's license and vehicle registration in hand, they hauled the trailer into Mexico the next day to begin their new life.

Jack headed to the less well-known east coast of the country, avoiding the big tourist areas of Mazatlán, Puerto Vallarta, and Acapulco on the west coast because of the greater possibility of being identified there. They decided to go to the Chetumal Bay area on the Yucatan Peninsula. About half-way there, they stopped to overnight in Tlaxcala, but the only place they could find to park their trailer was a motel. Lillie, who spoke some Spanish, went in to make arrangements for a room. What neither of them realized was that a *motel* in Mexico did not mean the same thing as in the States. The woman in the office asked Lillie how many hours she would need the room, and informed her that she would have to pay the house 25 percent of whatever she made. Lillie realized the motel was in fact a brothel used by the local prostitutes and she was expected to pay the madam her fee. After explaining she wasn't a hooker and haggling over the room rent for the whole night, Lillie and the madam agreed on a price. She went back to the truck and informed Jack that it was going to cost him $100 to sleep with her, "probably the most expensive piece of ass you've ever had."

The next morning, Jack and Lillie drove to Mahahual, a village north of Xcalak, where they found an almost deserted beach. They camped there for a week, cooking and sleeping in the trailer. It was tight at twenty-eight feet, but a lot like living on the boat they had sailed to San Francisco. During the day they loafed on the beach in the shade of the palm, sea grape, and almond trees and talked about how they would set up their lives. They ate a lot of beans and rice and got their protein from the sea, where most days Jack could take a swim and spear a grouper or grab a lobster off the reef. But the bugs got too bad, so they gave up and went to a trailer park in Xcalak. After paying for the first month, Jack won six more months by beating the park owner at chess.

Even with free rent, Jack knew he had to start making money. He saw his first opportunity while walking along a tourist beach in Playa del Carmen. Some of the locals had pushcarts full of the coconuts that had fallen on the beach. They were hacking the husks off the nuts with machetes and selling the milk to vacationing gringos. *I can go them one better*, he thought, and set out to do just that.

He collected his own pile of coconuts, and on Friday night loaded his stockpile into the truck bed. He packed them in ice and covered the load with a heavy tarp to cool them. On Saturday morning, the day a new group of tourists arrived, he drove to the resort area and set up shop a few hundred yards down the beach from the resort hotels. Arriving around midday, just as the overheated and thirsty new arrivals were taking their first walk on the beach, Jack put out his sign: "My coconuts won't give you the shits." When the gringos asked how he could make such a claim, he told them he didn't use a dirty machete to open the nuts like the other guys did. Instead, he used a portable electric drill, cleaning the bit with alcohol after each use. The milk inside the coconut was sterile, so there was no contamination. He handed every customer a still-wrapped straw that fit neatly into the hole he drilled in the nut.

"The milk was cold too," he told me proudly.

Jack said he consistently made money from this, but it was only on Saturdays. To supplement his income, he sold the names of companies other businesses needed to buy from, which he accessed from the twenty-one books of the Thomas Registry he had brought with him from Colorado. He had used this source in his own businesses in the States, and knew its value to companies that required various materials for their operations.

There was no Internet in those days, so this was a terrific resource for the local entrepreneurs. He also sold them Dun & Bradstreet ratings for $10, versus the $50 usually charged.

"After a while, I was generating $4,000 to $5,000 a month from these activities. That was a lot of money in Mexico at the time, and Lillie and I had a house built right on the beach. We lived with *los ricos.* You know, the rich people!"

"What strikes me in all this," I said, "is another consistent theme in your life. A while ago, I talked to you about your defiance and your need for revenge. There's another theme I'd like your reaction to."

He looked at me warily, and I assured him this wasn't nearly so heavy. "I'm just curious about your entrepreneurial side. You always seem to be involved in one venture or another, most of them completely different. First it was the little store you ran out of your locker at school. Then you had your own machine shop and Jack-for-hire international contracts and mercenary ventures. Now you tell me you cobbled together cold coconut milk and business information services. We haven't talked about it yet in our interviews, but I know you've also dredged for gold and run tropical river tours. What drives you to do all these unrelated things? There's no consistency to it."

"I can understand why it baffles you. Your life has been a steady, logical progression up the corporate ladder, and a lot of times I just needed enough money to eat. But there's more to it than simple necessity. I crave variety. I get bored easily and so I always want new things to do. It almost doesn't matter what they are, just so long as they're different. If it means developing new skills, researching obscure information, and relating to unconventional people, so much the better. But just as important, I get tremendous satisfaction from beating the system. Show me rules, constraints, or even laws that make no sense, and I'll try to get around them. Maybe that's related to the defiance we talked about the other day.

"But I wasn't the only one with entrepreneurial talents," he added. "Lillie had her own business too. She imported used clothing that she purchased from rag merchants in the US at ten cents a pound. They got it from the Salvation Army and other outfits like that. It was sorted by type—blouses, pants, and so forth—wrapped up in one-hundred-pound bundles, and put on container ships to Belize. Her total cost including shipping was $35 per bundle, and she sold most of them to the Mexican shopkeepers at $75. If she got two ten-bundle shipments a month, she cleared $800. She also had a little storefront where she sold directly to the public, and the markup was even higher."

"But you lived in Mexico. Why didn't you have the stuff shipped to some port along the coast? Isn't Chetumal Bay right next to Xcalak?"

"Well, for one thing, the bay is too shallow for commercial shipping. But that's not the real reason. The real reason is that it was illegal to ship clothing into Mexico at the time."

"So how did you get the stuff to your place in Xcalak?"

"We smuggled it. We had to avoid the customs officials who would have stolen it and sold what they didn't want for themselves. I know you're going to ask, so I'll tell you how we did it.

"There are lots of places you can cross the border from Mexico into Belize. The customs guys are only stationed on highways and bridges; 90 percent of the border is unpatrolled. We found a village on the Rio Hondo, which forms the border between the two countries. The locals there had figured out a way to make money helping smugglers like us cross the river. They had built a one-vehicle wooden barge they used to ferry cars or small trucks to the other side when the river was full, but in the dry season the water was only about a foot deep. The bottom was mud, so our truck would have sunk and gotten stuck. They solved this by piling two-by-twelve inch boards on both sides of the river, and pushing them into the water when someone needed to get across. The boards were Central American hardwood, so heavy that they sank and formed a platform on top of the mud you could drive on."

Jack told me that one night when they were in Belize picking up bundles of clothing, Lillie's store in Xcalak was broken into and cleaned out. The "coconut telegraph" told him who the thief was, and he went to the police. They investigated, but because the clothing wasn't in the thief's possession—he had moved it to his mother's place—there was nothing they could do.

"Two weeks later," he said, "both houses, his and his mother's, burned to the ground. Lillie's store was never touched again."

Then tragedy struck. One night, they were having some friends over for a dinner party and needed more soda.

"I was cooking," Jack said, "so Lillie said she'd go into town to get more. It was raining pretty hard, so she ran to the car, forgetting her glasses. I guess she figured she didn't need them for a short drive over roads she'd been on a hundred times before. She had no way of knowing that the streetlights on the stretch of road approaching a traffic circle were out, and so were the floodlights that normally shone on the obelisk in the center. I found out later that the lights on the other side of the circle were on, so it must have appeared to her that she hadn't gotten to the circle yet. She hit the curb at the perimeter of the circle, and her car went airborne and crashed into the obelisk. Lilly was killed."

Mexico

Jack had lost Shelly, and now he had lost Lillie. He sank into a profound depression, and says that if it hadn't been for his neighbors, he probably would have taken his own life.

"They checked on me constantly, bringing me food, not letting me be alone. But her presence was everywhere. The curtains she was sewing, her toothbrush lying crosswise on the holder, her clothes in the closet. The nights were dreadful. I dreamed she was there and reached out to an empty space on the bed. You can't imagine how bad it was."

He had tears in his eyes as he told me this. What could I say to a guy who still grieved after twenty-three years?

I had realized another thing about Jack as I'd listened to his story over the past six months. In spite of years of rejection, abuse, hard times, war, and personal tragedy, Jack always bounced back. He was a success on his own terms, and he had carved out, sometimes brutally, a decent (albeit unconventional) life for himself against the odds. In contrast, I knew others who had never been able to let go of bad things that happened in their lives. Their experiences weren't nearly as traumatic as Jack's, but they kept dwelling on them and playing the events over and over again in their minds. What made one person tough and resilient while another struggled constantly to heal?

In the depths of his grief, Jack heard from Pawnee Brown, a man he had helped escape a dicey situation when Pawnee was attempting to import cars into Belize. The Belizean customs officials had impounded the cars, but since Pawnee had been paid for the cars by customers of the brothel where he worked, he couldn't go back without them. Learning about his predicament at a gringo bar near the border that he and Lillie frequented, Jack had arranged transport for Pawnee into Guatemala. After that kindness, Pawnee contacted Jack from time to time, always hoping to return the favor. When he learned of Lillie's death, he knew he had found a way. He told Jack that he had this great idea for making money and asked for his help. He said the timing was perfect, since the rainy season had just ended. Gold would have been washed down from the Central American highlands and deposited in the creek beds, as it was every year. The particularly heavy rains that season meant that more gold than usual would be found. Pawnee told Jack that he'd handle everything, just to come to Guatemala and meet him at the brothel he now owned in Puerto Barrios. He also owned the bar that was attached to the girls' living quarters and had a house outside of town as well. When any of his girls needed a break, he would invite them to spend some time there. He didn't (usually) ask for anything in return, as he considered the girls legitimate employees, and giving them a little vacation was good for his brothel and bar businesses.

Pawnee was an adventurous, every-day-is-a-gift kind of guy who got that way after an extraordinary stroke of luck. He had been paralyzed from the neck down in a helicopter crash while serving in Korea, but during his stay in a VA hospital, a clumsy nurse accidentally twisted his neck while arranging his pillow.

Incredibly, he began to regain feeling and movement in his limbs, and with intense rehabilitation, he recovered almost completely. He told Jack that when the injury occurred, he had figured he was as good as dead. Now, with a new lease on life, he was up for just about anything. He also had a regular stream of income from his disability pay.

"I don't understand," I said. "Why would the VA continue to pay a guy who had recovered from his wartime injuries?"

"Because the VA believes his injury could recur," Jack told me, but I didn't believe it. I figured Pawnee was just scamming the government, something Jack would admire.

Pawnee and Jack drove into the interior toward the border with Honduras; and in the village where the road ended, they bought three horses, two to ride and one to carry their gear. They spent the next several weeks riding from one remote village to another, offering to buy whatever gold the locals had panned from the creeks for 50 percent of spot value. It was an attractive offer because the gold still had to be refined, and Jack and Pawnee would pay in cash as soon as they weighed it. As they arrived at each village, they asked if anyone had gold to sell. If the answer was yes, they found a clearing, set up a chair and card table, put their scale on it, and laid out the containers and chemicals needed to process the metal. Before starting business, Jack would place an empty beer can on a corner of the table and sit down. From cover some distance away, Pawnee would shoot the can off the table. It was their way of warning the locals not to try to steal the money they had brought to buy the gold, which Jack then stacked on the table in plain sight.

What the locals brought them was a pebbly mix of gold and creek bottom, so it had to be separated before the gold was weighed and paid for. The process, carried out in front of the seller, was to pour the mix into a beaker and fill it halfway with mercury. Jack then briskly agitated the mix, causing the impurities to float to the surface and the heavier gold to precipitate to the bottom. Once the impurities were poured off, the gold was separated from the mercury by straining it through a chamois. The mercury would flow through the cloth, while the gold remained on its surface. On average, the process yielded them one and a half to two ounces of relatively pure gold daily.

When they reached their goal of amassing about $40,000 worth, it was time to move on to the second part of the project and convert the gold into cash. They went back to the village where they had started, sold back the horses, and drove to Pawnee's house in Puerto Barrios for a good shower, some decent food, and the long-awaited company of some of Pawnee's employees. They rested up for a week and then took buses to the US/Mexican border town of Nuevo Laredo. After checking into a hotel, they went in search of hand-tooled cowboy boots, a typical tourist purchase, and brought them back to their room. They hung eight gold-filled sacks on the insides of the boots and put them on to make sure the boots fit and they could walk normally. Then they went out in their street shoes for dinner and some deliberately heavy drinking, returning to their room with a six-pack of beer at 1:00 a.m. They were still drunk when they got up at 5:00, sprayed each other with the last of the beer, put on their boots, and headed for the border. There weren't a lot of people around at that hour on a Sunday morning, and they walked unsteadily across, looking and smelling like a couple of gringos who had enjoyed a wild time in Mexico. The immigration officials were glad to send them on their way.

They took a bus to Houston, and Pawnee contacted his former dentist there, asking him where he got his gold crowns made. The dentist gave Pawnee a phone number and said he could use his name when he contacted the lab. Because of this reference, they were able to get connected with the lab's owner, who invited them in to discuss a possible purchase. When he saw what they had—eight small sacks of tiny nuggets he could melt down for crowns—he agreed to a price 10 percent lower than spot, to take into account the unknown amount of remaining impurities and as a fee for his services. Jack asked for payment in Canadian Gold Maple Leafs, and two days later, he and Pawnee had eighty-four gold coins. They had almost doubled what they had paid the locals for the nuggets, so they were each $10,000 richer.

The final step in the process involved an Indian doctor named Krishnel, from whom Jack had rented an apartment in Seattle when he was working at United Controls. He was a kinky guy who liked to be watched while he was having sex with his girlfriend, and for the two men, one thing inevitably led to another. Over the course of several sessions of watching each other copulate with different women, he and Jack became friends. Jack learned that among other interesting things about India's culture, the country had few controls over financial transactions except for the gold market, which was closely regulated. This had the effect of driving the price of gold up to about 50 percent above spot. He called Krishnel and asked if that was still true, and if so, did he think there were people in India who would be interested in purchasing Maple Leafs? Krishnel told him those coins had an intrinsic value over and above the already high price for gold, as investment vehicles for affluent Indians looking for ways to profit without the government's knowledge. He gave Jack his family's phone number in New Delhi and said if Jack could get the coins there, he was sure there would be a ready market.

Their challenge now was how to move almost $40,000 worth of gold coins across international borders. Over drinks one evening, Pawnee came up with a novel idea: fashion the coins into concha belts and hire a couple of hookers to wear them while accompanying him and Jack on the trip. Since Pawnee was accomplished in dealing with prostitutes, he took on the job of recruiting two women for the project. The hard part was finding hookers with passports. Jack's part was easy in comparison, as all he had to do was fabricate the belts. They figured that if they had the hookers dress as they normally did, they would look like what they were and nobody would question what appeared to be costume jewelry.

It worked, and they got through immigration and customs without incident, arriving in India early one morning. After checking into a hotel, Jack called Krishnel's family, and one of his brothers said he would send a car for them the next morning. In the meantime, he would call his well-to-do friends about the coins. The transactions, which included weighing the gold and some haggling, took most of the next day, but by 4:00 p.m. they had amassed a boxful of rupees. Krishnel's brother converted them into US dollars at his bank, and Pawnee and Jack returned to Central America. After paying the girls for their time, they were each almost another $10,000 richer. It had been a grand adventure, and was therapeutic in helping Jack with his grief over losing Lillie.

But he was now back in the house he and Lillie had shared, and the memories were still fresh. He knew he had to stay busy or he'd fall back into depression. So, true to form, he threw himself into a series of business ventures that lasted several years.

"Taking a page out of Pawnee's book," he told me, "I started importing used cars. I'd buy them three at a time at the Dallas Auto Auction, hook them together with tow bars, and haul them into Mexico behind my truck. Each car cost me about $500, and transportation was around $1000, including customs duties or bribes. I could sell them, on average, for about $2000, so by making a run every two weeks, I made around $40,000 a year. Sometimes I'd get special orders, like for used army vehicles or school buses, and I could make even more.

"One time, I learned through the ex-con grapevine that the Ohio State Police were switching from revolvers to semi-automatics, so on one of my Dallas runs, I took a side trip to Columbus. I made a bulk purchase of a hundred and fifty stainless steel .357 Magnums at $20 each. I hid them in the greasy, gritty parts of the cars I was importing—the Mexican customs guys don't want to get their hands dirty—and sold them for $100 apiece to the Chetumal police chief. He resold them to his officers. I don't know what he got for them, but I made $12,000 on the deal."

Learning the ins and outs of bringing things from the States into Mexico allowed Jack to expand his offerings. In subsequent years, he transported boats, ultralight aircraft, major appliances, whatever was in demand.

"I sold a lot of things to a lot of people, including to some who were involved in drug trafficking. I could get the equipment they needed, show them how to use it or fix it up so it did what they wanted it to do. I was a pretty good engineer, and I knew how to fly small airplanes and helicopters too."

"How did you learn to fly? Your experience in Vietnam was all on the ground, wasn't it?"

Jack told me his first experience flying a plane had been when a friend at military school invited him for a visit during the years when he wasn't going home. They'd been there a few days when Doug's wealthy parents took off for a week in Europe, leaving the boys in the care of the maid. It got boring after a couple of days, and the boys were looking for something fun to do. Doug's father had an airplane, a temptation too great to resist. They waited until the maid went into town to do some food shopping, and then pushed the plane out of the hangar and started the engine. Their idea was to drive it up and down the dirt strip behind the house. But they got going a little too fast approaching the end of the strip, and a gust lifted the plane about fifty feet off the ground. Worse, beyond the strip the ground dropped off steeply into a valley. Jack explained that once a plane's wheels leave the ground, it accelerates because of the lack of friction. They found themselves airborne and flying across the valley.

"I figured we were fucked. Fortunately, it was a Cessna 172, which was designed to be easy to fly. They actually used them to train new pilots. But neither of us had ever taken any lessons. All we had to go on was what we had seen in movies. We figured we better leave the throttle open so we'd keep going, and then started to experiment with turning and controlling our altitude. We managed to fly around for almost an hour, but somewhere in there it dawned on us that we were going to have to land the damned thing. We got it headed back to the strip, but Doug froze on the approach, so I had to do it. I didn't know any better, so I just throttled back and eased it closer and closer to the ground. I ended up clipping the top off some of the six-foot-high Johnson grass at the head of the strip, but once we got over it, I shut the engine off and we glided down. I'm amazed we didn't shit our pants."

Jack had discovered he had an instinctive feel for flying, and I understood this since I was the same way with sailing. The experience began a lifelong, and often profitable, love of flying.

"When I was in Seattle years later," he said, "I took flying lessons just so I could rent a plane and see the sun from time to time. The physics of flying are pretty straightforward, so I got the instruction manuals for other planes and learned how to fly them too.

"I learned about helicopters from a pilot I'd known in Vietnam. After the war he got hired to fly executives from their estates to their offices in the city so they wouldn't have to fight the traffic. But that wasn't enough air time to keep his license current, and he needed to log more hours. He invited me along on some of his flights and taught me how to fly. Helicopters are a lot harder than planes. The first time I took the controls, my buddy hovered the helicopter over a large cornfield and said, 'Just keep it over this field.' It was like patting myself on the head with one hand and making circles on my stomach with the other ... while standing on a beach ball."

He careened around uncontrollably at first and would have crashed if his buddy hadn't jumped in, but over the next several flights he acquired the skills. He never got a license to fly helicopters, but that didn't stop him from flying them in Mexico where enforcement of regulations covering small aircraft was lax.

"So now I understand how you learned to fly," I said, "and how that skill was valuable to the traffickers. But what was it like working with those people? From what I hear, they're a pretty brutal bunch."

"I worked with them for several years. They kept hiring me for more and more projects, and it got to the point where I was making so much money that I gave up everything else. Never once did I have a problem. They were the most direct and honest businesspeople I ever dealt with."

"But, Jack, they were organized criminals running drugs. How did you feel being associated with that?"

"I never had a problem with what they did as long as they weren't politicians. In my opinion, druggies are lazy, undisciplined losers with no self-respect. They're their own worst enemies, and the traffickers are just supplying a market, playing to their weakness. By making what they do illegal, we've turned them into criminals, just like we did with rumrunners during Prohibition." I could see that Jack was warming up for one of his rants. "Every liquor store owner would be a criminal now if that hadn't been repealed. And what about the most addictive drug out there? Nicotine! You want to talk about organized crime, take a look at Big Tobacco!"

If I let him go on with this, we would lose a lot of time, so I held up my hands. "Jack. Stop. Let's stick to the story. Tell me about one of the projects you did for these people."

He took a deep breath. "Right. Okay." He paused and then said in a calmer voice, "One of my clients was running cocaine through Mexico, and complained to me about how the police got half of the shipments he dropped out of an airplane into Chetumal Bay. I came up with the idea of stringing one-kilo waterproof packets of coke along a weighted line that had waterproof infrared strobe lights tied to it, one at each end and one in the middle. We stacked 150 or 200 of the packets in a box next to the door of the airplane. The weight went out first, and then as each packet hit the water, it pulled the next one out. The whole string went straight to the bottom. His guys on the ground waited until the police had searched the area and gone home empty-handed, then they went out in a skiff wearing night-vision goggles. They could see the flashing strobes, and used grappling hooks to snag the line and bring it up to the boat. If the police showed up again, they just threw everything back in the water and came back for it later. My client paid me $10,000 for solving his problem."

Then he told me about a much more ambitious project to design a submarine for transporting drugs across large bodies of water. It required assembling a number of advanced components, including an atomic battery stolen from a navigation buoy. The battery would be charged by a slow-fission reaction, and it in turn kept a bank of eight storage batteries charged. These batteries would power a motor that silently propelled the vessel at five to seven knots, submerged at sixty or seventy feet. GPS coordinates could be programmed into an autopilot, and the sub surfaced each night it would determine its position using a satellite navigation antenna. Waypoints could be input to guide the sub from Mexico to pick-up points along the eastern coast of the United States, and even in Europe. If it happened to be pinged by government sonar, the sub would immediately drop two hundred feet—or to just above the bottom—and speed up to forty knots for a short time, making a series of sharp course changes to evade detection. At the conclusion of each such sequence, it would lie dormant for twenty-four hours, then surface to reset its course and continue toward its final destination.

"I designed the sub and all its systems, but never built it. I told them I wanted $1 million, and they put off the decision. But they were impressed and paid me for the time I spent coming up with the idea. They kept hiring me for other work too," and he told me about one project they did ask him to execute: training their pilots to fly ultralight aircraft and to navigate at night using only a compass and landmarks.

"They wanted to get shipments of cocaine from several drop-offs along the Mexican coast to a collection point in Playa del Carmen. I helped them set up their routes. We cleared a dirt landing strip back in the bush, and then led the pilots in with ammo cans filled with sand and gravel that had been soaked in gasoline and diesel fuel. They burned like smudge pots. You know, like the ones they use in orange groves when there's a frost."

He said it was tricky, though, because the ultralights had to come in with the easterly trade winds behind them, rather than landing into the wind, the way a plane usually does. They had to do it this way so they could taxi straight to the end of the strip and offload onto a larger plane. Loaded, the big plane could only take off into the wind. The ultralights were on the ground for just a few minutes before they were off again.

It could be tricky for the pilots returning to their home bases as well. Trying to land into the wind with no cargo to give them weight was often difficult since the little planes were held aloft, soaring like condors on the volume of air passing under their wings. Throttling back didn't work, because the planes wouldn't settle to the ground. Instead, they began going backward out of control. In these situations, Jack instructed the pilots to buzz their comrades on the ground, who would then go out to the field, catch lines dropped by the pilots, and haul the planes down. The arrangement went on for six months, but the amount of cocaine the ultralights could carry was so small that the traffickers looked for other ways to transport larger amounts. But they paid Jack $5,000 for each week of working with their pilots, and the business relationship paid unexpected but welcome dividends in some of his later ventures.

"We've covered a lot of ground," I said. "How about we stop at this point and pick things up again next time."

The truth was that I was fatigued by interviewing on Skype. Both the audio and video were inconsistent, and I was trying to take notes. For his part, Jack was on a roll. All he had to do was keep chattering along, while I tried to keep up with his engineering jargon and explanations of situations that were completely foreign to me. Besides, it was a beautiful Maine afternoon. The brilliant, clear, deep blue sky was dotted with a few white cottony clouds, and a light breeze carried the smells of the woods and the lake up to our deck. The weekenders had gone home, and it was time for Susie and me to take a boat ride and enjoy the serenity.

Jack started our next conversation with a reflection, not a typical thing for him to do. "I've been thinking about our conversation last month. You know when you asked me how I felt working for drug traffickers? I just want you to know that I never moved any drugs myself. Not that I had any moral problem with it. I mean, I felt bad that the stuff messed up so many lives, but if those losers really wanted to go straight, they could have gotten help. Like alcoholics with AA, you know? No, the real reason I didn't handle any of the junk was it was too risky. Things go wrong, shipments get stolen, money doesn't get paid, somebody cuts it, whatever. If you get blamed, you're dead. But they don't kill you for training pilots."

"Thanks for clearing that up. I thought for a minute there you were going soft on me."

"Naaah, no way!" he said, but after this I did begin hearing more stories about how he helped other people, rather than just being out for himself. Sometimes this involved considerable risk. The last time he jumped in to help a friend, he ended up in prison.

He took a different kind of risk when he was approached by one of his neighbors on the beach at Xcalak. Don Edmundo was a legitimate businessman, so successful and well-known that he was in the race for governor of Quintana Roo, the Mexican state that comprises most of the Yucatan Peninsula. The man's seventeen-year-old son had gotten himself jailed in Belize for dealing drugs. Like a lot of rich people's kids, he had grown up privileged and spoiled, and probably thought himself untouchable. Perhaps he was in Quintana Roo, but Belize was another country, and they were cracking down on the trade. A kid strutting around acting like a big shot was an easy target for the police there.

"The don came to me about his son's predicament. We were pretty good friends, and he knew I had done a lot of risky things in my life. He never asked directly if I could get the kid out of jail—he was a politician, after all—but it was clear he would greatly appreciate whatever help I could give. He told me that his son was being held in Burl Boom prison west of Belize City. He had been there, and he described it as a low-security facility surrounded by a ten-foot-high chain-link fence with razor wire strung along the top. His son looked thin and gaunt after only one and a half months there, and the don was worried. I said I would try to help, and came back to him the next day with the scheme I had cooked up."

Jack's first step was to put several large wooden crates, similar to the ones he had used to transport chilled coconuts to Playa del Carmen, in the bed of his truck. He stowed the tools he thought he might need in one of the crates and covered the whole load with a heavy tarp. The next day, he entered Belize the same way he had when he and Lillie were smuggling bundles of clothing into Mexico, by driving across the planks at the Rio Hondo. He warned the locals in very specific terms to keep quiet about his crossing, and told them to expect him back that night. Smuggling clothes into the country was one thing. The worst thing that could have happened would be the loss of the bundles and paying a *mordida*. Crossing the border with a prison escapee would have much more serious consequences. Knowing Jack's connections with drug traffickers, the locals assured him they would say nothing.

Jack had a rough idea where the prison was, having heard about it when he was working on a short project in Belize City. Ex-cons are attuned to such things, he told me. He drove to the area, stopped at a cantina for a beer, and got into a casual conversation with the owner. He said he had heard there was a prison camp around there, and did that worry him? The man said no, they didn't keep violent criminals there; and anyway, he made money from the food and drinks he served to family members and lawyers visiting the prisoners. The place was just down the road, he said. Jack had another beer and drove on.

Five miles away he located the site on the edge of a swamp. The grounds were about the size of a football field, surrounded, as the don had said, by a ten-foot chain-link fence with razor wire along the top. At midday, it was oppressively hot and still, the air fetid with swamp gas from decomposing vegetation and the unmistakable stench of human waste in open latrines. There were insects everywhere, the biting ones hatching from a stagnant pond at the edge of the property. There was only one barracks, a wooden structure constructed from old rough-cut boards, about one hundred feet by thirty feet. Pieces of chain link fence were nailed to the exterior walls, covering the barracks windows.

"I only saw two guards, but they were armed with short-barreled pump-action twelve gauge shotguns that had pistol grips instead of stocks. These guns are designed to be fired from the hip, not aimed from the shoulder. They have cut-off barrels like that to spray a wide pattern of pellets at short range. You just shoot in the general direction of your target and you'll hit it."

Jack said that none of the prisoners appeared capable of launching an attack anyway. What few he saw were thin, filthy, and clothed in torn prison uniforms. They were stooped and shambling between the barracks and the latrine trenches, or just sitting in whatever shade they could find. Jack knew what the conditions were like in Central American prisons, and he figured many of the men were suffering not only from malnutrition but also dysentery. Their spirits had been broken too. It was standard for a prisoner to be kept segregated at one end of the barracks for the first ten days of his confinement and not be allowed to leave the building. Under the corrugated metal roof, the daytime temperature inside the barracks exceeded 115 degrees and water was restricted. When those surviving this ordeal were finally allowed out into the yard, they were so weakened and dehydrated, they posed no threat.

"I came back after dark and left my truck in the bush a couple hundred yards from the prison. I waited until the guards were out of sight, then walked up to the gate and put a bottle of cheap local Mezcal con Gusano on the ground just outside it. I knew that when the guards found it, they would think a relative had left it for them and proceed to enjoy the gift. I came back after midnight, and sure enough, the guards were asleep, leaning against the fence with the empty bottle between them. If they woke up, I was going to tell them my truck had broken down and I was looking for help. But they never stirred."

Jack walked along the fence until he was opposite the barracks, then cut through the links with bolt cutters. On the side of the barracks that faced away from the gate, he cut off the lower section of the fence covering one of the windows. He went over the sill and walked around inside, looking at the sleeping prisoners until he found the boy. He said it was relatively easy to spot him, because there was only one teenager in the room.

"I put my hand over his mouth to stifle any noise, whispered his father's name in his ear, and told him I was getting him out of there. He nodded that he understood, and we went out the window, crossed the yard, and slipped out through the opening I had cut in the fence. When we got to the truck, I put the kid into one of the big boxes in the back and covered it with the tarp. I drove away slowly to make as little noise as possible. But even if the guards had awakened and figured out what was happening, there wasn't much they could do about it. They didn't have a car and there weren't any phones out there. Hell, there wasn't even electricity. I went back the way I came, and once I got off the main road heading for the Rio Hondo village, I could relax a little. I splashed across the boards into Mexico and drove nonstop for six hours to the don's house in Xcalak. You can imagine the reunion, the whole family crying and giving each other *abrazos*. A week later, Don Edmundo gave me the deed to a house he owned in the best part of town. I still own it."

Jack needed a favor himself. His passport had expired, and it would have been unwise for him to approach the American Embassy in person. He asked the don if there was a print shop in town, and if so, could he use its equipment? Don Edmundo knew everyone, and he contacted the print shop owner to make the arrangements. In prison, Jack had met people who were experienced forgers, and when he had run his own print shop he'd had plenty of time to hone the skills he learned from them. The Mexican print shop would give him access to the type of card stock, pendulum art, raised hot stamping, and binding that he needed. And because of his foreign assignments, he knew of places with uncommon languages or alphabets. Combining these elements, he was able to fabricate an official-looking passport from a country that no longer existed. Creating such a document from a nonexistent country wasn't forgery, he told me. At least not at that time in Mexico.

The only thing remaining was to get the passport stamped, but that could be solved by bribing a Mexican immigration official. By comparing notes with other gringos, it wasn't hard for Jack to learn which official would appreciate a little extra cash as a fee for his service. The result was a Mexican stamp on a Rhodesian passport written in Afrikaans with Jack's photo in it. He deliberately visited a number of other Central American countries, collecting their stamps along the way and creating a travel record, in this case for a catatonic man in a Cleveland hospital named Thomas Johnson.

"How did you create this guy's identity?" I asked. "Did you just invent him, or was he a real person?"

"He was real. I wanted an identity I could use when I needed it, one that would stand up to scrutiny."

"How did you do it?"

"It's pretty complicated, if you want a clean ID. I've done it multiple times. You want to hear my tried and true method?"

"Absolutely," I said. "I'm sure it's one of your better stories." And I had to admit I was genuinely curious. How *did* one create an identity?

"Let's use Thomas Johnson as the example. You remember I told you I worked in a nursing homes when I was a kid, right? So I knew something about how they operated and I was able to take advantage of that. The first thing you have to do is find someone who's never going to be released, like that catatonic, someone about your own age who roughly matches your description."

"And how do you do that?"

"You start by calling nursing homes. But not just any nursing homes, only the wealthier ones that accept private insurance. You want to avoid any government programs because there are too many records that could be traced back to the real guy whose identity you're trying to assume."

"What do you say when you call?"

"I say, 'I'm calling about Mr. Johnson. His mom Molly asked me to call. He's about fifty, five-foot-eight, slender, light complexion.' Johnson's a common name, so sooner or later I'll find a nursing home with a Mr. Johnson. In the case of Thomas Johnson, it took a number of calls to find a guy who met that description, but finally a receptionist said to me, 'Oh, you must mean Thomas. Why do you want to know about him?' I told her I represented an insurance company, that Thomas's mother came to us because she wasn't happy with his current insurer, and that we're considering taking over his coverage. Then I make an appointment to come to their facility.

"The next step was getting a business card for a fictitious company. I've found 'The Rock' works well; everybody thinks it's Prudential. I had a print shop make up a hundred business cards using an alias, an address that was between two buildings, and a number from a pay phone... they had pay phones back then. I dressed in a suit and tie and carried a portfolio to the meeting, not a briefcase."

"Why not a briefcase?" I asked. "Most businessmen carry briefcases, you know."

"Because you can hold a portfolio open in front of you so only you can see what's in it. With a briefcase, you'd have to dummy up a bunch of papers and files so that when you opened it, it looked right.

"Anyway, I presented my card to the receptionist and told her I was there to discuss Thomas Johnson's situation because we are getting ready to take over his insurance. She sent me to accounting, where I gave them another card, explained my mission, and asked for information only they would have about the patient and his current insurance. What is Thomas's current condition and prognosis? How long has he been there? What was your billing to the insurer last year? How often do you get payments from them? What is the policy number? How much did his meds cost? Were they proprietary or OTC? As they gave me the answers, I jotted everything down in my portfolio. When we got to the information I should already have, I made a show of shuffling through my papers for Thomas's record and apologized for having forgotten to bring the file with me. I suggested they give my office a call, but since it was a pay phone, there was no answer. Then I pleaded for just a little more information. This was the critical moment, because if I didn't come off as sincere, I wouldn't get what I needed. In the end, most people gave it to me. I mean, I was there to help one of their patients, and if they believed The Rock would pay promptly and reliably, they wanted to cooperate. And the info is just standard boilerplate any insurance company would ask: date and place of birth, mother's and father's names, Social Security number, address of record, and so forth. Like I said before, it was important to find out if the patient was participating in *any* government-subsidized programs. If he was, I'd walk away from the deal because I didn't want an identity that could be traced."

"How do you know all this? It sounds complicated."

"A guy I worked with on one of my foreign assignments had been an insurance agent in a former life. He walked me through all the insurance questions and nursing-home procedures. But having all the information was only the beginning. Now I had to see Thomas so I could 'explain everything to him.' They called a nurse who took me to his room. I only spent a few minutes, because they guy was unresponsive, but that didn't mean he couldn't hear me. Legally, I had to talk to him. Then I went back to the accounting office and told them I'd have 'Carol' get back to them if we needed anything else."

"They never heard from you again, of course. But what did you do with all the info you had gathered?"

"I first had to find out if Thomas had any priors on his driver's license. Because of how long he'd been in the nursing home, I knew his license would have expired, and after seven years he wouldn't still be in the system — that was why I needed to know how long he'd been in the nursing home — but they keep records on priors. I always hired an attorney to check, and it he found any, I'd walk away from the deal. Seven years was also important for finding a job. Companies are required to keep payroll records for seven years. No pay stubs, no record.

"So I got a job in Thomas's name with a plumbing company — generic trades are best—and made up an address. I looked around for a neighborhood where there was a line of mailboxes, put in another one at the end of the line, and painted a number on it. The post office would deliver mail to that address. I wrote to the bureau of vital statistics requesting a copy of 'my' birth certificate and paid for it with a postal money order. The BVS mailed it to my dummy address.

"Then I got a driver's license from a state that wasn't Thomas's, just to add another layer of safety. I told them I had let my old one expire but now needed to start driving again. I went to Social Security and applied for a new card—I already had the number—and had it sent to my dummy address too. I wrote to military records in Tom's state and got a DD 214 which showed his discharge information. Now I had all the info I needed to get a passport."

"This is amazing. How long did it take you?"

"It took months, but at the end I had a clean ID, no skeletons. With it, I was able to build up a financial record: credit cards, bank accounts, even a credit rating. I *was* Thomas Johnson."

Nicaragua

*W*inter came early that year in Maine. It snowed on Halloween, reinforcing my resolve to get back to Siguaterra, at least for a visit. I justified it with needing to check on the property, equalize the batteries, turn on the fridge and TV, run the washing machine and dishwasher, make sure the well pump was operating properly, and take the car out for a few drives. While not as critical as the systems on a boat, land-based equipment needed tending to as well. Susie would not be happy if we got back in January and she didn't have her labor-saving appliances, access to news and the Internet, or the ability to drive to town on a road. We had a launch as well as the car, but going outside the reef to get to town when the trade winds kicked up four- or five-foot seas was not her idea of fun. Better that I take care of any problems in advance, and we agreed I should take three weeks on the island to do so. I would still get back in time for Thanksgiving.

There was another reason to go to Nicaragua: I wanted to get together with Jack and review where things stood with the book before Susie and I returned in January. She and I had decided we'd take an extended cruise back to Belize and take our time visiting the ports, cays, and atolls we had missed when helping out Betty and John. This would mean Jack and I would not have much time to review what I had written before we cast off for four or five months. If we could sit down now, without any distractions, we'd be able to cover a lot more ground. Since there were daily flights between the island and the capital, I suggested we meet in Managua for two or three days in the middle of my visit. We agreed on the dates, and Jack said he'd pick me up at the airport.

One of our friends on Siguaterra had been a flight attendant, and she recommended Jack and I stay at the hotel the airline crews frequented on trips to Managua. I figured if gringo ladies were comfortable there, the place was going to be in a safe neighborhood and would have all the requisite amenities: clean rooms, honest staff, good restaurant, cozy bar, and a pool. It turned out to be a good recommendation.

Jack and I didn't do any business on our first night together; we just relaxed in the bar, had dinner, and got caught up. We decided we'd start the next morning and go over what I had written so far, and agreed to meet for an early breakfast. Jack was waiting at the door of the restaurant when it opened at 5:30 and started calling my room every fifteen minutes until I pulled myself together and came downstairs.

After we ate we found a shaded open-air sitting area at the far end of a hallway where there wouldn't be any human traffic, just hummingbirds dipping into the multicolored flowers pouring out of their planters. We were able to resolve a lot of inconsistencies in the story, fill in some gaps, and get the timing of events straighter, but it wasn't easy. Jack-the-engineer wanted everything to be precise, thorough, and accurate. I, the liberal-arts guy, had to keep reminding him that poetic license was required to make the story readable, even if doing so compromised some of the details. My notes were rough and written in rapid chicken scratch, as disjointed as Jack's words were dyslexic. So we haggled good-naturedly for the better part of the day, and finally got things ironed out to the point where we had left off in our last Skype conversation, when Jack had told me how to create an identity. Then he continued with the story.

He said that after a year of grieving the loss of Lillie, his normal masculine urges reasserted themselves, and in 1990 he married a woman named Rosa from Quintana Roo State.

"The marriage lasted seven years," he told me, "until I caught her skimming money from my bank account and buying her boyfriend a taxicab. I threw her out."

Rosa was tenacious, however, and tried to take possession of Jack's house as part of the subsequent divorce settlement. As the proceedings went along, it was discovered that while the house was indeed owned by Jack, Jack was not the man Rosa had married. Thomas Johnson was her husband's legal name, the identity Jack had created after he helped Don Edmundo's son get out of prison in Belize. Johnson did not own the house, Jack did, and so Rosa was prevented from grabbing it. For spite, Rosa broke into the house and destroyed all the photos he had of Lillie and Shelly. Enraged, Jack struck back. He told Don Edmundo about the woman's avarice and how she had taken advantage of and hurt him. The don, who had won the election and now lived in the governor's mansion in Merida, took steps to be sure that Rosa never got more than menial labor as long as she stayed in Quintana Roo.

But Jack had to leave Xcalak when the Mexican Federales began working in earnest with the US Drug Enforcement Agency, targeting American expatriates they suspected of dealing drugs. Government agents were sent out to try to entrap the gringos by first offering pre-Columbian artifacts — possession of which was illegal in its own right—and then cocaine. Those entrapped were used as bargaining chips in diplomatic or trade exchanges with the United States.

"I knew I would be a suspect because of my connections, and sure enough one of the agents, a guy known as El Oso, tried to set me up. He showed me a little stone statue that he said came from Chichen Itza, but I refused to buy it. Then he offered me two kilos of cocaine. I said I'd have to think about that but would let him know. I checked with one of my former clients, and he knew about the guy, warned me to stay away from him. I wanted to teach the sonofabitch a lesson, though, so I played along. I picked him up in town, but said I was uncomfortable because somebody might see us making the transaction. I insisted we drive out into the bush. I took a rutted track into the jungle, then stopped the car. I reached behind me like I was pulling out my wallet, but pulled out a gun instead. I had it in a holster in the small of my back. I took the coke, then drove several miles farther into the jungle. I took his shoes and left him with a long walk home. I drove my car to El Oso's house and left it there. Then I took a taxi home and called the police to report a stolen vehicle."

Jack was gleeful about how he had tricked the guy, but he wasn't done yet. He gave the cocaine to the trafficker who had tipped him off and called in one last favor with Don Edmundo. The governor stepped in and had the agent arrested for stealing Jack's car. He was convicted and spent the next three years in a Quintana Roo state prison, but Jack knew he was a marked man. Sooner or later, El Oso would come after him, either personally or by sending friends. Rather than always having to look over his shoulder, he decided to wrap up his affairs in Mexico and relocate to Nicaragua.

Jack first went to Nicaragua in 1976 on one of his foreign

contracts, when he was hired to do a hospital engineering project in Granada. This Spanish colonial city sits on the shores of Lake Nicaragua about thirty miles south of the capital, Managua. It is distinguished by a big central plaza with centuries-old trees and gravel paths leading to fountains and statues of the conquistadors. A bandstand anchors one end of the plaza, and a few dozen folding chairs are arranged haphazardly on the lawn facing it. Across one of the avenues circling this park stands an eighteenth-century cathedral with uneven walls and rooflines, the result of earthquakes that have shaken the city over the three hundred years of its modern history. It is hushed and cool inside the cathedral, smelling faintly of incense and dotted with ranks of votive candles at the feet of robed saints. Jack said he took an English-language tour shortly after he arrived in Granada, and learned that the religious symbols in the cathedral were a blend of Catholic and pre-Columbian imagery. The early priests, his guide said, were so keen to attract the indigenous people that they not only incorporated their designs inside the church, they also allowed chickens to be sacrificed out front before the congregants went inside to celebrate Mass.

Most of Granada's streets were still cobblestone. There were horse-drawn carts and even small herds of goats. The local men regularly paid a goatherd to milk a nanny, believing that drinking a half cup of the still-warm liquid every morning would give them potency. The buildings fronting the streets appeared uninteresting, just bland stucco walls no more than two stories high — again because of earthquakes — and with no windows. At random intervals, however, there were iron gates that opened so cars could enter, and also allowed a view of the courtyards inside. These homes were called *quadros*, Jack said, with the living spaces arranged in a square facing inward, often with shaded galleries. The courtyards were full of flowers, and some even had central fountains.

"They may have looked plain on the outside," he said, "but inside where the families lived, it was really beautiful."

Jack also researched the lake. "Lake Nicaragua is 103 miles long, and that makes it the largest lake in Central America. If you look at a map, you'll see this huge freshwater lake separated from the Pacific by only a thin strip of land. There are hundreds of islands in the lake, some with volcanos on them. One is over a mile high and still active. You can see other volcanic mountains in the distance, but the climate at the level of the lake is like a tropical rain forest."

He told me that the shores of the lake are covered by thick vegetation, a result of the frequent rains. There are fourteen species of orchids alone, many aromatic and voluptuous in shape, colored yellow, cream, pink, and even black. Five-petaled hibiscus appear in hues of red, blue, orange, and white. Animal life around the lake is abundant as well. Bright green parrots with yellow napes fly in pairs across the morning and evening skies, huge-billed toucans perch in cashew trees, and long-necked white waterfowl stalk the shallows. Mammals range from tapirs and deer to mouse-sized marsupials, fearless little creatures that the locals try to keep around their homes because they frighten off the rats. Reptilian life is also well adapted to the lakeshore. Frogs and softball-sized toads serenade the night, but not so benign is the venomous viper known as the *barba amarilla* and the Central American boa constrictor. Locals fear this big snake, but resident gringos have been known to keep them in food storage areas to help control rodents. The crocodiles are not so welcome, since one of their favorite foods is dog.

"I knew a lady," Jack told me, "a little slip of a thing, who was walking her dog along the lakeshore one morning. The dog ran into a swampy area and a croc got hold of it. She went right into the water and wrestled the dog out of the croc's mouth, ran home with the dog bleeding all over her, wrapped it in a towel, and drove to the vet in Managua. The dog lived."

Not to be outdone this time, I countered with my own story. It was rare to be able to one-up Jack, and I didn't want to miss the opportunity.

"A friend of mine on Siguaterra has a big place on the water," I said. "The house looks like one of those mansions you see along the Intracoastal Waterway in Fort Lauderdale. George farms several acres of the property and he likes animals too. He keeps parrots and dogs as pets, has iguanas in the trees, and lets chickens and ducks wander around the property. He collects their eggs, and sometimes gives me a dozen. Anyway, in the evenings, these ducks liked to line up along the seawall and sleep there. He had twenty or more ducks at first, but began noticing fewer and fewer of them lining up each night. He didn't think much of it at first, but when there were only seven left, he had to find out what was going on. He went down to the shore at twilight and positioned himself so he could look along the seawall. Sure enough, a damn croc came swimming slowly along and stopped just below where the ducks were hunkered down. As he watched, the croc suddenly arched its back and snatched one of the ducks off the wall. The rest scattered, but ducks aren't real smart, so they'd go back night after night. George went down the next evening with a high-powered hunting rifle and riddled the croc with hollow point bullets."

There, I thought, *I can tell a violent story too!*

"Sounds like a guy I should meet," Jack said.

"I'll introduce you the next time you come for a visit," I promised. "You and George can talk guns and explosives, and try to outdo each other with your rants against the US government. I'll listen for the entertainment value."

Jack continued to tell me about Lake Nicaragua. At the lake's southern end, where it empties into the San Juan River, is an archipelago of 350 small islands. Geographically, the lake is in the far southwest corner of the country, but the river winds its way eastward 120 miles to the Caribbean Sea. It is navigable for small craft the whole way, and deep enough that Caribbean bull sharks are found in the lake's waters. The archipelago and river entrance are popular tourist destinations. When the skies are clear, the sunlight is so intense it stings. At night, the canopy of stars appears at first glance to be a huge cloud arching across the center of the sky. It takes a few minutes before vacationing city dwellers realize it is the Milky Way galaxy as it appeared before civilization's light pollution obscured it in populated areas.

It was in this Eden-like setting that Jack met and succumbed to Rosie, a waitress in the hotel restaurant where he was staying. At the conclusion of his hospital project, Jack returned to Seattle without knowing she was pregnant. After giving birth to a daughter she named Cory, Rosie contacted Jack and he accepted responsibility for the outcome of the affair. True to his code, he sent money to pay for the little girl's education, and to Rosie's credit, she sent her to a private school in Granada. He only saw his daughter for brief periods in the ensuing years, but made no secret about his support of her. Lillie did not allow his having had a child with another woman affect her. Theirs was a practical relationship, and in return Jack didn't pry into Lillie's behavior while he was away. Both were discreet, and any affairs were conducted away from home territory.

Dr. Ponce, the medical director of the hospital in Granada, had been impressed with Jack's work and contacted him again some years later. This time, Jack was offered the project of managing the engineering and construction of the doctor's weekend home on the lake. Having figured out from his earlier experience how to get work done in the area, and knowing the project would give him the opportunity to see Cory, Jack accepted. He did not go out with Rosie again, but he did visit her home a few times and got to know Cory's five siblings. Rosie tried to tap Jack for more money to support the others in her family, but he stayed focused on his natural child, making arrangements to pay the school directly for Cory's education.

Dr. Ponce hired Jack one last time in 1994 for a new hospital he was building in Managua. It was another happy coincidence, because by this time, Cory was finishing high school there and living with an aunt. Jack wanted to hire her part-time to handle the project's billing, but he went through the normal personnel routines of interviews and tests to avoid any accusations of nepotism. He did inform Dr. Ponce, however, and after he spent some time with Cory, the doctor was kind enough to recommend her to the university where she could continue her education.

Cory's boyfriend at the time, unbeknownst to her, was selling cocaine to their fellow students. Getting greedy, he came up with the idea of making even more money if he scammed his supplier, a woman known among the dealers as Cocha Blanca. He told her he could get the drug from another supplier at a better price than she was paying, and offered to buy it on her behalf. She gave him the money for two kilos, but he only bought one and foolishly pocketed half the money. Compounding his error, he cut the cocaine, first taking a half kilo for himself, and told Cocha Blanca that what he had gotten from the other supplier was no good. She naturally demanded her money back for the poor merchandise, but the boyfriend said he couldn't get it and accused Cory of having used some of the cocaine and cutting the rest. The woman contracted with a "collection agency" to go after Cory, and the girl began receiving threatening phone calls. When she told Jack what was going on, he immediately moved her to another apartment an hour and a half away from the city and had her stop attending classes.

But the collectors were good at their business, and in three days they phoned Cory to tell her they knew where she lived. Jack moved her again, but they found her after a week and this time demanded $45,000. The actual amount Cocha Blanca had lost was only $4,500, but the collectors had learned that Cory's father was a gringo, so they increased the amount by a factor of ten. To emphasize their point, the collectors came to the hospital where Jack and Cory worked and confronted her personally. She told them she didn't have that kind of money, and they told her to get it from her father or they would kill his little girl. They would call her one last time in three more days. Jack saw that he had no choice and arranged to get the money. He told Cory that when they called, she should tell them he had it and ask how he should make delivery. They gave her a time and location, and Jack went and waited there for hours before a wizened old Indian approached the car. Jack handed over the $45,000.

What the collectors didn't know was that hospital security had their visit to the hospital on tape, and they gave a copy of the recording to Jack. Now that he knew what they looked like, he set about finding them. Since he'd paid the extortion money, the threat to Cory was over and Jack could take his time planning how he would repay the people who had put his only child in jeopardy. He first visited Cory's boyfriend, put a gun to his head, and quickly learned where Cocha Blanca lived. He began watching her place from his car as drug deals were going down on the street, and after a week he knew who the regular players were. Making inquiries and showing these people the photos from the security tape, accompanied with ample amounts of cash, Jack was able to learn where the collectors lived as well.

The boyfriend died in an automobile accident shortly

thereafter, his car going over a cliff.

"How did that happen?" I asked, as if I didn't know.

"I dunno. Maybe he was drunk or on drugs and lost control of the car. Too bad, eh?"

The two collectors who had threatened Cory died as well, one when he picked up a flashlight lying on the street next to his car. The other was shot in his apartment. Cocha Blanca simply disappeared. Not much official attention was paid to these incidents, since such things happened to people in the drug trade all the time.

Although Jack didn't know it, one of the two collectors who met an untimely end was a US DEA informant, and he had given Cory's and Jack's names to the DEA. During the investigation into his death, this report surfaced and Cory was questioned. When she told Jack about it, he knew the DEA would soon come looking for him as well. He also knew they would uncover the arrest warrant for his parole violation and probably learn how he helped Lillie escape from Washington. It was time to make some new plans.

The urgency increased when an employee of the US embassy visited the hospital and began a "fishing expedition" with Dr. Ponce. How much did Jack make, the man wanted to know, and did he have any business dealings outside the hospital? Where did he live in the city? Any other family besides Cory? Dr. Ponce told Jack about the embassy's interest, Jack immediately resigned in order not to make any further problems for the doctor. He also wanted to make himself harder to locate.

Three weeks later, Jack's attorney, with whom he was staying, picked up a DEA letter from the mailbox at Jack's vacated apartment, informing him that his Guernsey bank account in the United Kingdom had been frozen by the agency. They had discovered the account contained $1.2 million, proceeds from the sale of Colorado property Jack had purchased soon after getting back from Vietnam. He had bought it using the money he had amassed from his military contract while in Vietnam, plus the profits he had made from manipulating the MPC while assigned there. The price in 1970 had been reasonable, even more so since the location was remote, off a dirt track going up into the mountains. Twenty years later, the property was adjacent to the future site of a ski resort, and the developer wanted to build condos on it. Jack sold it at a premium and squirreled the money away in a private numbered account in the Guernsey bank.

The DEA suspected, of course, that this much money had to have been laundered from Jack's presumed drug dealings. The agency wanted to use the frozen assets as an inducement for Jack to come forward and tell them what he knew about their informant's death, and about Central American drug trafficking in general. They even offered him immunity on his parole violation and not to pursue the charge for helping Lillie get out of Seattle. But Jack had learned from his jailhouse lawyer that if he refused to answer even one of their questions, the offer of immunity would be revoked and he would be sent back to prison. On the other hand, if he told them what he knew, his former clients in the trade would find and kill him, and probably Cory as well. Jack decided to go underground.

He contacted one of these former clients, described the situation he found himself in, and asked for help. Recognizing it was in his interest to help Jack, the man provided a place for him and Cory to stay. It was up the San Juan River, well inland from the Caribbean, five miles from any road, off the electric grid, and twenty-five miles from the nearest phone. One thousand kilos of cocaine were moving through this location every week, so his client's armed security provided another level of safety. Jack and Cory stayed there for a year, but then Cory was seen unintentionally looking through binoculars at a drug boat crew. Fearing the boat's captain might mistake this for surveillance and raise suspicions about them — and him — Jack's client advised him to pack up and move quickly.

They fled to Santa Cruz, a remote village near the Indo Maíz Biological Reserve, where they stayed hidden for another year. By this time, they were running short of money and Jack needed a source of income. He took most of the cash he had left, bought a used two and a half ton army truck, and began transporting produce — licorice, pineapples, and whatever other crops grew locally. Licorice was a particularly valuable commodity, and one day while driving a load of it through a remote stretch of jungle, Jack stopped fifty feet short of a tree lying across the road. His caution was rewarded when two armed men came out of the bush by the tree, far enough away that he had time to act. He reached under the seat, grabbed a hand grenade he had stashed there, and lobbed it left-handed at the robbers. After word of that incident got around, Jack had no further problems.

"You mean you carried a *hand grenade* in the truck with you?" I asked.

"Sure. I have a bunch of them. Would you like one? I'll bring it to you the next time I visit."

I said no thanks, but true to his word, he brought it anyway. When he presented it — in front of Susie, no less — I said to him, "This thing scares the shit out of me. I can't have it lying around the house. I wouldn't even know how to use it."

He apparently took this as a request for instruction, and proceeded to describe the army's time-tested method for pulling the pin and throwing a grenade.

"Jack. You don't understand. I don't want to learn how to kill someone with a hand grenade. You'll have to take it back with you."

He was clearly disappointed with my rejection of what he had thought was a great gift.

When Jack felt he was getting too well known in Santa Cruz, he moved to Santa Lastenia, an even more remote location, where he and Cory stayed for three months. But there was no opportunity to make any money in this tiny village, so they moved again, this time to San Carlos, where Lake Nicaragua empties into the San Juan River. Jack hoped that Dave, the young gringo he had met in a bar in Grenada years before, still had his boat repair shop in San Carlos and could use Jack's skills as a welder and metalworker. The town was the departure point for many of the river and lake tours, and the heavily used boats always needed maintenance or repair. A technically competent person who spoke English was a real plus, and Dave offered space in his *taller* to let Jack set up a small machine shop.

Jack was confident that he had moved enough times over the past two and a half years that his trail had gone cold, so he and Cory settled into San Carlos. Life there was uneventful, and Jack was able to make a decent living. Things went well until he needed to get his passport renewed again. At the end of the lengthy process, when he turned in the expired one, he was arrested for being in Nicaragua illegally. The immigration officials in Managua were sharp enough to realize that Rhodesia no longer existed and that Jack could not be the 105-year-old catatonic in Cleveland in whose name it had been issued.

Suspicious of this gringo, they contacted the US embassy, who matched Jack's passport photo with one on their Wanted List. The embassy reported him to the US Marshals, who arrested him for parole violation, aiding Lillie's flight, and as a person of interest in the killing of a DEA informant. They flew him to

Miami, where he was held in a federal facility for six weeks while they questioned and threatened him. He was again offered immunity from prosecution as well as participation in the federal witness protection program if he told them everything he knew about the drug trade, but Jack consistently refused. He did not trust the authorities to stand by their word, and had little faith in the WPP to protect him and Cory from the drug traffickers' retribution. The officers questioning him were so frustrated by his lack of cooperation that at the end of his final interview, they switched off the tape recorder and told Jack they were going to make an example out of him. He remembers their exact words: "We are going to butt-fuck you."

Once he was formally sentenced for parole violation (they couldn't prove anything else), Jack was "put on the bus". This was a common practice for getting reluctant witnesses to cooperate. He was shuttled around various penal facilities, all distant from one another, and each time requiring an early-morning rousing, no breakfast, long waits, hours on buses, no lunch, only to be delivered to the next prison after the mess hall had closed. After two months of this, Jack had gone from 180 to 150 pounds, but he still refused to give a deposition to the DEA. His teenage experience with Officer Wolfe and his previous imprisonment in the detonator affair had prepared him for rough treatment. Being on the bus only strengthened his resolve.

Jack's total time in custody was nine and a half months, one and a half months longer than the maximum his parole violation should have entailed, because his time in the Miami facility was not credited. The government was making good on its threat to punish Jack for not giving them the information they wanted, and they stretched out the incarceration for as long as they could. His last stop was in Arkansas, and by the time he got there he was in such a weakened condition (Cory said he'd aged twenty years) that he was excused from doing any prison work. He didn't know it at the time, but his bad treatment ultimately thwarted the government's last attempt at punishment. At the completion of his sentence, the Bureau of Prisons told Jack that if he had no parole plan to support himself when he was released, he would have to go back to a halfway house in Portland, the point of his original commitment. Jack's attorney used the Arkansas decision not to put him to work as an argument against this, since the whole point of the halfway house was to reintroduce former convicts to the workforce. Further, he informed them that Jack's daughter, who was living in Washington DC was willing to provide care and housing for her father. They had to release him.

Cory had married a young man she met when he came to San Carlos on a construction project, and she had accompanied him, pregnant, to Washington when he found a good paying job there. Son-in-law Frank came to pick Jack up at the bus station in Springfield, Arkansas, where the guards had dropped him off. Frank didn't recognize him. The robust, energetic man he had known at Lake Nicaragua was now haggard, had gray hair, and was wearing an oversize suit that hung on his skinny frame. He told Jack that he looked like an old homeless person, and in fact Frank had almost walked right past him as he entered the terminal. They drove back to DC, and Jack took up residence in Cory and Frank's apartment. He still had to complete an additional one and a half years of parole before he could get a driver's license or apply for a passport. In 2000, Jack finally got back to San Carlos and started his own machine shop there, vowing to become a permanent expatriate.

His business did well. Jack is a skilled machinist with an engineering degree, and can both design and fabricate precision metal parts. Although its reputation as a destination is growing,

San Carlos is still remote, and for the cruisers frequenting the place, finding parts for their boats can be difficult. Importing things from US suppliers is both lengthy and expensive, not to mention customs duties of up to 38 percent of their value. As a result, Jack has a steady stream of profitable projects. In 2006, he invested $70,000 to build the expanded shop he has today, and he makes enough money to purchase the machine tools (some costing $20,000 or more) he needs to grow his business. He has the best-equipped machine shop in the country outside of Managua, and sailors, tour-boat operators, and others needing custom metal work around Lake Nicaragua seek him out. He has air-conditioned his shop, hired and trained an apprentice, and has designed and built homes for himself and Cory, who came back to Nicaragua with her little girl when her marriage to Frank ran into difficulty.

In addition to his machine shop, Jack has other sources of income, one of which is competitive shooting. He is a crack shot and regularly wins long-range (1000+ meters) rifle competitions with purses of up to $10,000. His advantage over the other shooters is his ability to fabricate sniper-accuracy receivers and barrels in his shop, and then arrange his shooting on the range to coincide with a narrow time frame. He calculates the variations in temperature and humidity as the sun rises and the day heats up, determines the density of the air based on the firing range's height above sea level, and factors in the rotation of the earth, a real consideration at such long distances. Combining these elements with his high level of marksmanship, Jack consistently comes away with prize money.

He also works as a tour guide. When working for the cocaine traffickers, Jack had gained an intimate knowledge of the many small but navigable creeks in Mexico, Guatemala, and Nicaragua. He has turned this into a lucrative business. Speaking English gives him preference as a guide with the Brits, Americans, and Canadians, and he makes $100 a day for each one he takes up the exotic rain-forest waterways to see tropical wildflowers, iridescent butterflies, crocodiles, and howler monkeys. Normally, running such an operation is dangerous for a *norteamericano* because of the lock the local boatmen have on it. Challenging them not only risks the gringo outsider's boat, but also possibly his life. In Jack's case, however, the locals know who his friends are, and, wisely, don't interfere with him.

Satisfied at this point that we had made good progress on the book, Jack and I retired to neutral corners, he back to San Carlos and me to Siguaterra. In early January, Susie and I would be back to take *Mariposa* on a final cruise, so it would only be a few weeks before Jack and I could review the write-up of the corrections and the first draft of the new material we had just completed.

Belize Cruise

Figuring out what to wear on our annual winter flight to Managua required careful planning. Susie and I had to dress warmly enough for the early morning departure from Portland, Maine, where the temperature was typically in the teens (down jackets, wool knit hats, sweaters, sturdy shoes, gloves), and also be ready to step off the airplane in eighty-five degree tropical conditions (T-shirts, shorts, sandals). We felt, and probably looked, like circus clowns as we frantically packed and layered up in our bedroom at 3:00 on the morning of our departure. Once on the airplane we could peel off the heavy stuff, but then, where to stow it? And how to carry all of it, plus checked and carry-on luggage, through immigration and customs, fumbling all the while with passports and declarations? Jack met us as we finally emerged from the airport, and his friendship was never more appreciated than when we got into his air-conditioned car.

On the drive down to the river, I reminded Jack that we weren't going to have a lot of time to go over the draft. We had to uncover the boat, reconnect the electronics, make sure the heads flushed and the bilges pumped, switch on the engine and generator, unpickle the watermaker—the tasks seemed endless—and then provision the boat for a four-month cruise. The high tide was only two weeks away, which would have been plenty of time if everything worked. But we knew it wouldn't. After a boat sits idle for six months, connections corrode, seals dry out, batteries discharge, pumps clog. To complicate matters, there is this curious cascading effect when things go wrong on boats. As one problem is getting fixed, another one crops up. What should be a half-hour chore of clearing sludge from a bilge pump pickup turns into a half *day* of rewiring or replacing the bloody thing. And while working in the bilge, the leak in the engine's heat exchanger is spotted ... and so forth.

Jack understood. He was a sailor himself, and as an engineer he was the go-to guy on a Colombia River to Honolulu race he had participated in one year. Things go wrong when a boat just sits, but there are even more problems in the open sea. Out there, everything is in constant motion, flexing and torquing in the waves, and salt water is spraying every surface. Sails, spars, and rigging strain in thirty-knot winds. Things shift around below deck and in the bilges. Because of this, it's better to deal with problems that can be seen while still at the dock, and not have them compound the inevitable repairs that will be needed when underway. So Jack and I agreed we'd deal with as much of the book as we could before Susie and I left for Belize, and then pick things up again when we returned in May.

Belize's offshore atolls were of special interest to Susie and me. We'd been told they were unique in Atlantic waters, because they looked exactly like the atolls in the South Pacific: coral-head-studded lagoons surrounded by reefs that broke the seas, leaving calm water inside. But first we had to get out of the river, and if we didn't make the next high tide, we would lose a whole month. So preparations got hectic. Months' worth of meat had to be put in the freezer; canned goods, cases of beer, wine, rum, and gin packed into lockers and bilges; diesel oil and fuel filters stowed in the shop; propane tanks filled. And as much as we could, we also wanted to assure ourselves that the boat itself was seaworthy. Critical items like rigging, sails, engine, ground tackle, steering gear, navigation electronics, radios, and radar needed to be inspected and faults corrected. We knew from experience that it wasn't possible to get everything done before slipping the lines, but also recognized the wisdom in the sailor's old adage: if you wait until everything *is* done, you will never leave the dock. We just accepted that we would deal with whatever came up, as we had in the past. We had the gray hairs to prove it.

Getting *Mariposa* clear of the river into open water was always dicey. The boat's draft was six and a half feet, and the controlling depth of the sandbars at the mouth of the river (according to the charts) was five feet. But that depth was variable, dependent on tide, volume of water flowing out of the river, and whether the wind was blowing on or offshore. Also, occasional floods, tropical storms, and hurricanes could actually alter the underwater terrain. All these factors had to be taken into consideration to maximize the chances of gaining an additional foot and a half of depth. And although all the cruisers had their favorite GPS waypoints and compass headings, these variables meant each year's passage was different. Getting out of the river was therefore referred to as "passing the bar exam."

Susie and I always made our dash to freedom at the highest tide of the month, regardless of what day and time it occurred. That year, the late-January high was predicted for the early morning hours, so we cleared out of customs and immigration the day before. The other deep-draft boats had done the same, and we were all waiting at first light for just the right moment.

But this moment varied, depending on the source of information. There were a number of tide charts available to the sailors, and the times given for high water were not the same on all the charts. Sometimes even the day was different. Actually, this was fortunate, because if everyone thought that 07:37 was precisely the moment, it would have been chaos out on the bar when all the boats clumped together. Susie and I often waited a bit to see how everyone else fared, also figuring that the furrows dug by others' keels might help us get across. Then it would be our turn.

While *Mariposa*'s draft was admittedly a disadvantage, the boat's tonnage actually favored us. She weighed 56,000 pounds, and that, combined with speed, translated into momentum. Our tried and true procedure was to motor *up*stream a half mile or so, line the boat up on the GPS trace in the chartplotter, and put the throttle down full. As a result, by the time we got to the first sandbar—there were always at least three—we were making almost eight knots. In a twenty-five ton vessel, that was enough to let us bump comfortably over the first bar, hardly slowing us at all. The second took off a noticeable amount of speed; and by the time we hit the third bar, *Mariposa* was literally plowing through the sandy mud bottom. It was disconcerting to see the boat's wake, normally well astern, overtaking her. But the twenty-eight inch diameter bronze prop kept churning, and we never got stuck. Even so, clearing the last bar was a huge relief, and another occasion to crack open an early-morning beer to initiate the start of a new sailing season. We never would have had a drink this early back in Maine, but now Susie and I were reentering our cruising lifestyle, free of Puritan constraints. We savored the moment as well as the beers.

It was an easy beam reach north from the mouth of the San Juan River to Gracias a Dios, and then a straight shot northwest to Belize with the wind on *Mariposa*'s starboard quarter. Our destination was Placencia, a favorite among northwest Caribbean cruisers because of the protected harbor and the abundance of good bars, and restaurants, and yachting services there. But the winds were light as we got within striking distance, and we would have had to burn a lot of fuel to make it by four o'clock. Night falls fast at this latitude, and if anything went wrong to delay us, we would face either coming in after dark or sailing back and forth outside the harbor entrance until daylight.

Susie didn't like these options, and not wanting to contend with an anxious crew all day, I agreed to veer off our course and head due west for New Haven Bight. Isolated, protected on three sides by land and offshore by cays, this was a great anchorage. We'd be in by noon, take a swim, have lunch, maybe nap, and later have sundowners and make a leisurely dinner. From that perspective, arriving one day late in Placencia in exchange for a sunny spouse was an easy trade-off.

Mid-afternoon, we got a hail on the VHF from another boat approaching New Haven. It was Gail and Reg on *Tide's End*, friends from the river, and they had recognized *Mariposa's* distinctive hull from a distance. It would be nice to have their company, because it meant that Reg and I could explore the creeks around the bight in a dinghy while the ladies kept each other company. Later, we talked about having dinner together, but not knowing the security situation in New Haven, decided against it. Leaving one of our boats unguarded after dark would not have been prudent. Besides, there was a front approaching from the northwest, and we felt it would be wise to stay an extra day or two in the sheltered bight rather than bashing into four- to six-foot swells. We'd take turns having lunch aboard each other's boats while keeping an eye on the vacant one.

The morning weather report indicated that the front had intensified, and I decided to up anchor and move deeper into the protection of the Bight. There would be less fetch, so the water would be calmer there. It was a routine maneuver, one that Susie and I had done dozens of times: me in the bow handling the anchor and chain, she steering, shifting gears, and throttling according to my hand signals. We had learned long ago that trying to shout instructions between the bow pulpit and the cockpit was frustrating for both of us and, more importantly, completely ineffectual if the wind was snatching my words away.

I usually wore rigging gloves with well-padded palms and fingers (but fingertips exposed) when handling *Mariposa*'s eighty-pound anchor and three-eighths inch chain. But that day's drill was in flat calm water and we were only moving a few hundred yards, so I left the gloves in the cockpit. There was an electric windlass in the bow to haul up the chain and anchor, activated by a switch on the deck that I could operate by depressing it with my heel. This left my hands free to clean the mud off the chain, using the pulpit-mounted hose and salt-water pump, so it wouldn't stink up the locker where it piled up in front of the forward cabin. The windlass had a rotating drum with tooth-shaped indentations in it to secure the chain as it was lifted out of the water. All I had to do was press the switch, and hundreds of pounds of chain would be pulled off the bottom. At the very end, though, just as the anchor's shank started to come up through the roller mounted in the bow pulpit, I had to stop the windlass and go out to guide the anchor into its proper storage position.

I must have been careless this time, not making sure the chain was secure in the drum, because as I started to move forward, the chain jumped out of its teeth and the anchor started back down. Somehow, and I still don't understand how this happened, I got my left hand caught between the drum and the chain as it dropped back into the indentations. I don't remember doing it, but I must have lifted the chain up enough with my right hand to get the left one free, but the damage had been done. I looked down to see pieces of flesh missing from the underside of three of my fingers. There wasn't much blood—yet—and I found myself staring at white, exposed ligaments. It was a shock. I had never had a serious injury before, just superficial cuts, and only a couple of them had required stitches. After Novocain, no big deal, but there were no docs in New Haven Bight. And exposed ligaments or not, I still had to get the anchor down and dug in before the blow came. I grabbed a rag that happened to be lying on the deck (sloppy seamanship), wrapped it around my fingers, and got the anchor secured on deck.

I signaled Susie to power farther up in the Bight until I was happy with where the boat was lying, and had her stop. As soon as *Mariposa* started to drift back, I lowered the anchor and slowly paid out chain by controlling the clutch on the windlass drum. When I had about two hundred feet out, I had Susie power briefly in reverse to extend the chain straight on the bottom. Once properly aligned, I signaled another shot astern. When *Mariposa* held her position, I had Susie go back at half throttle for twenty seconds to bury the hook. I now felt we were safe for the coming front and could turn my attention to my fingers.

As I came into the cockpit, Susie asked why I had a rag wrapped around my hand.

Obviously, she hadn't heard me shout, "Oh shit!" when I looked at my fingers.

After I explained what had happened, she said we had to take a look at it and see what to do. We went below. Susie got out the first aid kit, and I carefully unwrapped the now bloody rag.

I almost passed out at the sight, but she said, "Do you think you need stitches?"

About the last thing I wanted to contemplate was somebody pushing a needle and thread into my un-anesthetized fingers, so I said, "As a start, let's rinse everything off with hydrogen peroxide and get the grit from the rag off. It will disinfect the cuts too. Maybe we can just keep rinsing it and keep it covered."

At some point during this process, a cheery hail came from the VHF. It was Reg.

"How's the holding up there? Should I come up too? You want to do sundowners later?"

Susie got on the radio. "Bill's had an accident. His fingers got caught in the windlass and we're trying to figure out how to deal with it."

Gail must have grabbed the mike. "Let me take a look," she said. "I'm coming over." Gail could be abrupt, and I was glad for any distraction from thinking about stitches.

"Sure," Susie said. "Are you a nurse or something?"

"I'll tell you about it when I get there. Let's go, Reg."

Five minutes later they were sitting with us in the main salon. Gail uncovered the bandage, and sure enough, Susie asked if I needed stitches.

"There's nothing to stitch," Gail said. "The pieces of skin that came off are gone and you can't pull the edges together."

"How do you know?" Susie asked.

I realized that neither Reg nor I were in this discussion. The women were going to decide what was going to happen to me. While they debated, I offered him a beer.

"I used to run a daycare center before Reg and I went sailing. Believe me, in twenty years of dealing with preschoolers, I saw plenty of injuries, a lot of them worse than this."

"What should we do?" Susie asked. "Should we just keep it clean with hydrogen peroxide until we get to Placencia and find a doctor?"

"Stop using the peroxide. It will only keep the wounds from healing. It's good to use to clean them at first, but it's corrosive to the skin. Do you have any antibiotics on board?"

"Sure, we have Cipro," I said, finally having something to contribute to the discussion. I had worked for Bayer, which developed Cipro. As a retiree, I could get as much as I wanted at no cost, so we had a good supply.

"Okay," Gail said, "here's what you do. Bandage the fingers and splint them so they can't bend. Change the bandages twice a day. Keep them dry. No swimming, and put a plastic bag over your hand when you shower. Take the Cipro so you don't get an infection. You don't need a doctor."

Thank God, I thought. *No stitches.*

We hunkered down in New Haven for three days as the front lingered, and we played a lot of cards with Reg and Gail. The morning of the fourth day dawned cloudless, with fifteen- to twenty-knot easterly trades reestablishing themselves, so we pulled up our anchors—I was super careful—and enjoyed a beam-reach sail north to Placencia. The seas had settled down to three- to five-foot swells, and we made six to seven and a half knots the whole way.

These kinds of ideal sailing conditions are rare. People who aren't sailors imagine that you just go out, raise the sails, and steer the boat in the direction you want to go. The reality is different. In the first place, your destination seems always to be located where the wind is coming from. And since sailboats don't go directly into the wind, you have to tack. This means zigging forty-five degrees away from the wind's source, then changing course and zagging back across the wind in the opposite direction. You make progress, but it's not in a straight line, so it takes a lot longer to get where you're going.

Furthermore, the longer you're out there, the more chance conditions will change. First there will not be enough wind, and then there will be so much that you have to shorten sail on a pitching deck. Seas can go from a comfortable three-foot roll on the quarter to six-footers crashing into the bow and almost stopping the boat.

Then, when you finally arrive at the entrance to your anchorage, which under these latter conditions always seems to be just a narrow break in the reef, the sun is so low that it reflects off the water's surface and half blinds you. Worse, it starts to get dark and you can't see anything. It's no wonder people buy power boats, but we sailors consider them artless, unequal to the challenge and incapable of appreciating the romance of the sea. Then, somewhere around midnight and facing six more hours of tacking back and forth in front of the harbor entrance, the romance fades and you begin to consider buying a trawler.

But *Mariposa* and *Tide's End* were fortunate, and we had our anchors securely down in Placencia before four o'clock, sails furled and cold beers opened. It wasn't easy getting the dinghy in the water and the outboard hung on its transom with only one hand, but it was time for Susie to have dinner ashore. No food to prepare, no dishes to wash. Besides, I wanted to brag to our fellow cruisers about anchoring *Mariposa* in New Haven with lacerated fingers.

We stayed in Placencia while my fingers healed, with Gail checking in on me from time to time. After the skin had closed up, she prescribed an exercise regimen to loosen the joints, which the splints had locked in a partial clench from the lack of movement. She had me lay my injured hand on a tabletop, palm down, and use the other hand to press down on the middle knuckles of the arched fingers. It was painful as the scar tissue on the underside stretched and the joint started to straighten, but she told me to do it twice a day, extending the fingers a little more each time.

"You'll have to do this for a couple of months or you won't ever be able to straighten out your fingers," she warned. "The joints will always be a little enlarged and you'll never be able to get the fingers completely straight. That shouldn't be a problem. But you'll probably have arthritis in those joints when you get older." Gail was always cheery this way when she was talking about health.

During the time we spent in New Haven together, Susie and I had learned that Gail loved ice cream, which our freezer was cold enough to keep frozen. So when Reg told us her birthday was two days away, we decided to throw a surprise party for her at the gelato shop in town. We also knew she liked to eat early, so we informed all the cruisers to gather there at eight o'clock on her special day.

Susie brought a chocolate cake she had attempted to bake in *Mariposa*'s oven. Because its temperature never got above 300 degrees, the result was rather dense, but it was great anyway with ice cream, especially with rum poured all over it. Lots of hugs and well wishes for Gail, and my thanks once again for having saved me from stitches.

While we were waiting for my fingers to heal, a sloop flying a German flag came into the Placencia anchorage. *Barmina* was captained by a single woman, and once she got her hook down, dinghy after dinghy motored over to welcome – and check out – our new neighbor. At six feet three inches tall, Lisa was an arresting figure, especially because unlike most tall women she was perfectly proportioned. She was also unusual in that she was a single-hander. This meant that she sailed and maintained her boat without any crew. Lisa had sailed her boat across the North Atlantic from Bremerhaven alone. It is not uncommon to find men single handing, but women are generally smarter than men in the risk-taking department. On a passage, for example, the sailor's judgment is impaired by getting only fifteen or twenty minute snatches of sleep for days on end. Confronted with an emergency, prompt and considered action must be taken. The fact that one person, no matter how experienced, simply can't do this consistently explains why so many solo sailors run up on reefs or find themselves on a collision course with a 200,000-ton container ship.

But Lisa was intrepid. She was an engineer — a *German* engineer — tremendously strong and proudly self-reliant. She not only sailed by herself, she also fed herself largely from the sea, collected rainwater for drinking, bathed in salt water, and even constructed a crude but working washing machine.

She assembled this contraption from an empty five-gallon paint can and a shaft of stainless steel tubing, to which she attached agitation vanes made from odd scraps of wood. To power it, Lisa constructed a paddle wheel that she hung over the side of her boat. As the boat moved through the water, the paddles turned, rotating the shaft, which stirred the vanes inside the can and washed her clothes.

Lisa was always fishing. She had two rod holders in the stern so she could troll while under way; and when at anchor, she would spearfish the reef while leaving a couple of baited hooks hanging off the transom. This persistence paid off. Lisa always had fish to eat, and never missed the opportunity to land another one. Once, when a large fish jerked a rod out of its holder on the rail, Lisa dove right in as if her body was attached to it. A minute later, she threw the rod back on deck with an eight-pound grouper at the end of the line.

Lisa was able to work all day on her boat and then shower, dress, and head ashore to hit the nightspots. This was when her predatory nature came to the fore, rather like a female vampire stalking the night for unwary males. Men foolish enough to think they could meet Lisa's challenge found themselves in for a night that left them completely drained, if not of blood, then of self-confidence as only a man can get when unable to match a vigorous woman's sexual stamina.

Because Lisa had no job or savings to draw on, she did need money for the staples she couldn't harvest from the sea, things like beans, rice or pasta, and long-lived items like unwashed eggs (they keep unrefrigerated for a month or more) and carrots or cabbages. Woman does not live by fish and sex alone. In order to earn cash, Lisa would enter into money-making ventures such as teaching people to snorkel or kite sail. She could also parlay her engineering expertise to help other sailors less adept, and she took bartered provisions in return. Being a very attractive woman, she could have traded sexual favors for food, but that would have lasted only until a few bloodless male bodies were found floating facedown down in the anchorage.

To teach kite sailing, Lisa showed participants how to strap a short, lightweight board to their feet, send a large rectangular kite aloft, and then attempt to control the kite with thin, strong cords. When the wind was up, the speeds achieved while skipping across the surface of the water — airborne as often as not — were truly remarkable. Learning the control aspect was difficult, though, because anticipating wind gusts wasn't possible, and sometimes the kite had to be doused quickly. It takes strength, quick reactions, stamina, and daring to master this sport, all of which Lisa had in abundance. Her challenge was finding folks crazy enough to try it, but she could be pretty convincing when she approached potential customers on the beach. How does a guy say no to a six-foot blonde-haired blue-eyed goddess in the briefest of bikinis inviting to teach him an exciting new sport?

Lisa demonstrated the technique by standing at the water's edge with her feet strapped to the board and jumping in just as the kite filled. Then she zipped around the bay, in effect throwing the gauntlet down in front of her potential customers. To finish the demonstration, she aimed the board back toward the beach and drove it right up on the sand, dousing the kite just before she was dragged into the sunbathers on their lounge chairs sipping cold Coronas. Every once in a while, though, a sudden gust would upset this calculated display of bravado. On one such occasion, Lisa misjudged things and was flung airborne into a dock house on a pier. Normally, such a mishap could result in serious injury, but in this case there was only minor damage ... to the dock house.

Accompanying Lisa on a passage was something taken on only by the unwitting. In one instance, a young Swiss girl was looking for a ride from Placencia to Isla Mujeres. Cruising sailors are often approached by backpackers and others with little money looking for a free ride, and this girl had identified two prospects: Lisa and a male Canadian sailor/musician. Prudently, or so she thought, the girl signed on with Lisa, and they started north.

We heard the rest of the story through the coconut telegraph, relayed by a couple who were buddy sailing with Lisa and the girl. They were older folks with liberal-arts educations who knew their limitations, and having an engineer nearby was good insurance. Further, sailing in company like this was a wise practice in waters where piracy was known. The two boats set out at the same time each day, made the same runs, stopped at the same anchorages, and remained in radio if not visual contact at all times. This was the same tried and true buddy sailing procedure we had employed with Betty and John.

Things were going fine, but then the Canadian fellow fell in with the other two boats. He was a nice kid, good looking and polite, and the Swiss girl was attracted to him. This wasn't lost on Lisa, and tensions started to build. The girl looked for excuses to be with the young man, swimming over to his boat in her own brief bikini, wangling invitations for a glass of wine in his cockpit, and otherwise seeking out his company. Lisa was pointedly not included.

Then one day the girl informed Lisa she wanted to jump ship and sail with the Canadian. Lisa refused, correctly saying that as captain, she was legally responsible for the girl at least until they could clear into the next country and redo the crew list. To emphasize her point, Lisa forbade the girl to leave her boat for any reason, and kept coming up with more tasks for her to perform. Tearful scenes ensued, and radio communications were filled with suggestions of involuntary servitude at the hands of a German guard. There were no reports of restraints, however.

The dilemma was finally resolved when the boats came into the anchorage at Xcalak, Mexico, and the three young people went together to clear into the country and amend their respective crew lists. Everyone was civil, but that night Lisa went out on the town to console herself at some of the clubs. Midway through the evening she met Nik, a six-foot eight-inch former Olympic basketball player from Holland who owned a resort in the area and was himself a powerful player in the nightclub scene. Equally challenged, they fell in together, and eventually Nik allowed Lisa to open a water sports school on the beach at his resort. At last report she was still there, intimidating male vacationers into scary water sports while raising their two children.

For Susie and me, the next few months were idyllic. My fingers healed, and we sailed out of Placencia to begin the leisurely exploration of the Belizean cruising grounds we had promised ourselves while helping out the waterless Betty and John. The string of cays and reefs running north-south off the mainland provided sheltered water, and the easterly breeze made sailing effortless. We stopped when and where we wanted, staying until the desire to see what else was out there prompted our next move. Mostly we were alone, amazed that such a sailor's paradise could be largely undiscovered. Occasionally we came into an anchorage where there were other cruisers. Some we knew, some were strangers, but regardless, an instant community invariably formed. Drinks and dinners were shared, sea stories swapped, music played, assistance offered and given, and then it was time to move on again.

We worked our way north, staying in the lee of the reef and cays, stopping each evening, until we eventually reached San Pedro, the northernmost of the Belize cays. This was where we had thought to part company with John and Betty three years ago. Now it would be our jumping-off point for a cruise out to the atolls, which paralleled the reefs twenty miles farther out to sea. We waited for a wind shift to the northeast, since that wind direction would get us southeast to the northernmost of the atolls without needing to tack. When the shift came, we went out through the break in the reef just south of San Pedro and enjoyed a lovely sail to our first stop, Turneffe Atoll.

We decided to anchor in the small bay at the south end of the atoll because we had heard that the all-inclusive resort there sometimes welcomed cruisers for dinner if they weren't completely booked. We took the dinghy to the resort's dock and tied up, expecting one of the staff to come out to greet us. Since it was a private resort, we didn't want to be presumptuous and just come ashore uninvited. The reception committee soon arrived in the form of two barking (not quite snarling) German shepherds charging down the dock toward us. We jumped back into the dinghy, pushing away from the dock.

"I guess they aren't going to invite us to dinner," Susie said, but then the dogs' handler came down the dock and calmed them. He was polite enough, and asked us if we knew that the resort was only for registered guests.

"Yes," I said. "We knew that, but we'd heard that sometimes you let cruisers come ashore for dinner and anchor overnight here. Would that be possible?"

He took his hand-held VHF off his belt, radioed the office, and after a brief exchange told us it would be okay. "Dinner starts at six o'clock. I'll meet you back here at quarter of and show you the way to the restaurant."

"Don't trouble yourself," I said, trying to be considerate. "Just give me a general idea of where it is and we'll find it."

"No, I'll meet you here on the dock. Please don't come ashore alone." He glanced at the dogs.

"Got it," I said, and we motored back to *Mariposa*.

We met at the appointed hour and were accompanied directly to the restaurant by the welcoming committee. The dogs stayed close. It was clear we weren't to wander around and we understood that, but all the same it felt a little threatening. When we stepped into the dining room at exactly six, the soup course was already being served. These folks ran a tight ship. The other diners looked at us as if to say, *What are you doing here?* and did not engage us in conversation beyond what was socially necessary. We were clearly interlopers in their exclusive realm, and our attire, while clean, was out of place amidst their finery. It was a bit off-putting to be received like that, after weeks of easygoing camaraderie among a bunch of "grotty yotties" (as we often referred to our fellow sailors), whose idea of formal wear was a clean T- shirt and shorts without holes in them.

The dinner was fresh grilled barracuda, a predator fish with firm flesh like tuna, but more delicately flavored. The first time we ate barracuda was after we caught one while trolling off the back of the boat. In truth, we had a Spanish mackerel on the line, but the barracuda swallowed it whole, so we ended up with a much bigger fish on the aft deck. We were concerned about eating it, though. Barracuda prey on reef fish, many of which are contaminated with a toxin that accumulates in their muscles. We had heard that if you eat one of those fish, it can make you sick. Locals call it break-bone disease because you feel as if every bone in your body has been broken.

We cleaned the barracuda and put it on ice. The next morning, we joined the daily Northwest Caribbean SSB radio net and asked the cruiser community if what we had heard was true. Would it be risky to eat our barracuda? The answer at first surprised us, but on reflection seemed logical: if the fish measured less than three feet, it could be eaten safely. Over that length, it was probably old enough to have accumulated too much toxin. It was impractical for us, but we also learned the locals' method of checking for edibility: cut the fish's head off and place it near an anthill. If the ants don't eat it, you shouldn't either.

Assuming the resort had employed this method — they certainly wouldn't risk a bunch of sick gringos — we enjoyed our dinner in spite of the cold shoulder. After dessert, we were met by our three escorts outside the restaurant, who walked us back to the dock and waited until we had cast off the dinghy and headed back to *Mariposa*. On the radio net the next morning, we informed our fellow cruisers about the "welcome" we had gotten from the Turneffe Gestapo. I doubt the restaurant got any more business from them, which probably suited the resort management just fine.

Our next stop going south was Lighthouse Atoll, remote and uninhabited except for the small community of sailors who were anchored there. As was often the case, as soon as our hook was down, a dinghy approached and we were invited for sundowners on a neighboring vessel. The couple on board had been at Lighthouse for a few weeks and were putting together a DVD about the reef. The husband said it was teeming with life because there was no one there to disturb it. He was a professional videographer and normally did his dives solo, but he invited me to join him the next morning.

The dive was spectacular. He had waited until the sun was high in the cloudless sky, so the light penetrated deep into the crystal-clear water and bathed the reef in shimmering waves. Near the surface, thickets of dark fan corals waved in the current. Farther down, trees of mottled tan elkhorn coral branched out five feet, and delicate stems of red fire coral warned of a dangerous touch. Strewn across the bottom were large brain corals, their convoluted white surfaces bearing their uncanny resemblance to what is inside our skulls. The sponges were equally dramatic, ranging in color from deep purple to pink, yellow, and green. It appeared that an adult could fit inside the largest of them, the barrel sponge, and so I got in one, buoyancy compensator, tank, hoses, and all. It was an odd sensation to be looking out over the top edge of the barrel, feeling softly surrounded by this living sea creature.

As we continued our descent, we saw tropical fish of every color and pattern — some with several colors and patterns — as if an Impressionist painter with a limitless palette had randomly daubed their bodies. For me, this is when thoughts of the Creator come unbidden, and I am struck simultaneously by the surreal experience of breathing almost normally 120 feet below the surface of the ocean, and by the awareness that if something went wrong down there I could easily die. This latter point was driven home when I realized my dive buddy, waterproof video cam in hand, had descended to this depth in search of lemon sharks. These predators, while not as dangerous as great whites, are known to attack humans occasionally. I had the illogical but nonetheless disquieting thought that he might have invited me on the dive as bait. Fortunately, nothing happened. We didn't even see a shark. But I didn't dive with him again.

Susie and I stayed a week at Lighthouse, snorkeling the coral heads that dotted the shallow lagoon and visiting with friends old and new as they came into the anchorage. Our departure was delayed a few more days as a weather front blew down from the States and reminded us why were there. Our only inconvenience was having to reanchor in the lee of the atoll so we wouldn't be rolled by seas coming from the north instead of their usually easterly direction. When the winds and seas had settled down, we sailed on to the southernmost of the atolls, named Glover Reef on most charts.

Of the three atolls, Glover was our favorite. Getting into the shelter of the lagoon was tricky, with lots of coral dotting the channel entrance. I stood in the bow pulpit and pointed directions while Susie steered us through the reef—again, no shouting, just hand signals. Inside, the water was calm, and the steady breeze promised to keep us cool. I dropped the hook in a sand patch, put on my mask and fins, and swam out, following the chain along the bottom until I was hovering over the anchor. I signaled Susie to put *Mariposa* in reverse and back her down at steadily increasing RPMs while I watched the chain tighten and the hook bury itself in the bottom. We gained a tremendous sense of security by following this procedure. *Mariposa's* anchor weighed eighty pounds and was attached to three hundred feet of chain, each link three-eighths of an inch thick. Once it was dug in and the proper scope let out, we knew we could sleep soundly. That evening, we came to rest two hundred yards off an uninhabited curve of pure white sand. Palm, sea grape, and almond trees lined the back of the beach, making a picture-postcard-perfect tropical anchorage.

Susie threw her sweaty, sunscreen-stained T-shirt and shorts on a cockpit cushion and jumped in to join me in the water. We enjoyed a long, cooling swim, came up the ladder (the one Jack had repaired), and rinsed off the salt with the freshwater cockpit shower. There was no point in dressing, so we sipped G and T's over ice au naturel as the setting sun turned the white sand to gold and the flycatchers skimmed just inches above the water, hunting for insects. That evening, we grilled two steaks from the mackerel-eating barracuda we had kept in the freezer, and made pasta pomodoro basilico and a cole slaw from green and red cabbage, carrots, and beets, all accompanied by a chilled bottle of pinot grigio. We had succeeded in transplanting our land-based dining and drinking style to a remote atoll in the middle of the Caribbean, and it was gratifying beyond words. What could have been put together by a twenty-minute trip to the supermarket and less than an hour in the Maine kitchen had required weeks to pull off on the boat. We clinked glasses, reflected on our extraordinary good fortune, and watched the waxing moon rise out of the water, turning the sea into a shimmering silver carpet.

With the stay at Glover, we had completed the cruise to Belize we had promised ourselves, and the May high tide was coming. It was time to head back to the river and get *Mariposa* secured for the hurricane season. We were farther south than San Pedro, so waited until the wind shifted well to the north of east so we could make Gracias a Dios without tacking. Once we rounded the cape, we sailed south on a beam reach and arrived at the anchorage across the bay from the San Juan River entrance several days before high water. Other deep-draft boats were congregating there, and everybody took advantage of the waiting time to begin the process of decommissioning. Evenings were spent socializing, recounting (with admitted exaggeration) the season's adventures, and swapping sea stories. The last night, a flotilla of a dozen dinghies rafted together in the center of the anchorage. We could all see our boats, so didn't worry about unwelcome boarders, and could drink, snack, and chat until dusk. The next morning we crossed the ten-mile bay and took the bar exam again.

Once we had cleared through immigration and customs and notified the port captain, I radioed Jack and told him we were heading upriver and could continue writing his story. When we arrived at the marina two days later, he was waiting for us with a chilled bottle of wine sitting on the Gauguin table. We got caught up, and he and I agreed to get back to work in the morning. After four months of being almost continuously afloat, I was ready for some time on terra firma. In addition, Susie had had plenty of her husband and was ready for some private time. We had a great relationship, but after months of being almost constantly together, she needed a few days of what a good friend and writer colleague calls "a marriage vacation."

Mariposa Sale

After we closed on the Siguaterra house in February 2010, Susie's nesting instincts kicked in. The sailing *had* been fun, hadn't it? But we'd *done* it for ten winters, right? Wasn't it time to start learning about our *new* locale, the people, the language? Aren't you getting a little tired of all that *work* on *Mariposa*? Now that we've done the Belize cruise, isn't it time to *sell* her? But only if you're really *ready* to give her up, of course....

I should have known this line of reasoning was inevitable. It reminded me of the lead-up to our marriage. Haven't you *ever* thought about having children? Who's going to look after us when we're *old?* Ever notice how *unhappy* those childless couples are? Wouldn't your dad be *proud* to have a grandson?

In both those cases, the outcome of the game was assured almost before it began. It took a while for me to break the code on this, whether it was about mating or boat ownership, and some guys never do. We think we are making the big decisions, when in fact our women have it all worked out and are guiding us along with gentle but unrelenting psychological pressure and a loving grip on our private parts. Of course, I would have a lot to say about the details, but there was no question about parting company with *Mariposa*. Sailors like me enjoy basking in their status as boat captains, but only the most oblivious don't realize who the fleet admirals are.

It took two years to find the buyer. The economy still hadn't recovered from the Great Recession, and nobody really needs a fifty-foot ketch. Someone with money was going to have to fall in love with the boat, entranced by some ingenuous notion about the romance of the sea and a naïve desire for adventure.

A fellow cruiser, an emergency room doctor from Australia on indefinite sabbatical, counseled us to build a website that concentrated on selling not just the boat, but the lifestyle. He said that's what attracted him to his boat, which he bought sight unseen, over the Internet. In addition to the standard and exhaustive description of the boat and all its gear and equipment—essential if we wanted to be taken seriously—he said to put up lots of pictures. And don't stop with the de rigueur photo of *Mariposa* under full sail and views of the boat's interior and above-deck layout. Include shots of the two of you enjoying dinghy trips up rain-forest rivers in the company of other intrepid explorers, and sipping sundowners in the cockpit with tanned, smiling friends. Write about your experiences: how you got into sailing in the first place, what you had to learn in order to be able to sail and navigate the boat, where you've cruised, things you would never have seen any other way. Make sure Susie tells her side of it too.

Our doctor friend must have known what he was talking about, because an orthopedic surgeon from Minnesota was among the first to contact us. Still, it took almost two years for him to get comfortable with leaving his practice in the hands of an associate, and to convince his wife that he wasn't just going through a midlife crisis. Then he called us back. If *Mariposa* was still available, he said, they were ready to come down to

Nicaragua and see her for themselves. I gave him some guidance on how best to fly from Minneapolis to Managua, and said if he would e-mail me his flight arrangements, I would meet him and his wife at the airport and take them down to the river.

I called Jack and asked if he'd lend me his air-conditioned car. I didn't want to subject these nice people to the heat and uncertainty of a two-hour-long ride through the countryside in a Nicaraguan taxi. Cabbies are city drivers, and if their cars break down in town, it's easy enough for the passengers to transfer to another cab. Not so in the bush, and I wanted the doctor and his wife to arrive at the marina cool and unfrazzled, with nothing to dampen their enthusiasm for the boat or the area. Jack said he'd play chauffeur, and that way I could chat with my prospective buyers without the distraction of avoiding head-on collisions with buses and eighteen-wheel semis passing on blind curves. He promised not to launch into any rants, and even make the effort to be pleasant to the doctor's wife.

The couple were easy to spot as they walked slowly out of the airport, gazing left and right, blinking in the glaring midday tropical sun. Managua doesn't attract many white gringo tourists, so the tall, trim, casually dressed but still distinguished-looking Dr. Jensen and his blond-haired, blue-eyed wife stood out in the crowd of small brown Latinos and overweight men in business suits talking on cellphones. The other giveaway was the swarm of cabbies who surrounded him and his wife, shouting "Taxi? Taxi?" while grabbing at their luggage. I rescued them from the maelstrom and led the way to the cool tranquility of Jack's car, idling in the parking lot with the AC on. Jack knew his way around, and we were out of the city in minutes.

The drive went better than I expected. Jack and Dr. Jensen hit it off right away, seeing parallels in their respective professions. Metal instruments were part of the surgeon's toolkit, and Jack knew the characteristics of metals and how to work them. He also had experience in health-care settings and with body parts from his time in the medical school morgue and on burial detail in Vietnam. With the doctor riding in the front seat with Jack driving, they quickly fell into medico/techno jargon, leaving Mrs. Jensen—Joanie, she asked me to call her—to chat about Susie's and my experiences as live-aboard sailors. She and Dr. Jensen—Tom—had chartered sailboats for a couple of weeks at a time in the eastern Caribbean and the Med, and at one time had a twenty-eight foot sloop-rigged Pearson weekender on one of the Minnesota lakes. But they had never organized themselves for months of independent living on a cruising sailboat, and had only been aboard vessels of *Mariposa*'s size and complexity at boat shows.

So we spent a lot of time talking about the galley and the heads, Joanie and I, and I wished Susie had been with us to more perceptively discuss the things that concern women. Joanie said she was also worried because every other time they had gone sailing, Tom had run up all the sails and heeled the boat over until the scuppers were in the water. I told her I started out the same way, and Tom would get over it after a few times struggling to shorten sails on a pitching, steeply angled, wet deck. If he had to do it at night, one time would be enough.

What do you do about food, she wanted to know, when you can't get to a supermarket for weeks on end? I explained how Susie and I had learned to provision *Mariposa* with four months of meat in the double freezers (supplemented with fish we caught by trolling while underway), canned fruits and vegetables in waterproof bins in the bilges, produce like cabbage, carrots, and squash that keep for weeks hanging in open-weave minihammocks strung across the galley, and dozens of eggs placed in their cardboard cartons and secured in closed lockers.

Joanie stopped me when I mentioned the eggs.

"Don't you have to put them in the refrigerator?" she asked.

"Well," I said, "these are unwashed eggs. You don't need to refrigerate them."

"You don't? Won't they go bad?"

"No, they won't. There's a natural substance from the hen that coats the eggs as they are being laid, and it makes them almost airtight for a couple of months. But do wash the eggs just before you use them, and crack each one individually into a cup to be sure it's okay."

The Q and A went on like this all the way down to the marina. Joanie had *lots* of questions.

I was able to overhear some of the conversation in the front seat too, and once the men had exhausted the technical subjects, it was apparent Tom was asking Jack what he knew about *Mariposa*. Jack said he had done a couple of projects for me, and described the boat in positive terms. I realized that Jack was doing his part with a low-key sales pitch to Tom while I was doing mine, patiently trying to ease Joanie's concerns. But we both knew that the important thing was getting them on the boat. *Mariposa* would sell herself.

We were greeted at the marina by the lodging staff, ready to take Tom and Joanie to the private bungalow I had reserved for them. Instead, they put their bags down in the middle of the reception area and said they wanted to go straight to the boat, which I took as a positive sign. We walked down the weathered wooden dock, going past a mixed bag of smaller powerboats and sailboats, some of them in pretty rough shape, and then there she was: fifty-six feet of gracefully curving lines, glowing warmly in the late afternoon sun. *Mariposa*'s six-foot bowsprit led aft onto a spacious teak-planked deck and a wood-trimmed pilothouse. Behind the house and two steps up was the cockpit and aft deck area. *Mariposa*'s tender, christened *Moth,* hung from the stern-mounted davits. Underneath it, the boat's transom was bordered with brightwork in the shape of a heart, a true "sweetheart stern." Two six-paned windows were set into the transom. From the front, *Mariposa* looked like a sturdy, well-designed cruising sailboat; from the back, she looked like a pirate ship. I told Tom and Joanie that on several occasions we had been asked to enter her in boat parades, and that was true.

We went aboard, and I took them on a fore-to-aft walking tour of *Mariposa*'s topsides, starting with the bow pulpit. An aft-facing teak seat was mounted in the curve of the pulpit's rail, and I had Tom sit on it so he could appreciate the full-length sweep of the decks, masts, pilothouse, and cockpit. I knew it was an impressive view, and it appeared to have the desired effect.

As we walked aft, I pointed out the anchor-handling windlass mounted in the bow well, the in-boom furling system for the mainsail and mizzen, and the windows surrounding three sides of the pilothouse, allowing for 180-degree visibility. I saved the cockpit for last, because in the ten years I'd owned the boat, it had never failed to elicit "oohs" and "aahs" when people first saw it. A solid teak, highly-varnished binnacle sat in the middle of the cockpit, and contained an array of navigation instruments arranged in a gentle curve. A matching varnished and spoked wheel completed the classic look of the helm. Cushioned seating curved three-quarters of the way around the teak-capped rail which enclosed the cockpit, and there were breaks giving access to the forward and aft decks.

I had Tom sit behind the wheel so he could appreciate the openness of the view forward, as impressive as the one from the bow pulpit looking aft. I also hoped that seated in the captain's position would impart the same sense of command that I felt when I sat there. I briefly described the navigation instruments in the binnacle, and the others which were set in a console atop the forward cockpit combing: electronic charts displayed on a plotter, distance-adjustable 360-degree radar, wind speed and direction indicator, GPS giving boat location and direction, and over-the-ground and through-the-water speed indicators. Then we went below.

Mariposa's interior was accessed via an eight-step curving companionway with a varnished banister. Entering the boat this way was like stepping inside a piece of fine furniture; wooden beams, paneling, doors, moldings, and drawers were everywhere. I led Tom and Joanie all the way forward, to the twin V-berths in the forepeak, and showed them the forward cabin's private head, sink, and shower. Just aft of it was the shop, which had a workbench and — this never failed to impress men — a vice, very unusual on a boat. Concealed behind a set of double doors in the shop — and this never failed to impress women — was a washer/dryer.

In the main saloon was a round varnished dinner table with seating for six. Across from the table was a brass-accented cast-iron woodstove, which also never failed to draw comments. I explained that if they should ever want to take the boat north, burning two paraffin and sawdust composition logs each night would keep them comfortable even if it was freezing outside. Susie and I had done it many times, finishing dinner in our underwear because it was so warm inside the boat.

Three steps up and aft of the main saloon was the pilothouse, with a second steering station and full complement of instruments. I pointed out how was nice it was to be able to safely sail the boat from this sheltered position in cold or rainy weather. The galley was in the pilothouse as well, with a double sink, stove/oven, two-door refrigerator, and deep side-by-side freezer compartments. Opposite the galley was a breakfast table with an inlaid green marble surface. The pilothouse was spacious, and the views out of the windows were expansive.

I hoped that I had saved the best for last. Aft of the pilothouse and down two steps was a carved wooden door leading into the master cabin. A king-size bed completely filled the back of the cabin, with the transom windows above it. I told them Susie and I would often just gaze out of these windows upon awakening, appreciating the natural beauty of our surroundings from our own private sanctuary. Behind another carved door was the master head, with sink, shower, and, of all things, a bathtub.

We went back into the galley and I pulled a chilled bottle of wine out of the fridge, suggesting we go up into the cockpit to enjoy sundowners while I answered any questions about what they had seen so far. Each answer seemed to generate more questions. Night fell, the frogs and toads began their nightly serenade, and I brought up another bottle of wine. We would have missed dinner if Susie hadn't come down the dock to warn us the restaurant kitchen was closing in ten minutes. (She and I had decided it would be better if I did the first showing alone.)

We closed the restaurant, once Susie and Joanie got going on domestic matters. Provisioning, cooking, cleaning, bathing, and washing hair were among the many subjects they discussed. Tom and I fell mostly silent (as often happens when women get to talking), and to be fair, Joanie's interests and concerns were well-founded. By the end of the evening, it was apparent Tom and Joanie were impressed with *Mariposa* and fascinated by our tales of the cruising lifestyle. I suggested a sea trial after we had breakfast the next morning, and they were all for it.

When Susie and I got back on the boat, we compared our impressions of the couple. Tom and Joanie seemed to have an easygoing, positive, and loving relationship. They had both lived in a second-world country like Nicaragua, and apparently knew how to navigate a different culture and language. They were intelligent and enthusiastic and could likely handle the misadventures that would befall them. Tom was an MD, and in addition to all the advantages that this conferred to them personally, it would also guarantee them fast friends. In addition, he obviously knew how to use and care for tools. For her part, Joanie was a nutritionist, so they would eat healthy, balanced diets. Together, they had done enough sailing to know they both loved it. Susie and I agreed that they looked like ideal candidates for the cruising lifestyle.

The next morning dawned clear and bright, with a steady eight- to twelve-knot breeze blowing. Ideal sailing conditions. Before we headed out, I pulled up the floorboards in the pilothouse and showed Tom the engine and generator — which I had had cleaned two days before — and the other major mechanicals, like the watermaker, battery charge controllers, hot water heater, and water pressure pump. I demonstrated my routine before starting the engine or generator: checking the levels and condition of oil, coolant, and transmission fluid. I told Tom that if he did buy the boat, he should *never* fail to do these things. Milky engine oil, for example, means water has gotten into it. Water doesn't compress, and starting a high-compression diesel engine with water present can literally cause the block to crack. Also, insufficient oil or coolant can cause the engine to overheat and seize. In either case, the engine is toast and the hassle and cost of replacing it, especially in Nicaragua, justified the minor inconvenience of doing the prestart checks.

I held my breath, as I never knew what would happen when I pressed the start button, but *Mariposa*'s engine kicked over on the second crank and ran smoothly. First test passed. We slipped the dock lines and motored out into the lake for the sea trial. Once we were in open water, I had Tom take the wheel so he could begin to get a feel for the boat ... and enjoy that sense of command. I showed him how to operate the transmission, always slowing to idle speed before shifting between forward and reverse, and how the joystick for the bow thruster worked. We made several gear changes and drove around in circles with the wheel cranked fully to starboard and then to port. I had Tom operate the thruster with the boat rudder amidships and the boat in reverse gear, showing him how it was possible to steer while moving backward by just tapping the joystick to one side or the other. Then it was time to run up the sails.

Tom knew the drill: fall off the wind, unfurl the genoa first, then raise the main and mizzen. Once the sails filled, switch off the engine. Marvel at the quiet, just the gentle rhythmic hiss of the hull breaching and sliding through the waves. As often as I had done it, I never lost my sense of wonder and peace. We were literally taking a ride on the wind, and judging from Tom and Joanie's silence, they were entranced too.

I had Tom put *Mariposa* through all the points of sail, tacking to port and to starboard, reaching, running, and jibing. The boat wasn't fast—she was built for comfort, not speed—but her momentum carried her smoothly through all the maneuvers. She was proving herself to be a true sailing vessel as well as a comfortable live-aboard home.

Before we went back to the dock, Susie and I demonstrated the anchoring procedure we had developed. I wanted to show Tom how to drop the hook in a controlled fashion, using the clutch on the windlass while Susie, with Joanie watching, slowly backed the boat down in reverse. We pointed out the advantages of me just giving hand signals from the anchor well forward with her at the controls. We raised the anchor in a similar fashion, the big electric windlass doing all the work while I hosed the mud off the chain as it came up from the bottom, using the saltwater pump in the bow. When we were all back in the cockpit, Susie commented that mastering the anchoring drill was, to her, the most important part of cruising. Once the hook was well set, she said, you could relax, have a swim, shower, enjoy sundowners, and make dinner comfortably. You could also go to sleep and not worry about the anchor dragging and putting the boat on a reef in the middle of the night.

When we had *Mariposa* securely back in her slip at the marina, Tom asked if he and Joanie could have some private time at lunch to talk things over. He suggested he and I meet back at the boat at four o'clock, and he'd let me know if they wanted to proceed with a purchase. At the appointed hour, he and I went below and sat in the main saloon. I had switched on the air conditioner, a piece of equipment I had forgotten to mention earlier. Now I was glad I hadn't, because coming down the companionway out of the tropical heat and humidity and into *Mariposa*'s cool interior was a delightful surprise. We sat with two iced teas, and Tom came right to the point: he and Joanie wanted to buy the boat. He seemed apologetic that the offer he was making was not at the full asking price of $280,000, but rather $250,000. I countered that would be acceptable if he took ownership of the boat in "as is, where is" condition. We shook hands, and the negotiation was over almost as soon as it began. I think we were both stunned at how easy and natural it was, and I suggested we forget about the iced tea and round up our wives for a celebratory beer at the bar. They were as surprised and delighted as Tom and I were.

Of course, there were a myriad of details to be ironed out. We agreed that we should sign a contract spelling out not only the agreed-upon price, but how and when payment would be made, delivery taken, and ownership transferred. *Mariposa* was a US Coast Guard documented vessel, and that meant formal government paperwork had to be completed. I offered to draft the contract, and if it was okay with Tom, I would ask Jack, as a knowledgeable businessman, to review it and help finalize terms acceptable to both of us. Tom was comfortable with Jack, so he agreed.

The next morning, as I was sitting at the Gauguin table drafting the contract, I was approached by a short, stocky, pugnacious-looking lady with close-cropped dark hair who had run into Susie and Joanie in the ladies' room and overheard their conversation. She said she wanted to congratulate me on the sale, but also wanted to pick my brain about places we had cruised in the Caribbean. It turned out that she had single-handed her thirty-six-foot sloop from southern California, down the west coast of Mexico, through the Panama Canal, and up the east coast of Panama, finally taking a break in the fresh water of the San Juan River. Like most experienced sailors, Tricia was seeking local knowledge before heading out again.

I had called and asked Jack to come over to the marina, and he showed up while Tricia and I were talking. I introduced them and watched, fascinated, as they sized each other up. I had never seen Jack interact with a single female before, and this lady was his match in blunt outspokenness. They challenged and bantered, thrusted and parried with each other, and I wondered if Tricia showed the same sort of spunk that had attracted Jack to Lillie all those years ago.

At one point, Jack made a foolish comment about putting lipstick on a pig. "But it's still a pig," he said, and Tricia took exception. "I'll never marry you if you keep talking like that," she said, and the implication was clear. If Jack wanted to make time with this woman, he'd have to watch his words. Jack wasn't sure how to respond to her statement. I could hear the wheels turning as he shifted his glance from one side to the other. *If I say something like "I never asked you to marry me," that could imply I don't find her attractive. But if I apologize for having offended her, then I'll look unsure of myself. Either way, my chances of getting into her pants will be worse.*

"So, Bill," he said, hoping to escape the dilemma he'd put himself in, "I guess you'd like my help finalizing this contract with Tom. I can talk with both of you and work out the deal points, but I don't have any way of getting it typed up."

Tricia jumped in. "Tell you what, Bill," she said. "You share your knowledge of the cruising grounds with me, show me charts, give me waypoints, and I'll type up the contract." Perhaps she too was looking for a way to salvage a potential relationship with Jack. *If I type up the contract, it will mean I'll have more contact with this guy as we go back and forth between Bill and Tom. It'll give me the chance to see if he's really as dumb as that comment he made.*

"Well, thanks, guys," I said. "I really appreciate your help. Now, why don't you go fight somewhere else so I can get back to drafting this contract?"

"How about a liquado?" Jack said to Tricia, perhaps as a peace offering, and I was reminded of the offer of a cup of coffee he had made to Lillie after he'd splashed her dress on the corner in Seattle. Were Jack's old courting instincts resurfacing after all these years? Where might this relationship go?

"Okay, but I'm still not going to marry you," she said grudgingly, and they went off to a different table. The lovely Lydia came over to take their orders. *Careful, Jack,* I thought. *Don't let her see you staring at the girl's chest. And, Lydia, don't you dare cock your head to one side and ask him if he wants* "algo mas?"

As Jack and Tricia pulled things together on the contract over the next few days, they were in regular contact with me and Tom, and with each other. It was all very cordial, and we formed our own little community. When we hit the occasional sticking point,

Tricia assumed the role of mediator and helped us get things resolved. Jack then captured the language, and she typed it up.

When the final version was ready, we all gathered at the Gauguin table. Susie and Joanie were with us, as they were also signatories to the contract, and Jack and Tricia signed as witnesses. Everybody got something to drink in celebration, and Tricia said we should have a photo to commemorate the occasion. She produced her camera, set up the shot (with palm trees and river in the background), and asked one of the other cruisers to take the group shot. As we lined up shoulder to shoulder, he said, predictably, "Say cheese!"

"Forget that," Tricia said. "Stick yer tits out!"

I was shocked—and, I have to admit, amused—hearing a woman make a statement like that in public, and was again reminded of Lillie's outspokenness. How would Jack react? Was there a relationship in their future?

Redemption

The deal cut, Tom, Joanie, Susie, and I could relax. They had a million questions about the details of living on a sailboat and the cruising lifestyle, and we responded as completely as we could while trying not to embellish the stories too much. They were fascinated, as if we were describing a totally new world, filled with unfamiliar terms and extraordinary experiences. We told them about our own early days with the boat, and the steep learning curve we had been on. We had read books and subscribed to magazines about cruising, gone to boat shows, attended seminars, and taken classes on diesel mechanics, weather, and seamanship. I even got a captain's license from the US Coast Guard, learning (among *many* other things) about which vessels had the right of way over others under different circumstances, the lights and shapes displayed by ships on the open sea and in inland waters, and the challenges to sailboat navigation presented by the interaction of wind, points of sail, tides, and currents.

"I'm curious, Bill," Tom said as we began one of these conversations. "How did you get started with sailing in the first place?"

"I was eight years old," I said, "and my parents had a summer place on a lake in northwestern New Jersey. There were a lot of sailboats on the lake, and my buddies and I thought it would be fun to try it ourselves. I talked my mother into giving us an old bedsheet, which we folded into the shape of a triangle. We tacked the edge of the sheet to a sapling, drilled a hole in the front seat of our rowboat, and stuck the sapling into it. Then we tied a piece of clothesline to the back corner of the sheet and pushed the boat out onto the lake. The sheet filled with wind, and off we went.

"It was glorious sailing down that lake, but we realized when we reached the end that we had no idea how to get back. We didn't know anything about tacking, and even if we had, a flat-bottomed rowboat doesn't go upwind. We had to wait for a powerboater to take pity on us and tow us back home.

"But my parents saw how excited I was by the experience and bought me a used eight-foot pram with a proper mast, sail, rudder, and centerboard to see if I was going to stay interested in sailing. They couldn't get me out of the thing, and when I was fourteen they bought me a sixteen-foot Comet class sloop. I raced the boat on weekends and took it out whenever there was a decent breeze. I got to know the lake so well, I even went sailing at night.

"So all the elements were there: the sense of adventure, the magic of riding the wind, the accomplishment of becoming a good sailor, the excitement in the eyes of the girls when they said, 'Oh, you have a *sailboat*?' I was hooked. As an Aussie friend once told me, the rot had set in early.

"Over the years, the boats got bigger, the sails got longer, the destinations farther. It became apparent you could actually live on a boat and, if properly fitted out, sail it anywhere in the world. Marriage, family, and career intervened, but Susie and I kept the dream alive. We chartered sailboats in the Caribbean–Susie passed the sailing test in the Virgin Islands before we married—in New England, the Gulf of Mexico, and the Med. The experience of sailing a lot of different boats gave us a pretty good idea of what we wanted, and nine months after I retired we found *Mariposa*."

Susie jumped in at this point, not willing to let the Virgin Islands test go unchallenged. "I knew what you were doing with that first charter," she said. "You weren't about to settle down with someone who didn't like sailing. Thank God I wasn't sick. But I had my tests too."

"Oh, yeah?" said Joanie. "What did Bill have to do to win your heart?"

"It didn't start well. He came to a meeting of a social-service club I belonged to in Chicago, not because of any charitable instincts but because he had been told there were a lot of young, unattached females in the club. Everybody went to dinner after the meeting, and as my girlfriend and I were finding our seats at the table, he barged in and told her, 'You sit over there,' and pointed vaguely down the table, so he could take the chair next to me. So there I was, stuck with this old bald guy in a business suit. He was a good conversationalist, though, and by the end of the evening I had given him my phone number. He said he was leaving the next day for a month-long business trip in Italy, but would call me when he got back. I wondered if I'd ever hear from him again.

"But six weeks later he did call and asked if I remembered him. When I said yes, he asked me out to dinner. I figured what the hell, it's only dinner, and we arranged for him to pick me up at Crate and Barrel, where I was working three evenings a week. He came into the store wearing a leather jacket and carrying a helmet, and said he'd parked his bike just outside. I thought,

This old dude may not be such a fuddy-duddy after all. He took me straight to his apartment, saying we'd have an aperitif before going out to dinner. I was wary, naturally, but he seemed like a gentleman and I was curious. The drink he offered me was from a numbered bottle of vintage Palo Cortado sherry. I had never drunk sherry before.

"Then we went to a Mexican restaurant. Bill he told me he had lived in Mexico City and if I had any questions about the menu, I should just ask him. Then he ordered and chatted up the waiter in Spanish. I thought, *Hmm, a guy with international experience who speaks more than one language. Hmm.*

"After we'd had a few more dates and Bill had proven himself trustworthy, I invited him to my place for dinner. He was complimentary of the coffee chicken recipe I had pulled out of some magazine, thinking it would seem exotic. We still joke today about how awful it was. Then he had me over for dinner, and that was it. Along with everything else, he could cook! I decided to take him to meet my parents.

"My father was uncharacteristically quiet—I had never brought a man home before, just boys—but when Bill found out my parents had met in Italy during the war, he spoke to them about their experiences … in Italian. My father loosened up, and at the end of what turned out to be an enjoyable visit, my mother took me aside. She said, 'If you don't marry him, I will!' It took me two and a half years to convince him."

"So, you've had a long history with each other," Tom said. "And with sailing. Did you have any other boats before you bought *Mariposa*?"

"After I sold the Comet," I answered, "I didn't have a boat for years. But because I was into sailing, I looked for other people who did. I was working in New York City and was able to connect with a group of guys who raced their boats on Long

Island Sound. It was good experience because some of the boats were pretty good sized, forty to fifty feet. I even did some overnight races, and that introduced me to the beauty and challenges of nighttime navigation.

"Susie and I kept chartering too, and one of those charters was with Caribbean Sailing Yachts in Saint Vincent. I liked the boats they were building for charter service and ended up buying a thirty-seven-foot cutter from them. I put it into CSY's fleet under a purchase/leaseback arrangement, and we sailed the Windward Islands for two weeks every year.

"I sailed her up to Connecticut at the end of the contract, but the winds on Long Island Sound were too light to move a boat designed for the strong Caribbean trade winds. I donated her to an organization teaching city kids to sail and took a tax write off. Then I bought an O'Day 22, but the boat was so light and tender that it couldn't handle anything over ten or twelve knots. I upgraded to a Pearson 28, which turned out to be a great day sailer and weekender for the Sound.

"A career move took me to the Midwest, but I just couldn't relate to inland lake sailing, even though I'd started sailing on a lake. I guess being on blue water had spoiled me. Anyway, I didn't have a boat for twenty years. Then I took a job in Pittsburgh, and of all things we bought a steel-hulled houseboat and cruised the Allegheny, Monongahela, and Ohio Rivers for ten years. It was great for the kids, and I felt connected enough to the sea, albeit 1500 miles downstream, to be okay with it. Even though I never went more than 140 miles from home, the fact that I *could* have gotten out into open water made all the difference. And then I retired and bought *Mariposa*."

"That's a great story," Joanie said. "But I'll bet you've had some anxious moments too. What's the scariest thing that happened to you when you were out sailing?"

Susie shot me a look, and I knew I was going to have to own up to one of the stupidest things I had ever done on the water. It happened on one of our trips south, after summering in New England and sailing down to Annapolis for the boat show in mid-October. We always went to the show, not because we were looking for another boat, but because every major marine equipment supplier had an exhibit there. The people manning the exhibits were knowledgeable, their advice was free, and the prices were discounted. Once the show broke up, cruisers like us made a mad dash down the Chesapeake to Norfolk, Virginia, where the Intracoastal Waterway started.

Known as the Ditch, the ICW meanders through sounds, harbors, rivers, and canals as it makes its way behind the strand of barrier islands along the East Coast. The image most people have of the ICW is that it's completely built up with waterfront homes, marinas, condos, and golf courses. It looks that way in some places, but not on the Waccamaw River in South Carolina, considered by many to be the prettiest part of the trip. This river is the aquatic equivalent of Longfellow's forest primeval: miles of deep tannin-stained water curving through untouched forests and swamps. The vegetation is so lush and exotic that you half expect to encounter a brontosaurus around the next bend in the river. There are side creeks you can anchor in, and then not see another human for days. It's just you, the water, and the wildlife: bobcats stalking, eagles soaring, alligators basking, birds singing, owls hooting, and katydids rasping. Being on an ocean-going sailboat in the midst of this untouched river environment, sipping merlot and grilling steaks as evening softly falls, is a wonderfully surreal experience.

It was happenstance that brought us to the Waccamaw that day, as typically we would passage the East Coast offshore, using the Ditch only to avoid the laborious process of crabbing our way around the big capes—Hatteras, Fear, and Canaveral. This particular day started out normally enough. It was late October and already brisk, even in South Carolina. We'd had a tranquil night anchored in a cove off St. Helena Sound, kept warm by the composition logs we burned in the woodstove. It was forty degrees outside, but in the confined space of the sailboat, it was cozy.

In the morning, we ran the generator for an hour or so to charge up the batteries, then hauled up the anchor and headed out to sea. We plotted a course for the entrance to St. Catherine Sound sixty nautical miles farther down the coast. It would be a full day's sail; cars may go sixty miles an hour, but sixty miles *a day* is pretty good for a sailboat. The sailing conditions were perfect. The day was brisk but sunny, the sea a saturated sapphire blue, the bow wave of the boat a continuous curl of white froth, and the only sound a muted splash as the wind let *Mariposa* have her way with the sea. We made a steady seven to seven and a half knots the whole way.

Somewhere in the middle of the trip, Susie said, "I smell smoke. Don't you smell it?"

"Yeah," I said, "but we're not far offshore and the folks on land probably have their fireplaces going. It's cool enough to want a fire. And the wind's coming off the shore. That's what you're smelling."

This seemed to satisfy her, at least for a while.

But a couple of hours later, Susie said again, "I still smell smoke. Why don't you go below and just have a look around?"

Susie's always been a worrier, and I, the experienced captain, pooh-poohed her concern. "Look, the stove's been out since last night," I said. "You're just smelling the fires on shore."

Then, as we approached the sea buoy off St. Catherine's, the scent grew stronger. This time Susie wouldn't accept my explanation and insisted I go below.

"Maybe you're right, it's just fireplaces, but I don't see any houses around," she said. "How about you just humor me?"

As soon as I went down the companionway, I knew we were in trouble. The lower stairs leading from the pilothouse to the main saloon were on fire, flames about a foot high.

This was serious. Our sailboat, like most modern cruisers, is constructed of fiberglass, a composite of matting, resin, and plastic. Exposed to enough heat, it melts and then burns. It is said that there is nothing faster than a frightened man with a bucket on a sinking boat, but I'd lay odds that the blur I became racing to the fire extinguisher was comparable.

The extinguisher knocked down the flames, thank God, but it would take over an hour of pressing wet towels to the smoking timbers before they seemed cool. While this was going on, the boat was under full sail and heading into a shallow sound with tricky channels. Running aground and burning to the waterline was only one of the scenarios I envisioned. Bursting into flame in the middle of the night while tied up in a marina next to fifty other plastic boats was another. So we opted for dropping the hook, causing the boat to come head to wind, and furled the sails. Finally, we had some time to metabolize the adrenaline pounding our hearts and determine our next move.

After another hour, I was satisfied there were no more smoking embers and could turn my attention to finding the source of the fire and making sure it wouldn't spark another one. I suspected the generator, as it was the only electrical thing that had been on that day, even though it had only been for an hour and a half at six in the morning. It didn't take long to find the tangle of wires coming out of a mass of melted insulation the size of a golf ball on the side of the generator. A short in the grounding cable must have occurred, allowing an overload of current to produce enough heat to ignite the wooden timber to which it was stapled. So long as I didn't try to switch on the generator, we shouldn't have any further problems. Even so, we decided to motor upstream, duck into a cove, and anchor away from any other boats. We both needed a drink, but opted instead for two-hour overnight watches so there would always be one of us awake, in case the fire reignited. Susie's look in the morning said it all; there was no need for an "I told you so."

As enjoyable (or embarrassing) as it was to regale Tom and Joanie with our sea stories, I had to get back together with Jack. We were close to finishing our interviews, and we both wanted to wrap up the story so we could take a couple of steps back from the details and contemplate what we had created in toto. We needed to avoid all distractions and stay focused, so agreed to meet at Jack's shop and put in whatever time it took. I wasn't totally surprised to arrive the next morning and find Tricia with him.

"I was just leaving," she said, clearly unsettled at having been discovered in what looked like a compromising situation. I hadn't thought anything of it when I hadn't seen her dinghy tied up at the marina the night before, but now it made perfect sense. "I only stopped by to give Jack his copy of the signed contract," she added, looking at the floor. This was uncharacteristic behavior for Tricia.

Jack jumped in to the rescue. "Yeah. We wanted to make sure everything was in order. Looks good, Trish. Thanks for bringing it over."

I resisted the temptation to pull down the outside corner of my right eye, as the Europeans do to communicate cynical disbelief. "Great," I said, also a little uncomfortable. "Thanks again for all your help. You have given me the second happiest day in a sailor's life." We all knew that was the day when you *sold* your boat.

After Trisha left, I said to Jack, "*Now,* what have you got to say for yourself?" I was obviously quoting Officer Wolfe's fateful words, and he got a kick out of it. But Trisha apparently didn't want more than a passing relationship with Jack, and shortly thereafter she set sail — alone — for her next adventure.

I wish I could say that Tom and Joanie sailed off into the sunset to enjoy a life of fun, friendship, and adventure on *Mariposa,* but it wasn't to be. The first inkling Susie and I got that their enthusiasm might cloud their judgment was when they told us about their plans for the next fall's cruise. They were going to jump on the boat, go straight down the river, and sail north to meet one of their sons (with girlfriend) for some scuba diving at Isla de Providencia. I told them I understood their excitement, but suggested they should spend a couple of weeks out in the lake to get to know the boat first.

"You know," I said, "try out different sail combinations, practice maneuvering under power, anchor, deploy and stow the dink, get familiar with the navigation instruments, run the watermaker. Cook, sleep, shower, toilet, just generally get used to living aboard. It's sheltered water on the lake, and if anything goes wrong, help is close by."

I thought about warning them more strongly about moving too fast, but I couldn't bring myself to quote the mariner's wisdom: "There are old sailors and bold sailors, but no old, bold sailors." All of the money was not yet in the bank.

They were thankful for the advice, but it was clear they had the bit in their teeth and would not be dissuaded. I figured the coconut telegraph would let us know how they were doing, and it did.

Cruising friends began telling us of *Mariposa's* mishaps almost as soon as Tom and Joanie started out the next October. They sailed out to the islands without incident, but as soon as the kids came on board, things began to go wrong. The girlfriend almost ran them out of water by taking frequent, long showers. Then the watermaker got cranky, and they had to go back into port to refill their tanks. Two women using hairdryers drew down the batteries too far, and they were constantly running the generator to recharge them. Tom didn't remember to let the engine RPMs drop to idle before shifting gears, and the transmission started making grinding noises. One night they forgot to haul the dinghy up into the davits. When a squall came in from an unexpected direction and their anchor broke loose, they had to try to reanchor with a dinghy full of rainwater dragging off the transom. Not engineered for this type of stress, the davits twisted and could no longer be used. They had to tow the dinghy behind the boat for the rest of the season, slowing their progress by a full knot. That didn't seem like much until they couldn't make an anchorage before dark one night.

Tom and Joanie managed to muddle through their shortened cruising season and brought *Mariposa* back to the river early. "Bloodied but not bowed" was how they characterized their experience, but I was dismayed to learn that they tried to blame Jack for a bad job on the davits. They tried a second cruise a year later, but the mishaps so unnerved Joanie that she abandoned ship and flew back to Minnesota. There were rumors of affairs by both parties, and ultimately the marriage failed. On a final phone call, a disheartened Tom said to me, "I swung for the fences but whiffed it. I'm afraid the adventure is over." He put *Mariposa* up for sale, and Jack tells me the boat is languishing at the dock in San Carlos.

"She looks rough," he told me. "Somehow, the bow pulpit got

torqued too. The brightwork is peeling and there's moss growing on the deck. The sail covers are all mildewy. God knows what's going on inside. Maybe you should make a low-ball offer, fix her up, and sell her again. You could make some money."

Good old Jack, ever the entrepreneur, I thought. I told him to go ahead and buy the boat if he wanted. I didn't want any part of it.

Susie and I are still stunned. Tom and Joanie had looked like they came from Central Casting, they seemed so perfect for the role of live-aboard cruisers. How could a doctor who used tools constantly in his medical career not care for the mechanical systems on a boat? How could a couple who seemed such a great team fall apart so quickly? In the end, we had to acknowledge the wisdom of a fellow cruiser — the same guy who advised millionaires on investments — when he said simply: "They just got in over their heads."

After Tricia took off that morning, Jack and I were able to refocus on his story. He told me the pleasant days running his machine shop and enjoying his daughter's and little granddaughter's company had been interrupted by an accident involving Cory's eldest half-brother, Miguel.

Miguel had gone to the United States when Cory was six and spent twenty years there without ever making a visit back home. He learned English and held construction jobs in and around Wilmington, Delaware, paid his taxes, and stayed out of trouble. Then, not paying attention to traffic one day in 2003, he stepped off a curb and into the path of a city bus. His injuries were severe: 25 percent of the frontal and parietal lobes of his brain were crushed by the impact, and he spent nine months in the hospital, the first three in an induced coma. When he came out of it, he was declared totally disabled, unable to walk or talk, incontinent, and with the mind of a ten-year-old. He was able to smile and gesture with his hands, but was otherwise helpless.

As the only person in the family fluent in the language and bureaucratic culture of the United States, Jack went to Delaware with Cory to negotiate a settlement on Miguel's behalf. They considered bringing legal action against Wilmington's mass transit department for what could have been a five- to ten-million dollar award, but quickly realized that the city would tie things up in the courts for a decade or more. They decided to pursue more immediate remedies through the workers' compensation insurance system.

In addition to Miguel's normal benefits, there was also the possibility of Jack obtaining a contract to take care of him as a personal-care attendant. Since Jack had worked around nursing and convalescent homes when he was younger, he had obtained a PCA to smooth his access to patient records. If he could renew it now, it would mean Miguel could live at home with him, rather than being sent to a state-run institution. Having seen firsthand how people were often neglected and even mistreated in such places, he could not in good conscience allow Miguel to be transferred to one. So he took the tests and renewed his PCA, and Cory applied for and was awarded guardianship under Delaware law. They moved into Miguel's apartment and had him brought there when he was released from the hospital.

The first six months were particularly difficult, and until Miguel gained bladder and bowel control, Jack had to change his diapers and clean him up. He also took Miguel to physical therapy five days a week for months, until it was judged that he was not going to make any more progress. He was still eligible for more than a year of workers' comp benefits, however, and Jack got the PCA contract for the same length of time, or until a final settlement was worked out. But the insurance company wanted to limit its costs and sought to conjoin their benefits with Miguel's medical assistance. The company knew that if it could come up with a way to disallow one benefit, it would disallow both. It took Jack a year and $25,000 in legal fees to work through these issues, but in the end the family prevailed. The court's decision hinged on the fact that paying Jack and Cory to care for Miguel would be cheaper than putting him in a nursing home at the state's expense. The final settlement was an insurance annuity of $1.4 million, payments from which would continue until Miguel's death. As part of the deal, Jack's PCA contract was extended to ten years.

Workers' comp has requirements, however, and in order to continue receiving benefits, Miguel must now have a physical exam performed by an MD in the United States every six months. If by some stretch he were to pass the exam, he would have to be available to work in Delaware. Miguel, naturally enough, didn't want to remain in the States; he wanted to be back in his home country and close to his family. Jack's and Cory's lives were centered in Nicaragua too, so Jack had to come up with a way to first close things out in Delaware and then physically move Miguel. He had Cory sublet Miguel's apartment to one of his construction buddies, also a Nicaraguan who was sympathetic to their situation. This solved the first problem, since subletting allowed Miguel to retain his US address.

The bigger challenge was how to get Miguel out of the States. Jack knew the owner of a hotel near the border in Laredo, Texas, where he used to stay when he was importing cars into Mexico. Fortunately, the man was still in business. Linked to his hotel, he had a sideline helping smuggle Central Americans into the States, and Jack asked him if it would be possible to reverse the process and get someone *into* Mexico. He agreed to help if Jack could get Miguel there.

Now Jack had to deal with transporting a severely disabled man from Delaware to the Mexican border. He bought a used pickup and drove the 1600 miles, stopping three nights at handicap-access motels and ordering takeout meals for dinner. In the mornings, Jack brought food back from the motels' breakfast buffets before they checked out. Lunch and bathroom breaks while on the road were difficult and time consuming, but they made it to Laredo without incident. They checked in at Jack's old motel, and the owner told them that some coyotes they could make arrangements with were coming north in a few days.

It wasn't cheap because of the extra effort it would take to sneak a man in a wheelchair over the border, but the coyotes managed it, delivering Miguel to Jack at an agreed-upon location in the outskirts of Nuevo Laredo, Mexico. The drive south from there was difficult, because now they were traveling in Latin America and did not have the well-maintained US roads and US conveniences. It took them over a week to get to Jack's place on Lake Nicaragua, but he had finally gotten Miguel back home.

As for the six-month physicals, Jack takes Miguel to a doctor in Managua. Dr. Martinez is a friend and colleague of Dr. Ponce, and Jack regularly takes both men out shooting. He also does gunsmithing for Dr. Martinez as a favor, and when Jack told him about Miguel's dilemma, the doctor offered to help. He has a brother with his own medical practice in Miami, and Dr. Martinez sends his brother the results of Miguel's exams. The brother in turn submits them over his signature to Delaware, and Miguel continues to receive his benefits. Jack must get physicals himself in order to maintain his PCA payments, but since he needs to go the States on business anyway, he has them done when he is there.

Miguel continues to live with Jack, who takes him to his twice-weekly two-hour therapy sessions, and both his physical and cognitive functions are improving. This progress contradicts what the physical therapists in Delaware had said, but Jack figures their judgment had been compromised by clients trying to avoid the expense of providing Miguel with further treatment.

Jack is getting older now, so is preparing for what happens when he is gone. He has retained the services of a gringo in his fifties to look after Miguel, and will send the man to the same school in the States that he attended to get his PCA license. Just before Jack's ten-year contract expires, Cory will select him to replace Jack. This person's annual physicals will be done by the same doctor who does Miguel's, and he will forward them to his brother in Miami to be submitted to the insurance company. In this way, Jack can keep the money flowing even after his death.

"I am amazed," I said, "that you have gone to all this trouble for a guy you barely know. I mean, cleaning up his poop, setting it up so it looks like he's still in the States, smuggling him into Mexico, driving him to Nicaragua, faking US physicals for him. Why have you done it?"

"Well, look," Jack said, "the guy is family to Cory, and family is big in Latin America. Besides, I want her to take over the business when I can't work anymore. I want her to feel obligated to me for taking care of him."

This sounded like vintage, calculating Jack, but I thought there was more to it. Yes, there was his abiding commitment to flaunt authority and beat a system that had so badly treated him, but that didn't address his visceral reaction when Miguel was threatened with institutionalization. It was against his code to allow it to happen, and he'd done what he had to do—disgusting, risky, manipulative, whatever—to prevent it. But I thought there also might have been an element of atonement. Jack had done a lot of truly awful and violent things in his life, and maybe he saw aiding Miguel as a way to make up for some of it. Not that he'd admit such a thing, even if he were aware of it, so I didn't share these thoughts with him.

Although his life has settled into a comfortable routine, Jack still gets calls for special assignments from time to time. Dr. Ponce recently asked him if he could bring a former Nicaraguan president back to the country to face corruption charges. The US-educated official had amassed, as many Central American heads of state did, a small fortune by taking payoffs, skimming foreign aid, and stealing land from the unsophisticated country people. In one such land grab, the ex-president stole one hundred square miles from a poor, indigenous group, not realizing that rich Nicaraguans, many of them doctors, actually owned twenty-five of those square miles.

After his term ended, the man fled to Panama to avoid prosecution and was now enjoying a luxurious retirement in the permanent springtime of the country's mountain highlands. His villa was surrounded by fourteen-foot walls and protected by a dozen armed guards. The compound could only be accessed by two bridges over a shallow, dry moat. The ex-president also had a private airstrip nearby, where he kept a plane for those occasions when he wanted a change of scene or needed to attend to his finances in the capital.

But the *ricos* he stole land from wanted to put him on trial, and Dr. Ponce had assembled a group of them to finance his return. Ponce's group offered Jack $1 million to bring him back— $500,000 when he left on the mission and another $500,000 upon delivering the ex-president to the Nicaraguan authorities. They gave him $50,000 up front to assemble his team and determine how it could be done. Jack took three trusted friends with him to Panama to scope out the project. He used a helicopter owned by one of the *ricos* to fly up the mountain valleys below the Panamanian radar, and they located the villa and the airstrip using information the group had gleaned from their sources in the country.

The scheme Jack concocted was to pump heavier-than-air nitrous oxide into the compound through tubes run over the walls at night. (This sounded so preposterous that I made a note to challenge Jack about it in the future, but we were so close to the end of his story — and my interview patience — that I let it go.) He said the gas would put the guards to sleep or make them so groggy that the raiders could break into the compound, spirit the ex-president out, and get him over to the airstrip. There were a number of private planes moored there, and they planned to preselect one close to the runway and take out the lock and tumblers on the door so it could be opened with a penknife. Once they got their target aboard, they would start the plane and fly him back to Nicaragua. Jack said I would be surprised how many of these private planes lacked ignition keys.

What further investigation revealed was daunting, however. Earlier in his career, the ex-president had attended the School of the Americas at Fort Benning, Georgia, and still had ties to the US military. During his time in office, he had allowed American troops to train in his country during some unrest there, and some rabble-rousers were actually killed in these exercises. In return, he was able to demand that the US government protect him, and in fact the guards at the villa were American soldiers. Jack decided it was just too risky to take on well-trained US troops and backed away from the project. The *ricos* allowed him to keep the remainder of the $50,000 for his efforts, and he put the money into a trust for his granddaughter's college education.

At sixty-nine-years-old, Jack now considers his shop to be a hobby business, and he personally handles only the projects that interest him. He is training an apprentice to run the shop and in the basics of marketing and purchasing. Cory is being prepared to manage the financial and administrative sides of the business, and soon Jack will semiretire. He no longer needs to worry about money (although he would love to get his hands on that $1.2 million in the Guernsey bank), and can focus on travel, creature comforts, attending to valued friendships, and making sure Cory, Miguel, and his granddaughter are taken care of. He is, in effect, creating the environment he never had as a child or teenager, but now can finally provide for and enjoy with his own family.

He has never lost his concern for animals either, going all the way back to his military school days and the jobs he held at racetracks as a pony boy. Today, instead of ground squirrels and horses, he is focused on dogs, and recalls with fondness the pair of half wolves fifteen-month-old Shelly used to toddle between, fists gripping their ruffs, on walks down the beach in Portland. The animals would unfailingly turn her around at the edge of their territory and bring her back home. This strong trait of protectiveness for their human family explains why Jack has stayed with the breed, even when their hunting instincts cause neighbors to lose chickens or even larger animals. He likes to tell the story of one of them treeing a young man for hours when he approached the dog's kill, one of his family's goats. If one of his half wolves—he always has at least three, among parents, siblings, or offspring—is ailing or injured, he will go to great lengths to help it, including driving four hours in the middle of the night to his vet in Managua. The dogs' unconditional loyalty to him reflects Jack's own code when it comes to his trusted friends, and he never worries about anyone coming on his property uninvited.

Meeting Jack now is to encounter a redeemed man getting acquainted with advancing age, taking a daily nap, mentoring a promising young machinist, and indulging his daughter's uncertainty about taking over the business. He patiently allows his five-year-old granddaughter to follow him around his shop, letting her help with things that are safe and answering her incessant questions. He smiles and laughs a lot, and invites people he respects for a steak dinner and intelligent conversation at his home. He treats his domestic help kindly, and never stints on their medical care if they are sick or injured. But Jack is not exactly in his dotage, as he still gets carried away in rants about the government and the sorry state of today's values and culture. Most significantly, if a friend who has won his trust is wronged and needs him, Jack is still capable of extraordinary violence. It just doesn't show on the surface as much as it used to.

Appendix

In order to make Jack's story flow smoothly, a number of omissions were necessary. Making these omissions pained Jack, because as an engineer he wanted everything to be complete and precise. He often went into maddeningly exquisite detail when relating certain incidents or experiences. I had to tell him, for example, that most readers probably wouldn't care if the chicken feathers he put into his clothes that cold Maine morning were stuffed with the quills up or down. Or that the exact diameter of the metal chips coming off the lathe in the shop in Colorado was one and a quarter inches and not one and one eighth. But it didn't matter what I said. He'd just go blithely on ... and on ... and on.

Which is not to say that there aren't readers who revel in this level of detail, so I have collected the aforementioned omissions in this appendix. For those of you who want to know what a sucker rod is, or how to doctor an AK-47 assault rifle clip, read on!

Sucker Rods

After leaving Flippy to explore her lesbianism in Los Angeles, Jack headed for the Texas oil patch, where he'd heard there was work. He found a job, he told me, on a workover rig, stacking sucker rods. I didn't know what a workover rig was, but decided

I didn't want to spend half an hour hearing his impassioned technical explanation. I fell for the sucker rods, though. Even though I knew I was in for it, I asked, "What the hell are sucker rods?"

He explained that they were forty-foot hollow rods, one inch to one and an eighth inch in diameter, flared at the ends to one and three quarters inches, and threaded male and female so they could be attached to each other. The rods ran down a well casing all the way to the level of the oil, where a pumping mechanism with one-way valves was attached to the bottom rod. The up-and-down motion of a machine at the wellhead caused a column of oil to be sucked up the pipe all the way to the surface.

Periodic maintenance was required to repair or replace the pump's valves, and to accomplish that, the pump had to be pulled up from the bottom of the well. Jack was stationed on an open platform on the top of the rig, and as each length of sucker rod emerged, the men at the wellhead unscrewed it from the one below. Once it was loose, Jack pressed down on the top of the rod with all his weight, causing it to bow slightly. When he released the pressure, the rod snapped straight, and this motion caused it to jump a few inches into the air. The men below could then shove the rod into a rack where it would be stored until the pump was repaired. Then the whole affair was reassembled rod by rod and lowered back down the well.

The pay was good, but the work was dangerous, as these rods each weighed 230 pounds. A wrong move could knock Jack off his platform, and even though he wore a safety harness, he'd have a free fall of several feet before he crashed into the steel framework of the rig. It was cold up there too, with forty-mile-an-hour winds dropping the temperatures into the midteens. Jack's muscles got so stiff, he was afraid he wouldn't be quick enough to catch himself if he started to fall.

In addition, the hazing to which the old hands subjected the newcomers was intolerable. Newcomers were referred to as maggots in the oil workers' hierarchy—one could advance to worm, then to finger, and finally to hand—and constantly had tricks played on them. In Jack's case, as a maggot, he was sent into a sludge pool and told to "clear the intake pipe." The location of the pipe was indicated only vaguely, the viscous liquid in the pool was too turbid to see through, and his waders weren't high enough to prevent to sludge from running down into his boots. He slogged around in the pool until he saw the men laughing and jabbing each other in the ribs. Only then did he realize he had been treated to the oil-field equivalent of the snipe-hunt trick played on first-time hunters.

He bailed out of this hazardous and demeaning environment after a month and a half and headed for Colorado to look for a job working inside.

Improvised Weaponry

During his time in Vietnam, Jack was often presented with situations that allowed him to combine his knowledge of munitions with his native inventiveness. In one instance, he was air-dropped four cases of hand grenades, only to find that they had been assembled without detonators. Normally, such grenades would be useless, but in Jack's hands they became improvised shape charges. While a grenade throws shrapnel in every direction when it explodes, a shape charge can be aimed. To construct one, the explosive inner linings of several grenades had to be taken out. Since Jack knew the linings were compounded of a material that melted at a certain temperature, he immersed the grenades in a double boiler. After five minutes, he removed them and carefully poured out the explosives. Next, he took copper sheeting and formed it into a cone by wrapping it around a bottle with a gradually narrowing neck. He placed the cone in a steel tube and packed the explosives in the space between the cone and the inner lining of the tube. When the charge was detonated, the explosion was contained by the tube and directed outward by the cone for about twenty-five yards. The blast also turned the copper into super-heated plasma. If it hit a transport vehicle, molten copper would spray all around the interior. A shape charge that hits an armored vehicle couldn't penetrate it, but was devastating nonetheless. It had the same effect as a hollow-point bullet, with the steel on the inside shattering in all directions from the point of impact. Regardless of the vehicle they were riding in, enemy soldiers were killed or wounded.

Shotgun shells were useful too. Although not normally considered battlefield weapons, shotguns were used by MPs in POW camps, and occasionally Jack could get some of the ammunition. He opened the crimped end of the shells, removed the lead shot, and poured out the gunpowder. Taking bamboo tubes that had a coating of nails glued to their exterior, he packed the gunpowder inside the tubes and smeared pig feces all over the outside. A firecracker served as the detonator, so the tube acted like a crude hand grenade. A VC soldier hit by any of the nails would invariably develop an infected wound and be incapacitated without antibiotic treatment.

Captured ammunition for the AK-47 assault rifles the VC carried could also be sabotaged. Jack removed the bullets from the rounds in the clips and poured the gunpowder out, just as he did with the shotgun shells. He replaced the gunpowder with highly explosive detonation cord and put the bullets back in. The clips with the modified ammo were left randomly along trails where there had been recent fighting. VC soldiers, thinking the clips had been dropped in the chaos of the action, loaded them into their rifles. When the AKs were fired, the detonation cords would explode, blowing up the rifles and seriously injuring or killing the soldiers.

There! Wasn't that extra material illuminating?

BC

ACKNOWLEDGEMENTS

The seed for this book was planted by my brother-in-law, David Witt. When his sister Susie and I began cruising, we regaled him with both our sailing experiences and stories of the odd collection of people we met. He said, "You have *got* to write a book about this!" Later, when it was in draft form, he provided numerous and valuable suggestions for improvements. So thank you, David.

Susie's and David's mom Rose Marie Witt provided continuous encouragement, further suggestions, and an edit. She's an avid reader with wide-ranging tastes, so I took her advice seriously. The title of the book also reflects her input. Many thanks to Rose as well.

And of course, my thanks to Susie for her prodding me when I got lazy, and for listening to me read sections of the book I wasn't sure I had handled well. I even incorporated some of her ideas, difficult as they may have been for a husband to hear. She also let me commandeer our better computer for endless hours, forsaking her music in the process.

Titia Bozuwa, an accomplished author in her own right, invited me to join a series of writing seminars she hosted each year. Her unfailingly constructive criticism, along with that of the other participants, served to change, shape, expand and ultimately improve the story I was endeavoring to tell.

Bett Barrett, also an accomplished author, was the leader of those seminars and also my always patient, insightful and thoroughly professional editor. Like a good coach, she encouraged me to do my best and gently but insistently guided my efforts. She even

Bill Goodwin

did the research I should have done, making corrections so the story made sense historically.

Manny Menezes and Roger Moore, both Vietnam veterans, helped me greatly with that portion of the book. I wasn't there, so their knowledge of the realities of the conflict were invaluable in getting the details right. Thanks, guys.

And finally, thanks to the protagonist of the story, who for obvious reasons cannot be named. His willingness to share the extraordinary events of his life are the substance of this book.

B.G.

CPSIA information can be obtained at www.ICGtesting.com
Printed in the USA
BVOW08s0417051215

429410BV00001B/1/P